INTO THE HOUSE OF THE ANCESTORS

Inside the New Africa

Karl Maier

John Wiley & Sons, Inc.
New York • Chichester • Weinheim • Brisbane • Singapore • Toronto

For Sarah

This text is printed on acid-free paper.

Published by John Wiley & Sons, Inc.

Library of Congress Cataloging-in-Publication Data
Maier, Karl
    Into the house of the ancestors : inside the new Africa/Karl
    Maier.
        p. cm. $2362-9610$ $10/00$
        Includes index
        ISBN 0-471-13547-X (cloth : alk. paper)
        1. Africa, Sub-Saharan—Politics and government—1960– 2. Africa,
    Sub-Saharan—Social conditions—1960– I. Title.
    DT352.8.M35   1997
    967.03'2—DC21   97-26809

Printed in the United States of America

10 9 8 7 6 5 4 3 2 1

Contents

The great powers of the world have done wonders in giving the world an industrial and military look, but the great gift still has to come from Africa—giving the world a more human face.
—Steve Biko, 1971

Preface

A commotion in the dark corridor outside my train compartment awoke me from a sound sleep at 2:00 A.M. We had reached the Swiss-Italian border, and the Italian police were rudely questioning an African woman about the legitimacy of her European passport. A bright flashlight was brought to bear on the document, and one officer repeatedly scratched the passport with his fingernail to test its authenticity. "It's new, an English one," he yelled out the window skeptically to a couple of immigration officials who were chatting with two border guards armed with machine guns. After a few more minutes of questions, the police reluctantly told the woman that she was free to go. She hoisted her large blue bag and wandered toward my compartment, the only one in the car with its door open. Everyone else was asleep. After a few minutes of hesitation, she leaned in and asked me if I would move my feet so she could sit down.

I am ashamed to say that my initial reaction was as cold as the night air; I had another five hours ahead of me and wanted as much room as possible to stretch out. A few moments later the woman's accent registered in my still groggy brain. She was definitely West African and I was fairly certain she was Nigerian, probably from the sprawling commercial capital Lagos where I had lived for two years. Suddenly many of the faces of Nigerians who had welcomed me warmly into their homes, offices, and lives flashed through my mind, and rediscovering my manners I quickly scooted over. She lifted the bag up to the luggage rack above our seats, sat down, and wiped the sweat from her brow. It was the dead of the European winter, but she was hot from lugging her bag around and undergoing the grilling from the Italian immigration authorities.

Fully awake now, I asked her where she was from, and at first, no doubt wary of yet another query about her nationality, she mumbled that she was British. Yes, but originally, I asked again. She smiled and replied louder, "Nigeria." From Lagos, I bet. Yes, she said, how did I know? I used to live in Lagos myself. What part of the city are you from? I asked. Ikorodu, came the reply. I told her how I remembered the huge night market on Ikorodu Road where thousands of tiny kerosene lamps on the market stalls bathed the entire four-lane thoroughfare in a soft yellow light. She smiled. So you enjoyed Nigeria, she said confidently. Were you there on business? No, I was a journalist. Oh, the army boys don't much like journalists, do they? No, I said, I suppose they don't, but then again, they don't seem to like anybody these days. "That's right," she grunted. "Terrible people."

Do you mind me asking what you are doing here? I ventured cautiously, not wanting her to think I was prying. Trading, she said. Buying textiles and leather goods, such as shoes and purses, in Zurich and Milan, and returning to sell them in London. "Two-two months," she added in the Nigerian way of saying she made such trips every two months. But isn't it difficult wandering around in the middle of night, dealing with these border guards? "My three children and I need the money. Life in Britain is expensive." How did she like Zurich? The people there were for the most part polite, she said. How about Milan? "Ruffians," she hissed, clicking her tongue disgustedly.

I asked her if she ever returned to Nigeria, and she said yes, as often as she could. She had been back several months before, visiting relatives. Did she want to return to live there or were her children too integrated into British culture to leave? I asked. "British culture," she snorted dismissively. "I want nothing to do with British culture." It reminded me of the time Mahatma Gandhi was asked what he thought about Western civilization, and he responded, "I didn't know they had any."

She said she was eager to return to live in Nigeria, but that under the current military regime, she doubted it would be possible anytime soon. "Life there is no good. Nigerians are hardworking people, you have seen that yourself, but these military boys won't let the people survive. They chop [steal] all the money. Maybe when the army leaves, then I can go back. But when will they leave? No one knows."

We went on talking for much of the next two hours, about everything from finer points of West Africa's traditional pepper soup, for which the word "hot" does not begin to do justice, to where she was able to purchase ingredients for Nigerian dishes in London, such as yams, manioc (cassava) flour which is known as *gari,* and palm oil. It turned out there was little she could not find in London. Off and on we both fell asleep as the train ambled toward Milan, and off and on we talked. What would she do when the train arrived? She explained that the waiting room at the station would open at 4:00 A.M. She would sit there until about 7:00 A.M., and then she would find a cheap hotel to set up her temporary office for the next three days of shopping in Milan before returning to Britain.

The train slowed to a crawl, and as she gathered up her bag we exchanged our good-byes, agreeing that it would be nice to meet one day on Ikorodu Road when things were better in Nigeria. I watched out the window as she climbed down from the car and stood momentarily on the platform as if she were lost. She threw the bag over her shoulder and headed for the stairs that would take her to an empty room and a three-hour wait for a cheap hotel to open. Before disappearing into the chilly night, she turned around and saw me looking out the window, and she smiled. As our train pulled out of the station that morning, it struck me how inadequate the stereotype is of Africa as the fragile continent. I have spent half of my adult life in sub-Saharan Africa as a journalist, and if there is one thing I have learned about Africans, if one can generalize for a moment about 500 million people, it is that they are anything but fragile.

They have accomplished what many other indigenous groups that felt the icy touch of European civilization—the Incas and the Aztecs in the Americas, for example—failed to do. They survived, and with a great deal of their culture, however bruised and battered, intact.

I have been asked often by westerners why in the world I have chosen to live for all those years in Africa, with its wars and famines, its horrible diseases such as malaria, yellow fever, the *Ebola* virus, river blindness, and many others, all the chaos and violence that appear on Western television screens like unending snippets from one long nightmarish film of the coming apocalypse. Of course, had there been CNN during World War I filming the mustard gas attacks, had the television cameras been poking through the fences of the concentration camps and into the gas chambers of World War II, or had there been footage of Africa's own holocaust, the Atlantic and Arab slave trade, perhaps the West would exercise a bit more humility in its judgment of Africa's current crisis. Certainly future historians, if they are truthful, will rate the violence of twentieth-century Africa as relatively mild indeed compared to the slaughter that Europe has experienced and imposed on others.

My answer to the question, however, is twofold. I freely admit to having succumbed to an overwhelming sense of admiration for the courage and sheer determination with which so many Africans seek to overcome their difficulties. In general, Africans are among the most hospitable and direct people I have met anywhere. It is true that I have had my brushes with trouble; I have been shot at, detained, threatened, and I came within hours of dying from malaria. But it is also true that never have I been more welcomed into people's homes or treated with more respect.

Africa is a place of constant surprise and seemingly limitless energy. It is perpetual motion. West African market women will insult you unless you get into the spirit of things and bargain with them, and then will click their tongues if you give in too easily to their bantering. It is a place where a family that is barely surviving in a refugee camp will insist that a visitor have a drink of water, a bite to eat, even share the meat of their last chicken, or issue a heartfelt apology for having nothing to offer. Every day that I am out of Africa, I miss it.

When I was first approached to write a book about the land and people whom the world today regards as sub-Saharan Africa, I felt a great deal of apprehension. How can one generalize intelligently about a continent with such a rich variety of cultures, languages, and religious systems? What do people in the far northeastern Horn of Africa have in common with someone in the central highlands of Angola in the far southwest? Indeed, as Professor Ali Mazrui of Kenya has pointed out, the entire geographical definition of Africa was an imposition of European mapmakers. He was not speaking about the carve-up of Africa by the European powers at the Berlin Conference in 1884–85, an exercise that had dire consequences for the fortunes of the independent nation-states that emerged from the end of colonial rule eighty years later. His question was, where did the boundaries of Africa end and those of Europe or Asia begin? Who said, for example, that the Arabian peninsula was not part of

Africa? The physical separation of the two occurred only in the nineteenth century with the building of the Suez Canal, and the geology, language, and culture of northeastern Africa and Arabia are remarkably similar. But European mapmakers said the two were separate, and they became so.

Conscious of such caveats, I pushed ahead with the assignment. The purpose of this book is neither to sanitize the image of sub-Saharan Africa nor to soft-pedal its problems. Rather, my goal is to provide a balanced picture of how its peoples are summoning their tremendous inner vitality, their cultures, their religions, and their capacity to adapt to a rapidly changing world around them. In doing so, I hope to reveal the strength of purpose and self-pride with which Africans are arming themselves to overcome the immense challenges they face as they head into the twenty-first century.

Today there is a new mood in the air. The era of "big-man" politics is fading, tyrants are no longer tolerated so easily as they once were, and the issue of responsible government is back on the African agenda. Part of the credit goes to the emergence of a new generation of African leaders who are too young to have experienced colonial rule and are no longer prepared to follow the ways of the first postindependence rulers. There have been many setbacks and false starts, but sub-Saharan Africa of today looks and feels very different now than it did even ten years ago. At least half of all countries are undergoing political and economic reform programs. Printed and electronic media are generally freer than ever before, and public criticism of a head of state no longer ensures an extended stay in prison.

Demands for change are growing louder. "All over Africa, ordinary people are in revolt against a leadership whose performance has become life-threatening," wrote Claude Ake, the Nigerian social scientist who died tragically in a 1996 plane crash. "They link their misery to leadership performance and they are convinced that their condition will not improve until they empower themselves to intervene in public life for the improvement of their own lives. That is how they come to call for a second independence from their own leaders, asserting the need for the colonial revolution to be followed by a democratic revolution."[1]

This book attempts to celebrate the spirit of Africa by portraying the lives of people all over the continent who are making Herculean efforts, often exposing themselves to great personal danger, to forge a better future for their peoples, to start that great trek, however much against the prevailing wind, toward true freedom. The focus is placed deliberately on the extraordinary endeavors of very ordinary people, from an agricultural worker who pioneered a new school of modern sculpture in Zimbabwe to a priest and an elderly widow who risked their lives to save Tutsis during the Rwandan genocide. For if positive change is to be lasting, it will be carried out by people from all walks of life and not simply those in the seats of power. As the thoughtful British historian Basil Davidson has argued, "mass participation" was "at the heart of all those African societies which proved stable and progressive before the destructive impact of the overseas slave trade and colonial dispossession made itself felt."[2]

Already, in their own small ways, people are building from the ground up. The work and lives of the book's protagonists are chosen because they address the key challenges Africa faces today: war and peace, health, education, ethnic tolerance, local community development, the reassertion of African art and culture, and the fight for effective and honest government. The tools with which they engage their battle vary. A young woman Zulu chief strives to modernize her traditional powers, to innovate the past so to speak, in the hope of ensuring prosperity for her followers. Villagers in Mozambique have used their centuries-old rural beliefs to defend themselves against civil war. Traditional healers, nurses, and social workers are uniting in Zimbabwe and South Africa to fight the AIDS epidemic. Adults play big brothers to help former child soldiers deal with the trauma of war in Sierra Leone. Church leaders, businessmen, and university professors foster regional autonomy amid the collapse of the nation-state in what was Zaire. A medical doctor turned human rights activist braves threats and extended jail terms to challenge the military regime in Nigeria.

The common motivation of the central characters in the pages that follow is their conscious decision to take up the struggle to restore the moral order of Africa for the good of the greater community. They are armed not with weapons of war but with a determination to provide African solutions to African problems, to reclaim their self-worth and self-purpose. They are the modern day freedom fighters in Africa's second revolution.

Glorious Light

The air tingled with excitement as the first crimson rays of sunlight announced the dawn over the rolling hills outside the South African city of Durban on the shores of the Indian Ocean. A motorcade escorted by dozens of armed soldiers and police officers roared up a knoll overlooking a tightly packed township to deliver Nelson Mandela to the Ohlange High School and his long-awaited appointment with history. The day was April 27, 1994, and Mandela had chosen to cast his vote in South Africa's first all-race elections at the site of the tomb of the founding president of the African National Congress, John Dube.

As Mandela ambled in his long, slow strides toward the cemetery, he paused to shake the hand of a young white soldier armed with an R-4 automatic rifle. "It's an honor for me to meet you," he said. "You must have had to get up very early. I'm very sorry." The trooper, who just a few years before would have been under orders to regard Mandela as the most dangerous man alive, stood there dumbfounded. "Thank you, sir," he stammered, "but it's my job." Mandela held his hand for a moment and said it did not matter, he was very grateful anyway.

After laying a wreath at the tomb, Mandela walked down toward the school where a phalanx of three hundred photographers and television crews were jostling with each other for the ideal position to capture the most famous vote in African history. As the ruckus was going on, Mandela went around shaking the hand of every police officer and soldier he could find, asking warmly how they were and saying how nice it was to meet them. "Thank you very much for your good work," he told the commanding officer, a white police colonel, who responded, "You take care of yourself." Mandela thanked him for the advice.

From there, Mandela strode up the steps into the schoolhouse, cast his vote in secrecy, and reappeared outside to do it again for the cameras. "An unforgettable occasion," he said with his wide, disarming smile. "We are moving from an era of resistance, division, oppression, turmoil and conflict and starting a new era of hope, reconciliation and nation-building." When asked who he had voted for, Mandela said with a mischievous laugh, "I have been agonizing over that decision for a long time." For twenty-seven years, Mandela had been a prisoner in the jails of South Africa's apartheid rulers because he believed that the African majority should enjoy their full democratic rights. During that time he emerged as the premier symbol of the struggle for freedom and equality of Africans on the continent and throughout the diaspora, in distant places like the United States and Brazil, where his likeness is painted on the walls of homes in cities such as Salvador and Rio de Janeiro.

If he harbored any bitterness at his long incarceration, his years of working in the lime mines outside the cold, windswept prison on Robben Island, he never showed it. Long shunned by the West as a Communist—former British Prime Minister Margaret Thatcher once described him as the leader of "a typical terrorist organization"— Mandela walked out of jail in February 1990 and said, let bygones be bygones. His vote four years later marked the final stage of Africa's emergence from the shadow of colonial occupation. It was as if Mandela were the human manifestation of the inscription written on John Dube's tombstone: "Out of the darkness into the glorious light."

No one who witnessed that scene, or indeed Mandela's rise from being the world's most famous prisoner to becoming head of state of Africa's most powerful country, could forget the incredible dignity and humility that enveloped him. The uncanny ability of "the old man," the *madiba*, as he is commonly known, to make those around him feel better about themselves was often described as "Mandela magic." Much has been written about the iron will and sacrifice to free his people from subjugation; but his genius, and one of the many reasons he evokes such admiration around the world, is his ability to bring African values to bear on the problems of the late twentieth century—values such as the preeminence of the interests of the community over those of the individual, respect for traditional culture, and an at times unbelievable capacity for forgiveness.

Four years before South Africa's elections, another elderly man, like Mandela a tall, dignified septuagenarian, explained why the people in the neighboring country of Zimbabwe felt so little bitterness toward the whites living there. The whites had arrived a century before under the command of the British imperialist Cecil Rhodes, stole the people's land, their cattle and their minerals, and ruled over them in the racially segregated country called Rhodesia until finally capitulating after a horrific liberation war in which tens of thousands died. Mike Hove, a former diplomat and author, sat one afternoon in the living room of his home in the city of Bulawayo and described how his father was among many who had extended hospitality to those white pioneers, provided them with shelter, and crouched with them around the campfires sharing their evening meals of caterpillar stew and beer. Only later, when the whites launched their campaign of theft and forced their erstwhile African hosts into "native reserves," did they resist. It was not surprising, he said, that one hundred years later, the Ndebele and Shona people could live together with the whites in relative tranquility in the modern nation of Zimbabwe. The concept of forgiveness was central to the African character, Hove said. "In African religion, your relationship with the creator is only as good as your relationship with your foe. So if two brothers fight, they would have to go and appease the spirits. In this part of the country, the ceremony is very simple. You take some ash from a container. One brother takes part of the ash, and the other brother does the same, and they eat it. Once they have gone through that cleansing ceremony, they would be reconciled to God through our ancestors. The idea of forgiveness is part of life. One who refuses to forgive the person who has offended him becomes an outcast; he is not human anymore."

As the millennium approaches, Africa is in dire need of a renewed injection of the values outlined by Hove and symbolized by "Mandela magic" if the continent is to pull itself out of its political and economic crisis. Professor Ali Mazrui has suggested that the rampant instability, corruption, and dictatorial government which have turned the dreams of freedom and independence into a nightmare are the result of a curse pronounced by the ancestors on the living for ignoring Africa's past and the cultural values bred over the centuries. "It is the compact between Africa and the twentieth century and its terms are all wrong," he has written. "They involve turning Africa's back on previous centuries—an attempt to 'modernize' without consulting cultural continuities, an attempt to start the process of 'dis-Africanizing' Africa."[1] To lift the curse, Africa must take the good from its past to meet the demands of the future. Africans must reclaim the sense of history and purpose of which colonialism dispossessed them. Simply aping the Americans and Europeans, promoting "dis-Africanization" and Westernization, is doomed to fail.

The European carve-up of Africa at the Berlin Conference—a massive exercise in international piracy whose goal was to create moneymaking colonies—bequeathed to the founding fathers of modern Africa a deformed heritage. When Kwame Nkrumah of Ghana, Jomo Kenyatta of Kenya, Tanzania's Julius Nyerere, Kenneth Kaunda in Zambia, and the Senegalese poet Léopold Senghor led their countries to independence, they inherited a haphazard patchwork of often unworkable nation-states still dependent on the capitals of the former occupiers. The charismatic Nkrumah, who guided Ghana to independence in 1957, once proclaimed, "Seek ye first the political kingdom and all else will follow." But all else did not follow. The struggle of Africa's people to reclaim their birthright, to pursue their lives in relative security and with a reasonable hope of delivering a better future to their children, was just beginning, and it was to experience many reverses.

Uhuru—freedom—remains a mirage on the horizon, dancing away disconcertingly into the distance just as it appears within reach. Africa's infant mortality rate remains alarmingly high, at seventy-five per thousand, and even in Uganda, the economic success story of the 1990s, one in five children die before their fifth birthday. Africa's contribution to total world trade is declining rapidly, to about 1 percent, millions of people have fled their homes to escape famine and war, and hundreds of thousands more have migrated to Europe and the United States to avoid oppressive governments and the lack of economic opportunity. Of the world's severely indebted poor countries, twenty-five are in Africa. By the year 2000, half of Africa's people, 300 million people, will live in abject poverty, with little or no access to basic health care, sanitation, and clean water.

Such statistics find apparent confirmation in the horrific pictures of African war and pestilence carried daily on global television networks. International aid agencies escalate their propaganda campaigns, flashing ever more graphic scenes of tearful children living in squalid refugee camps or polluted urban shanty towns, and urging the public to respond with credit card donations. The message is, Save a life by sending money to poor dependent Africa. This portrait is a distortion. Actually, Africa often sends more money to the West than the other way around. All the assistance Africa receives from the international aid agencies, the United Nations, and the big industrial nation governments, some $10 billion a year, just about covers the payments African countries owe on their foreign debts, mainly to the West. If just one of every four or five dollars Africa pays to the banks and creditors was destined instead for primary education, every African child could find a place in school.[2] The same thing could be accomplished by cutting by one-third the region's annual $8 million military bill, much of which again is paid to the West.

Yet blaming Africa's myriad problems on the outside world will simply not do any more, and it is very rare to hear Africans living in Africa offering such excuses. Even without the constraints of the unbalanced economic relationship with the West, African countries have their own very urgent problems to sort out, and only they can do it. Just as Mandela was casting his ballot and leading his country out of the darkness of apartheid, a blanket of horror was falling on the tiny central African nation of Rwanda. The government, led by extremists of the Hutu people, organized the genocide of between one-half to a million of its citizens, members of the Tutsi minority and Hutu moderates. A few months later, the military rulers of Nigeria jailed the winner of that country's first elections in a decade, apparently setting Africa's most populous and potentially most promising nation on the road toward violent confrontation.

While civil wars rage today in Somalia, Sudan, and Rwanda's neighbor, Burundi, and claim thousands of lives, a tenuous peace is hanging literally by a thread in Angola, the scene of a twenty-year conflict. One can count on one hand the number of countries that have witnessed since independence a peaceful handover of power from one government to the next. Even rarer are the leaders who own up to their mistakes in office, such as Nyerere who, when he bowed out gracefully as president of Tanzania in 1985, declared in his farewell speech, "I failed. Let's admit it."

Decades after the end of colonial occupation, Africa still casts about for answers to the question of which way ahead, of how the continent can harness its vast natural resources and the undying energy and ingenuity of its people to reverse its breathtaking decline. The wreckage of foreign models imported largely from Europe litters the landscape like a line of rusting hulks. The nation-states left by the colonial powers have proved to be alien structures, unwieldy at best and in some cases outright unworkable. Multiparty systems too often have unleashed debilitating contests between politicians who are prepared to stoke the fires of ethnic rivalry, no matter what the cost, to win power. The socialist one-party states, so popular in the years immediately following independence, ended up as overbearing monoliths, hanging like millstones around Africa's neck, stifling initiative and fostering corruption.

Now, at the urging of western institutions such as the World Bank, the model of the rapidly industrializing so-called Asian "tigers," countries such as Singapore, South Korea, and Taiwan, has become the latest fad, but that too is likely to fare little better than its predecessors unless it is built on solid local foundations. Professor Mazrui has a point when he attributes the demise of Africa to a curse of the ancestors. Since independence, Africa has jettisoned its past. When the Europeans withdrew, power was not returned to the traditional chiefs and kings from whom it was taken by force, but to rulers who believed almost exclusively in the superiority of western institutions. Too many of these modern leaders are not interested in seeking lessons from their precolonial forefathers. Incredibly, not one professes a public belief in indigenous African religions, for example. The vast majority are Christians, Muslims, or Marxists. They accepted the nation-states and in large part the political and economic institutions created by the European colonizers, as well as the notion that Africa's history before the slave trade and full-scale foreign occupation had little to teach the present and future generations. If Africa was to modernize, it world have to embrace "civilization" in a distinctly alien form. As Basil Davidson put it in his critique of the nation-state, *The Black Man's Burden*, "Africa would be free: except, of course, that in terms of political and literate culture, Africa would cease to be Africa."[3]

An African political order did exist before the slave trade carried off millions of Africa's sons and daughters to the Americas and the Arab world and the subsequent occupation by the imperial powers. Whether in the stateless nomadic groups that herded their livestock across the vast savannahs of the continent or in more complex centralized systems, such as the Ashante state in Ghana or the Shona kingdoms in what is today Zimbabwe, in the eyes of their citizens, these regimes were legitimate. There was a moral order to life, a belief by most of the peoples that they had a stake in it. It was certainly not the case that European civilization at the time was fundamentally more advanced than that of Africa, except of course in the technology of firearms. As Ronald Segal has argued in his pioneering work, *The Black Diaspora,* there is something to be said for the notion that any society which pillages another for its people might be considered the more backward one, at least morally. "In fact, since even the more conventional criteria of cultural advance encompass standards of personal security and civil justice as well as material wealth and the extent of territory under centralized administration, the difference may well have been in favor of Black Africa."[4]

Millions of ordinary Africans are looking for a new path. They have beat a hasty retreat from the morass of onerous strictures and regulations dictated by governments that enforce them when it is convenient, and they have sought solace in their own cultures, their clans, and their families. The rich mosaic of indigenous religions remains a vibrant force, not only in Africa but also in the Caribbean and in Brazil. In every village and urban neighborhood, the work of traditional healers and spiritual leaders continues. Even Islam and Christianity have to a large extent been Africanized. To millions, the nation-states and the governments that represent them are burdensome foreign impositions, some of their more notorious leaders, such as Mobutu and Nigeria's General Sani Abacha, merely taking up where the foreign rules left off.

Today, Africa's national frontiers are violated every day by men, women, and children who circumvent the formal borders to carry on with their business activities and family responsibilities as best they can. The lack of a secure environment in which to work, crumbling infrastructures and educational institutions, and the dearth of confidence that investments today will bring rewards tomorrow have pushed the bulk of Africa's economic activity underground into the so-called informal market. It is perhaps not registered in the annual calculations of gross national product but it is the true engine of day-to-day life all the same. There is perhaps no greater testament to the continent-wide vote of no-confidence in the formal institutions of state and government than the propensity to turn to the informal market.

Claude Ake pointed out that 60 percent of sub-Saharan Africa's people are still rural, and they define their values and interests not in terms of individuality but of communality:

... freedom is embedded in the realities of communal life; people worry less about their rights and how to secure them than finding their station and its duties and they see no freedom in mere individualism. Their sense of freedom is not framed by tensions between the individual and the collectivity or the prospects of securing immunities against the collectivity. Nor is it defined in terms of autonomy or opposition but rather in terms of co-operation and in the embeddedness of the individual in an organic whole ... Participation rests not on the assumption of individuality but on the social nature of being and the organic character of society. Always, it is as much a matter of taking part as of sharing, sharing the burdens and rewards of community membership. It does not simply enjoin rights, it secures concrete benefits. It is not simply an occasional opportunity to signify approval or disapproval of people who exercise power on our behalf; it entails the exercise of power, however small or symbolic.[5]

It would be unrealistic to argue that the nations of Africa attempt to turn back the clock to some past idyll to seek their salvation. After all, if the precolonial order was so healthy, it should have stood up more effectively against foreign interference. If all traditional chiefs were so concerned about the fate of their people, why did so many willingly participate in the slave trade? And yet, it is just as unrealistic to maintain that Africa's future generations have nothing to learn from their forefathers. When Africa finally begins its march toward prosperity and security, as it almost certainly will one day, the key ingredients will come not from Washington, London, or Tokyo; they will be homegrown. In any society, representative government and economic development must sprout from deep roots in the soil of local culture because only in that way will its people feel that they are part of it, that they have contributed to it, and that they have a reasonable chance of benefitting from it.

However disadvantaged at independence, however deep the spiritual wounds of the slave trade, however illogical the colonial borders, and however tight a grip the former imperial powers maintain over the economies, postindependent Africa should be in much better shape. The political leaders who took over from the colonial authorities were not forced to pursue policies of extravagant self-enrichment at the expense of their people and ultimately their countries. There were and are other choices to be made, other paths to be followed.

The momentum for change is building. A new generation of leaders, including Ugandan President Yoweri Museveni and the *madiba* himself, Mandela, is pushing aside the old discredited and often corrupt postcolonial leadership. They are laying the groundwork for the emergence of an arc of good government and prosperity stretching from Eritrea in the northeast down through Central Africa and linking up with South Africa.

The elder statesman Nyerere now sees hope on the horizon. "A new leadership is developing in Africa . . . the military phase is out. I think the single-party phase is out," Nyerere said in August 1996.[6] The reasons for such optimism are many. The end of the cold war has freed Africa from a distracting and often painful involvement in the ideological battles between East and West; a majority of African countries have initiated reform programs to open up their economies to the outside world; and the twisted apartheid system of racial domination in South Africa has given way to a multiracial democracy that enjoys widespread legitimacy. The challenges of massive unemployment, poor education for the majority, and worsening levels of crime are daunting, but the change in South Africa gives new hope for southern Africa, with a potential market of 130 million people and a treasure trove of essential resources—from coal to diamonds, gold, hydroelectric power, oil, and vast tracts of arable land.

The eighteen-year civil war in Mozambique, surely one of Africa's most destructive conflicts in the continent's poorest country, came to an end with United Nations–monitored elections taking place in an atmosphere of remarkable calm. Millions of civilians have been able to return to their homes in relative peace while the former armed adversaries, the Frelimo government and the Renamo rebels, face each other in parliament rather than on the battlefield.

Likewise, decades-old dictatorships have fallen in a number of countries, from Mali in West Africa to Malawi in the east, and tiny Benin has witnessed a peaceful transition from one elected government to another. Uganda has risen swiftly from the ashes left by the cruel dictatorship of Idi Amin and the ravages of the Acquired Immune Deficiency Syndrome (AIDS) and in Ethiopia and Eritrea, which were decimated in the 1980s by civil war and famine, there is relative peace.

The collapse of Mobutu sese Seko's kleptocracy in Zaire has removed a painful, embarrassing wound from Africa's collective consciousness. His ruinous administration, his support from the major Western powers, his sponsorship of a motley array of movements dedicated to undermining his neighbors, and his close involvement with those who led the genocide in Rwanda finally caught up with him. The lightning quick rebellion led by Laurent Désiré Kabila which drove out Mobutu in May 1997 and renamed Zaire the Democratic Republic of Congo is part of a political revolution sweeping across the face of Africa. The ease with which Kabila's army sliced through the Congo was due to two factors: popular revulsion at Mobutu's rule and pan-African support for the rebel cause. An unprecedented coalition of a dozen African countries, from Angola and Eritrea to South Africa and Zimbabwe, galvanized by Museveni and Rwanda's vice president and defense minister, Paul Kagame, decided it was time that Africa took its destiny in its own hands. They armed and trained Kabila's fighters and provided officers and troops to support them, and in six months they brought down the old tyrant. As Museveni commented after Mobutu's ouster, "The big hole in the middle of Africa has been filled up and now we can build roads from east to west. We want a common market from east to west and from South Africa to the west."[7]

A dream, perhaps, but there is the sense that the end of Mobutu's Zaire heralds a second chance for Africa. Within weeks of Mobutu's downfall, democracy activists in Kenya reignited their campaign against the authoritarian government of President Daniel Arap Moi, whom they immediately dubbed "Moi-butu."

Mandela put the new feeling of optimism this way. "I am convinced that our region and our continent have set out along the new road of lasting peace, democracy and social and economic development. The time has come for Africa to take full responsibility for her woes and use the immense collective wisdom it possesses to make a reality of the ideal of the African renaissance, whose time has come."[8]

New Roads Taken

From its robust market women reigning like queens over expansive open-air shops to the legions of tiny village children walking miles each morning to rural schools, from the crowds of lithe, muscular fishermen pushing wooden boats like stilettos out into the choppy morning seas to the tall, elegant nomads driving vast herds of cattle and goats across the savannahs, Africa is constantly on the move, always prepared to astonish, to amaze, and to leave anyone who cares to look close enough gasping in wonder at the sheer energy of life on display. Its people show a remarkable ability to transform themselves, to adapt as situations demand, and to embark in search of new solutions. That resilience explains in part their success at surviving, and in many cases thriving, despite the harsh economic and political climate that envelopes most of the continent.

Every day, from all walks of life spring modern-day pacesetters who are pointing the way toward a progressive future. They symbolize the best qualities of the African personality: compassion, innovation, belief in the preeminence of the community over the individual, artistic brilliance, and the talent to face and overcome obstacles and to take advantage of opportunities that have come their way. Unfortunately, the obstacles, whether in the form of poor educational facilities, lack of money to start a business, or stifling bureaucracy and corrupt governments, too often outweigh the opportunities. Yet when the breaks do come, it is rare to find that someone has not moved quickly to capitalize on them.

Chinua Achebe, the astute Nigerian writer, has ascribed the tragedy of his country, and by extension of the whole of Africa, to "simply and squarely a failure of leadership."[1] He is referring, of course, to the political leaders who filled the shoes of the departing European governors at independence and eagerly took up residence in the same colonial state houses vacated by their predecessors. The basic structures of the European-created nation-states remain unchanged, designed more to exploit their citizens than to serve them. The new rulers slipped easily into the patterns of the old: denial of human and democratic rights, corruption, divide and rule tactics. Left out of the equation have been the ordinary citizens who form a great reservoir of human initiative which Africa so desperately needs to tap. As Achebe's countryman, Professor Adebayo Adedeji, the former executive secretary of the United Nations Economic Commission for Africa, has put it, "What has become embarrassingly clear, after three decades and more after the attainment of independence by the majority of African countries, is that the generality of our people have been excluded from any significant contribution to the determination of national directions."[2]

Enterprising contributors to the general welfare do exist everywhere in Africa, however. They may not be in the presidential palaces or parliaments, and their impact may not always make newspaper headlines. Yet in their own small ways, they have decided to cast off the debilitating pall of resignation that Africa's so-called Big Man leaders, its poverty and underdevelopment, and its recent history of civil wars and ethnic strife have done so much to promote.

This chapter describes the lives of four outstanding African pioneers: a Zimbabwean sculptor; a Nigerian computer specialist; a university professor caring for the elderly in Ghana; and a young South African medical doctor thrust into the role of Zulu chief. They have become trailblazers, convinced that Africa can make its own way on its own terms.

JORAM MARIGA never left home without his pocket knife. When he was not working as a government agricultural worker, he could usually be found whittling away on some piece of scrapwood that he picked up while riding his motorcycle along the myriad trails that wind through the majestic mountains of eastern Zimbabwe. He was always cutting, chipping, slicing, and shaping wood, something he and his brothers had been doing since they were teenagers. Enjoyment of crafts, of working with the hands, ran in the family. His mother Edina was particularly gifted at pottery, but it was Mariga's father Sindoga who stirred their interest in carving. "We grew up loving to carve, and I did it just to please myself," Mariga says. He taught his two best friends, Robert and Titus, to carve, too.

Mariga was a worker for the Ministry of Agriculture in the mid-1950s in Nyanga, a picturesque region of stunning peaks, forests, lakes, and waterfalls straddling the border with Mozambique, to help small farmers improve their crop production. As he journeyed up and down the hills on his government-issued BSA 350 cc motorcycle, it became apparent that what the area and its farmers needed most were roads. "There were only tracks and only a few were big enough to be called roads. It was difficult for the small farmers to bring their produce to the markets." Mariga took charge of a work gang of forty men and two tractors to clear a road to the district administrator's office. "The tractors just plowed along, pushing all the stones to one side. I never thought anything about them. They were rocks."

Then, one cool sunny day in August 1958, at the base of a rocky outcrop known as a *kopje*, the grader blades chipped off a piece of a remarkable stone that caught Mariga's eye. "I admired the color of that small stone. It was greenish, and when you picked it up, you could feel that it was slippery, like soap. I didn't know what it was, and I had never seen anything like it. If you looked through it facing the rays of the sun, it was a little bit translucent." Only later did he learn that he had found a piece of soapstone. Mariga continued with the job of clearing the road that day, but he could not stop fiddling with the stone. As usual, when it was time for a break, out came his knife. "I decided, since it is so slippery, why can't I use my pocket knife on it? And when I did, the knife was able to cut it easily."

From that moment on, Mariga, at the age of thirty-one, became obsessed with stone carving, a fixation that over the next four decades would spawn one of the most exciting movements in modern African art. It took years and almost a divine amount of luck and coincidence to develop, but when it did, the sculpture from Zimbabwe would be exhibited all over the world and would fetch tens of thousands of dollars per piece on the international market. The sculptors themselves were transformed from largely illiterate farmers and unemployed workers to ambassadors for their country and their continent.

To hear Mariga, now a graying but still energetic seventy-year-old, tell the story, the beginning of the sculpture movement was the most natural thing in the world. That is not to suggest that Mariga is a humble man. A glow of personal satisfaction fills his face when he insists that the details of each stage of the art's development be remembered accurately. He is filled with pride, too, when he describes how the new movement's ultimate goal is to preserve Zimbabwean culture.

What he does not dwell on, however, is the fact that the phenomenal success of the sculpture movement is due in large part to his own persistence and unique love of carving, a passion he developed way before he knew that it might bring any monetary rewards. "When I found it was possible to carve this type of stone, I said to myself, 'Why not roam about in the nearby area and find a much bigger piece?' I was lucky, because right in the same area I discovered a deposit of that soapstone. I found one piece weighing over five pounds, so I tied it to the back of my BSA 350 and dragged it home. That is how it began. Every Sunday, I would leave my house and look for more stone. And then I began carving. I tried all sorts of things—utensils, bowls, and small figures. During that time I began carving octagonal bowls."

Mariga and his friends Titus and Robert continued to carve, mainly to pass the time. Most of their pieces ended up with friends and relatives since Mariga never thought they were worth anything. Titus had other ideas, however. He hauled some of the wood carvings over to Troutbeck, a popular tourist area, to see if he could find anyone to buy them. At the time, African art and curios were not the popular consumer items that they would become two decades later. Zimbabwe was still known as Rhodesia, a racially segregated British colony run by a tiny minority of bigoted whites whose forefathers had been part of a column of invaders from South Africa led by the British empire builder, Cecil Rhodes, eighty years before in search of gold and land. A more reactionary place would have been difficult to find. By all accounts, Rhodesia in the 1950s was a cultural backwater, except for traditional African dance, music, and crafts, which the white rulers discouraged as best they could.

Even the spectacular granite stone ruins at Great Zimbabwe in the southeast of the country outside the city of Masvingo were attributed to the work of foreigners. Africans could not have built them, the reasoning went. At its height, Great Zimbabwe served as the capital of a Shona empire ruled over by the sovereign Mwene Mutapa in the fourteenth and fifteenth centuries. *Dzimba Dzemabwe*, or the house of stone, was the largest stone structure in sub-Saharan Africa. The breadth of its international trading network is suggested by the fragments of Chinese dishes from the Ming dynasty that archeologists have found at the site. Among the artifacts uncovered at Great Zimbabwe were ceremonial birds, which after independence Zimbabwe adopted as its national symbol. The birds were carved out of soapstone.

As luck would have it, when Titus reached Troutbeck, he met Pat Pearce, the wife of a local white farmer in the Nyanga area who was working with peasant women to produce and market carpets and crafts to earn some extra money for their families. Pearce was obviously unusual among whites for her interest in African culture. (She was later deported to England as a political undesirable by Ian Smith's hard-line Rhodesian Front government in 1971.) But when Pearce saw the wooden pieces, she immediately bought a few and asked Titus where he had learned to carve. Joram Mariga, he said. Could Titus put her in contact with Mariga? He said he would try, but Mariga was not too keen on talking with outsiders.

By then, the political situation in Rhodesia was heating up, with the first significant stirrings of African nationalism in more than half a century facing an intensified clampdown by the white minority government. As the atmosphere worsened, Mariga, like many Africans, wanted as little to do with whites as possible. He was noncommittal when Titus pestered him about showing some of his work to Pearce.

"That was a time when politics was leading to fighting," he says. "People were quarreling about political things, and I was not interested. I didn't want to be involved. I decided I would try to talk to her without meeting her face-to-face. So I went over to the Star Store, which was nearby, and asked for the telephone directory. I found a number for Mr. and Mrs. Pearce, one-six-one-two. I rang her up, and she asked me what my carvings were made of. I told her stone. She said, 'No, there is not a single person in Rhodesia who carves in stone,'" Mariga recalls, still with a hint of irritation at her skepticism. "I replied, 'Well, that is what you know, but I have things made out of stone right in front of me.'"

Pearce used to drive to the area once a week with two of her friends who were helping local women with their crafts, and they agreed to meet. Mariga showed her some of his stone pieces, and she asked if she could take a few back to her home. "The following morning she rang the Star Store and asked someone to fetch me. When I picked up the phone, she asked if I could go with her to Salisbury. I said, 'Yes, but no. Yes, because I don't see why I cannot go with you, but no because I am employed. I can't go without permission.'" The permission Mariga needed was not only for time off work, but to travel with a white woman whom he did not know. Luck intervened again when the "native commissioner," a Mr. Reed, who happened to be somewhat enlightened, approved the trip.

What Mariga had no way of knowing at the time was that just before he discovered the malleability of soapstone, the Rhodesian government had decided to set up a national art gallery in Salisbury, as Zimbabwe's capital Harare was then known, to display the works of the European masters. The authorities hired an eccentric Mexican-born Briton, Frank McEwen, a highly respected authority on art, as a consultant on building the gallery. McEwen's parents were both art collectors, and as a young boy he had been exposed to West African sculpture in the form of statues from Nigeria and Ghana, which his father owned. When studying at the Sorbonne in the 1930s, he befriended artists then at the Ecole de Paris, such as Picasso and Matisse, whose works had been deeply influenced by West African sculpture.

West Africa was the birthplace of a sculptural tradition in sub-Saharan Africa that dates back at least two and a half millennia. Terracotta figures discovered at a tin mine in the northern Nigerian village of Nok are believed to have been produced around 450 B.C. Ranging between four inches and four feet in height, the human faces portrayed in the figures are large and highly stylized, while the rest of the body and the limbs are generally simplistic.[3]

Another major sculptural style that produced terracotta and bronze casting, and one that many believe was a successor to the Nok, emerged sometime around the sixth century A.D. in the southern Nigerian city of Ifè, the spiritual home of the Yoruba people. Together, the Nok and Ifè traditions were the only two known in Africa that attempted to produce human forms in terracotta sculpture in near life-size proportions.[4]

African art began to make a major impression on the world scene by 1904–05. Among the first to impress Europeans were the so-called Benin Bronzes, which had been seized by the British Royal Navy when it sacked the city of Benin in southern Nigeria in 1897. Soon after, African masks and carvings caught the imagination of some of the major European artists of the day. Maurice Vlaminck wrote that when he showed André Derain a mask he had received as a gift, Derain was "speechless" and "stunned." Derain bought the mask from him and showed it to Picasso and Matisse. For some specialists, this and other similar encounters with African carvings and sculptures exposed these artists to novel forms of expressionism, style, and asymmetry, which sparked the beginning of the revolution in twentieth-century European art.[5] Picasso's *Demoiselles d'Avignon* of 1907 has been seen as a major first signpost of Africa's impact on his technique.[6] Another of McEwen's acquaintances at the Ecole, Georges Braque, once said that African masks had "opened a new horizon for me."[7]

Fifty years later, a new revolution in African art was about to be unveiled to the world. When the British Queen Mother inaugurated the Rhodes National Gallery in 1957, McEwen became its first director. He had come to Africa in search of art "still little contaminated by the West," and personally funded a workshop at the new gallery for Africans to experiment with painting—a radical, and to some a subversive, concept in Rhodesia. The gallery's inaugural exhibition, entitled "From Rembrandt to Picasso," contained a small section that placed works by Picasso and other Parisian artists next to African carvings to demonstrate the impact of African art on the European masters.[8]

As soon as Pearce and Mariga arrived in Salisbury in April 1962, they went to see McEwen at the national gallery. McEwen looked over a few of Mariga's pieces and bought a bowl for £10 (about $20). "This stimulated me a lot," Mariga remembers. "My salary during that time was about seven pounds per month, so it was quite a lot of money to me. From that day, I decided to use any free weekends and public holidays to sculpt." The next year he made the jump into stylized art with his soapstone piece *Tall Man*.

His immediate quandary, though, was how to scour the Nyanga Hills for more soapstone while avoiding close encounters with the local wildlife. "Around Mika hills there were nice stones, but there was only one village in the area, and there used to be all sorts of animals, like lions. It was impossible for a person to go alone." He talked his friend Eric into taking up sculpting as well, but they had no transport to move the bigger pieces. Mariga overcame that problem by convincing a driver at a local bus company to use his vehicle to bring them down from the hills. "At first he asked, 'Are you mad?' Then he agreed, and said he would bring them as far as the Star Store. From there, Eric and I used our bikes to bring them home—one-two, one-two."

Later that year, Mariga founded a stone-sculpting school in Nyanga, and it grew quickly to include forty-six people. "They were mainly young farmers who had not done very well in their studies. It gave them something to do." Some of those early students eventually became master sculptors, including people such as Chispen Chakanyuka, and Mariga's nephew John Takawira, who was once arrested while carrying a load of rocks by Rhodesian policemen who thought he was planning violent subversive activities. One can only imagine how they responded when he explained he needed them for his sculpting classes. John's younger brothers Bernard and Lazarus later joined him among Zimbabwe's artistic elite.

Using his contacts abroad, including Picasso's promoter Daniel-Henry Kahnweiler,[9] McEwen was able to attract the attention of the international art community to the development of stone sculpture in Rhodesia. At home, the movement spread like a bush fire. "Everyone was whispering the gospel of stone sculpture," Mariga says.

His student Chakanyuka left the Nyanga school to return home and became the major source of inspiration to a second colony in northern Zimbabwe, situated in a remote spot atop the Zambezi river valley escarpment. It is called *Tengenenge,* which in Shona means "the beginning of the beginning." The community sprang up at the edge of an old chrome mine owned by Tom Bloomfield, a chubby white tobacco farmer. Rhodesia's declaration of unilateral independence from Britain in 1964—in the mistaken belief that it would ensure the continuance of white rule for one thousand years—and the international sanctions that followed in response had bankrupt Bloomfield and left his tobacco workers jobless.

Chakanyuka suggested the alternative of stone carving, and he knew just where to find a virtually unlimited supply of the type of stone, such as black serpentine, they needed. The *Tengenenge* school started in an area that was a stronghold of the nationalist guerrillas loyal to the Zimbabwe African National Union (Zanu), whose leader, Robert Mugabe, would become the country's first elected prime minister at independence in 1980, and later state president. Yet the colony was never attacked during the war. (It has continued functioning into the 1990s.)

Mariga remained in Nyanga until 1972 and was eventually asked to teach classes in crafts at the Young Farmers Association of Manicaland province. He retired in 1988 to work full time as a sculptor. McEwen left Rhodesia in 1973, and the sculpture movement flagged during the last years of the independence war, before picking up again after the first democratically elected government took power in 1980.

Originally, the movement was dubbed "Shona sculpture," reflecting the culture of Zimbabwe's biggest ethnic group, and it illustrated the heavy influence of traditional religious preoccupations with the ancestral spirits, taboos, and the Shona supreme god *Mwari.* Yet it included artists from neighboring countries, such as Mozambique, Malawi, and Zambia, and the name it acquired after independence, "Zimbabwean sculpture," like "Shona sculpture" before it, has always been somewhat of a misnomer. The sculpture movement has skyrocketed in popularity, especially abroad. Exhibitions of the sculptures have toured the major world capitals, and even though some of the best sculptors are illiterate and work in their bare feet in the bush, some of them have become fabulously wealthy. Pieces can fetch up to $50,000 on the world market.

With the increase in fame and potential for economic gain, however, has come a flood of lesser artists who mass-produce crafts for the tourist market. There has been a virtual explosion of tourist-oriented crafts, including everything from the imitation stone sculpture known as "airport art" to painting, weaving, and pottery. That this is the case should be little surprise.

Like much of Africa, Zimbabwe has taken the medicine of "structural adjustment," a catchall name for the strict austerity measures designed by international creditors such as the World Bank and the International Monetary Fund, to deal with mounting foreign debt and worsening balance-of-payments situations. Since the mid-1980s, the Mugabe government began to reverse its economic course, moving from more socialist to largely free market policies. It lifted food subsidies, cut expenditure on health and education, removed tariffs on foreign imports, and reduced government payrolls. However much the reforms have been lauded by international creditors, the overall result for the large majority of Zimbabweans has been a sharp decline in living standards, with higher prices, unemployment, and homelessness. The craft industry, much of it still informal, became an avenue of survival for the poor. Dozens of little roadside craft colonies and retailers have sprung up all over the country in recent years to cater to visiting tourists from Europe and South Africa.

Such developments in part explain the desire of the more serious sculptors to move toward using harder stone to prevent the airport artists from copying their work. Mariga, for example, has been especially keen to work with harder rock, and he was among the first to use lilac-colored lepidolite and leopard stone. The artists also share a fear of the creeping Westernization of Zimbabwean society and an obsession with preserving their culture in stone. "There has been a big change in recent years. Many of the young sculptors are falling under European influence," Mariga says. "There is a lot of this airport art. They are copying white people."

The sculptors in Zimbabwe have always differed from their counterparts in the West, in that they never make sketches beforehand, and unlike their ancient cousins in the Nok and Ifè traditions, they do not add material to the rock. Instead, they approach the stone directly and carve from the outside in. Many believe that the shape of the sculpture is already in each stone and that the process of sculpting is simply one of liberating the form hidden inside.

From a distance, Mariga's home in an eastern suburb of Harare looks like a rock quarry, and on closer inspection an outdoor art gallery. The driveway is filled with blocks of rock and sculptures. What used to be the garage has been converted into an open-air workshop, where Mariga's wife Maude and his son Walter work on their latest pieces. Chisels and hammers beat out a constant rhythm of creativity. "Maude is also sculpting, and some of her pieces resemble my work. Of course, everybody knows that like begets like," Mariga says. "But if you look carefully, for instance, at the eyes, the ears, the nose, the mouth, they are not similar to my work. This is her own style."

Individual style is so important to the sculptors, and it is one of the reasons they so bitterly resent the airport art. No two pieces should be copied, and the harder the stone one uses, the safer it is from the poachers, the more lasting one's work will be, the more immortal the message, the more enduring the culture. The pride springs to life again when Mariga talks about his son. "Straight away Walter started to sculpt in hard stones. He has some in leopard stone, springstone, and now he has gone into working with dolomite, which is very hard."

Mariga's works are remarkably practical in their approach. Unlike some of his contemporaries, he does not seem to dwell too much on the spiritual world, although it is there, as evidenced by a tall piece in green serpentine, with an elongated head and rough flowing lines down its left side, which he calls *Communicating with the Earth Spirit.* When asked if he ever portrays spirits, he literally snaps back, "Have you ever seen a spirit? I don't know what one looks like."

Standing in front of another piece in springstone with an exaggeratedly long snout, he says, laughing, "It means somebody who talks too much. I have indicated someone who talks a bit with the long mouth." Another is a figure crouched down as if it were expecting to receive a beating. "This one here I have called *Take Cover*. It's in the hiding position. Next to these two, I have *Tatenda*, which means 'thank you' in Shona. It's an animal which has come across an enemy but managed to escape. So you see its two hands are clasped together in order to thank God."

Mwari, the Shona god, is a common theme in Mariga's works. One piece, which depicts the pain of drought that has been a constant and recurring enemy to Zimbabwe's farmers, is called *Mwarianiasum—God Is with Us*. "I did it for the drought. For a couple of years there was no food for quite a lot of people. But then the following season was a better one. So, first of all the person was thin, but then with the good season the stomach started to swell up." He moves along and bows down to another piece, explaining in detail like a teacher what he has in mind. "That is called *Moriavarusoka*. You can see this is the mother, and the son, they are standing together and the mother is holding the son. At the back here are the feet of the father. My son says that these feet have never worn shoes. They are typical natural feet."

Mariga's own brand of naturalism is pivotal to his sculpture. Despite what to an outsider appear to be extraordinarily big heads, to Mariga this represents reality, a reality that must be depicted accurately for future generations. He explains his thinking this way: "The sense of the mouth must be big enough. I discourage my wife and children from carving tiny little mouths. The reason why is that the people in Zimbabwe and the whole of Africa live on *sadza* [corn meal porridge] and *nyama* [meat]. So the mouth should be big enough. Although sculptures are stones, if we were to be given the powers of God to put some brains in this sculpture, we would need a fair amount of room to put in the brain. All sculptures should have big heads, eyes, ears, nose, because say God could put life into these sculptures, we would need to have things that make for a good life— more room for the brain, reasonably big eyes for them to see, and fair ears for them to hear. For in Zimbabwe sculpture, if we want to show the way we Shona people feel and the way we live, we should have sculptures with big eyes, big mouth, big everything. And also limbs should be tied together with the body so that they don't chip off. As soon as we start to sculpt, we are making history, so we don't want to confuse the coming generation by telling them that there was a generation of people who were a composition of heads only.

"Or that there was," he finishes with a mischievous smirk, "a generation of people living in Zimbabwe with tiny mouths only good for sucking juice."

HALF A CONTINENT away in the giant West African nation of Nigeria, Seni Williams is a different sort of creator—one who works in the complex world of silicon chips, megabytes, and microprocessors. Williams is a world-class computer software developer in the most unlikely of settings, Lagos, the sprawling Nigerian commercial capital. Lagos has never been known as a friendly environment for the growth of high-technology industry, and in recent years, of any industry at all. After a decade of steep economic decline, due in part to the collapse of the world oil market in the early 1980s and in part to the greediness of its own rulers, Lagos's infrastructure has imploded. Any company operating there must contend with power cuts, water shortages, high crime rates, and a telephone system that creaks on the best of days. A 1990 World Bank study of 179 firms found that 92 percent supplied their own electricity, 63 percent dug their own wells, and 37 percent relied on their radio and telephone systems. Yet in such an atmosphere, Williams and his computer company, TARA, are thriving.

The reason is relatively simple. The economic instability of Nigeria, which closely mirrors its political crisis, has forced Williams to develop a highly flexible software package for his main clients in the banking sector precisely because they never know what is going to happen from day to day. And they have to be ready. The so-called Nigerian factor, that great spirit of chaos which has thwarted the best-laid plans of most businesspeople, helped to push TARA to the front ranks of software development. "In Nigeria, you can never predict tomorrow or what the Central Bank is going to do," Williams says. "This is the key thing. Tomorrow the Central Bank, through their own disorder, may just say, 'We want to know all the people who have this, that, and the other profile.' And if you do not give it to them in the next forty-eight hours, they will shut you down. The 'Nigerian factor' is the ability to change like a chameleon. Survive. It's a Nigerian trait. But now that is becoming a global requirement."

For most of his life, Williams, a shy, soft-spoken man in his forties, remained relatively shielded from the problems of Nigeria. Born into a wealthy family, his accountant father sent him to boarding school in Britain, and by the age of twelve he was already working with computers. He was a natural. After graduating from university, Williams was hired by the international computer firm ICL. He later moved on to Price Waterhouse and eventually joined a consulting firm in Boston, where he met his future American wife, Diane. He could have remained in the United States or Britain, as tens of thousands of educated Nigerians and Africans have done, but he felt he needed a challenge. After twenty-three years abroad, Williams decided to return to Africa. Consulting jobs took him to Ivory Coast, Swaziland, Kenya, and Cameroon, before he settled in Lagos.

"It was partly out of parental pressure, but also I did not really like the concept of living in the UK anymore," Williams says in the living room of his Lagos home, which routinely suffers power outages and water shortages. "I had had enough, and I felt it was a good time to come." He laughs at his own naïveté. "Tactically it was the wrong time for anybody to think about coming back here. It was 1983, the beginning of the end for Nigeria. It was the end of the oil boom, the collapse of everything. And we basically came back into a revision of military rule. We sort of saw the last of the civilians, and it has been military rule since. But Diane really encouraged us to stay and make what we could of the place. I think it was a very good decision."

Seni and Diane bought an existing local computer-consulting company, TARA, which was in effect broke but had a valuable list of clients, especially in the banking sector. "As far as we could see, it did not look like a computer company, but it was still carrying out related work. We set about infusing a computer culture in the company and building up a systems integration firm that deals not only in software but in all the different aspects of the computer industry to deliver solutions to people. That is why we find ourselves in communications, networking, software. We sell a bit of hardware, not very much. But we are a very big computer user ourselves. We put together complete working systems, and models of systems."

Three years after their takeover of TARA came their big break, the signature of a cooperation agreement with the California-based Oracle Corporation, the number two software company in the world. The deal allowed TARA access to Oracle's valuable software and pushed it to think ahead. "Oracle changed TARA. Oracle never rests, it just keeps changing and changing, and I think that has driven us along. The momentum that Oracle gave TARA culturally is that this is a business that never sleeps. Either you keep up or fall behind. So, as a company, we were forced to keep up with what was going on internationally."

Nigeria's banks enjoy a well-deserved reputation for being among the most mismanaged in the world. Frequent changes of the banking rules by the military regime make the concept of planning a dubious one. For TARA, that meant that it has been forced to take the Oracle software and improve upon it, with the premium on simplicity and flexibility. As it turns out, rather than proving an impediment to success as it has with so many other industries, Nigeria actually has provided the right environment for TARA, both in the demands of the banking sector and cheap labor costs. "To do what we did here would literally cost millions of dollars in the United States. We have cheaper labor, computer programmers, designers. Typically the price for a software person here is about four thousand dollars per annum. In the States the same quality of person goes for eighty thousand, and you need about fifteen to twenty of them to build anything very large, and you need them for some years. You also have to invest in infrastructure. And in our case, Oracle has made a sizable investment, four hundred thousand to five hundred thousand, to buy the software that we use. We got that for nothing."

But there are many downsides to working in Nigeria. Besides the problems of ensuring a constant supply of electricity, much of TARA's equipment needs have to be imported, and for years tariffs on computers were extremely high. And because computers have been regarded by the Central Bank as nonessential items, obtaining the necessary foreign exchange in times of hard currency rationing has been difficult. Ironically, that too played into Williams's hands. At first, TARA wrote software for specific banks, but quickly realized it needed a product for the general market. That brought the company into fierce competition with international banks until the "Nigerian factor" kicked in. When the value of the national currency, the *naira*, plummeted, foreign software packages became too expensive for local banks to purchase. "As the private banks grew in number here, the exchange rate got worse and worse. What it did provide was a growing market and one that was more favorably disposed to buying local products because of the cost of importing competitive systems." Soon TARA's products were serving 20 percent of the domestic banking industry.

Under pressure from the needs of its Nigerian clients, and armed with Oracle's software base, TARA continued to develop until it produced a system called Auto-Bank. Fortunately, banking outside the country, in Africa as well as in Europe and the United States, was undergoing tremendous change as well. After a major contract in Slovakia, TARA expanded into Ghana, Benin, and Sierra Leone, and the giant American company ATT has been collaborating in developing the system for the United States. "The attraction of our system is the fact that we do not fix a particular kind of account that you can have," Williams says. "A bank can decide to create a new type of account and they don't have to reprogram the system. What we allow banks to do is dynamically create their own accounts. It may be for just one person. They can tailor their products much more closely to their customer."

Although Williams does not say so, it seems clear that part of what has made him so successful in Nigeria dissuades other potential competitors who lack trust in the stability of the system and the capriciousness of the military rulers. Few businesspeople are willing to make the investment of several million dollars, or to borrow the capital that is necessary to "reach critical mass, to break out of the retaining wall," as he puts it.

There are other problems. In education as in business as in market trading, Nigeria has become a society of short-term desperation, in which the desire for immediate gratification has outstripped the commitment to long-term development. "There is no training or retraining of people for tomorrow," Williams points out. "Everyone is just stagnating. Young Nigerians have been bitten by the same bug. At my company, I will say, Okay, pick anywhere in the world you want and go on a training course. They aren't interested. You have to force these people to go on training because they feel that once they have a certain amount of knowledge, that's it. The ability to recover your investment is just unknown. The computer industry is a business in which every six months you have to dump everything you knew and start again. I think the motivational factors for people to keep learning, and relearning, are just not there. When they go back home, there is no power, there is no water, there is noise, there is pollution, there is a security problem that is immense, just to get home in one piece. Then they come to work, there is traffic, and there are the same problems. It's continual assault on people."

These impediments have created a cultural problem, Williams believes. "A trader settles down at the end of the road selling oranges, and within two days another trader is selling exactly the same thing, and then there are three, four, five, a whole row of them. The only thing that happens is that the price goes down, so none of them win, and they all end up with a surplus. Yet two streets away there is nobody selling oranges. Nigerians are myopic."

When Williams looks at his potential market, his ambitions are clearly Pan-African. TARA cannot survive if it relies solely on the Nigerian market because that market is too small for the company to recover its investment in hardware and training. "There is the whole of Africa," he says. "We say to ourselves, what if our banking system was running in every single branch in every single bank in Africa? You don't need America, you don't need Europe. Because Africa is by far a big enough market. We see tremendous potential for the right kind of product in the right kind of price range. With PCs and the software which is available for not very much money, this is the right time to strike."

LIKE SENI WILLIAMS, when Nana Apt maps out her strategy for the future, she looks to Africa. Her concern is not so much with modern technology and potential markets, but their impact on society's weaker members. Hers is the business of compassion. Apt, a fifty-year-old sociology lecturer at the University of Legon on the edge of the Ghanaian capital, Accra, is obsessed with devising ways to ensure the care of the fountains of cultural wisdom, the elderly, who are being discarded in Africa's headlong rush to capitalist economics and Western materialism.

"Many governments and many people, when you talk of aging, say, 'This is not a problem. In Africa we look after the elderly.' But these people are simply not looking at reality," says Apt, a former president of the African Gerontological Society and founding member of the Ghanaian chapter of Help Age, a nongovernmental organization that cares for the aged. She is right. The worsening plight of the elderly can be seen in the streets of cities all across Africa. What would have been unthinkable just a decade ago has become a fact of daily life. Growing numbers of old people have become homeless derelicts, wandering around in apparent confusion at the modern buildings sprouting up and the cars and trucks whizzing past them.

Africa used to be one of the world's best places to grow old. Those who reached an advanced age were secure in the knowledge that the young would take care of them. That insurance policy was summed up in the Ghanaian proverb: "If your elders take care of you while cutting your teeth, you must in turn take care of them when they are losing theirs." For centuries, advanced age has been regarded in traditional religious terms as a blessing, and the elderly were revered as sacred, the holders of wisdom and culture, the crucial link between the living and the ancestors. Expressions for the elderly in West African languages often mean "he or she who knows" or "he or she who has vision." The aged held high status as mediators in family and village conflicts, and as experts on social problems, folklore, and family and ethnic traditions. They assumed senior positions on family councils, and in marriage, birth, and funeral ceremonies. They were the educators—and young Africa an immense classroom. Growing up in Africa was simply not complete without an extended stay with one's grandparents to learn the knowledge and the secrets that only years could provide. Within the African community, the aged held pride of place. A typical household consisted of multiple generations, creating a symbiotic relationship summed up by the proverb of the Akan people: "The hand of the child cannot reach the shelf nor can the hand of the elder get through the neck of the gourd on the shelf."

African attitudes toward the responsibility of caring for the aged drew on three basic principles: social recognition, reciprocity, and family solidarity. To ignore the elderly was to commit an unpardonable act of ingratitude, and the Western practice of placing one's parents in old-age homes was considered abhorrent, even barbaric. There was, of course, good reason for the moral stand. If children took care of their parents, grandparents, and aunts and uncles, then they too would be looked after by their offspring and relatives. Africa devised a privatized social security system and positioned it where it could be most effective and most caring: in the family and the community.

It is known as "the extended family," and in Africa it is the most important institution, for better or worse. In recent years, the extended family's reputation has taken a beating, decried by those, many Africans included, who believe that Africa must imitate the European and American models socially, culturally, politically, and above all economically, if it is to emerge from decades of economic decline and political crisis. The extended family, it is said, holds back individual initiative, such as the case of the young educated professional who could succeed if it were not necessary to send all his money back to his village relatives, and it promotes such ghastly trends as nepotism in the state bureaucracies. For the most part, that is all true.

But the extended family is also the bedrock of Africa's enduring humanity, battered, yes, but still holding on, which the Western world has all but lost, to the regret of increasing numbers of its people, in the insatiable drive for individualism. Besides, the extended family is capable of Herculean tasks. In 1983, when Nigeria ordered the overnight expulsion of at least 1 million Ghanaians, for example, they returned without the aid of the United Nations or any international relief agencies and disappeared back into their communities within weeks. Without the extended family, Ghana would have been the site of a major humanitarian disaster, most probably with tens of thousands of people remaining dependent on international food assistance for a generation. Anywhere else in the world, such an achievement would have been almost unthinkable. In many countries today, the extended family is the last line of defense against the wave of orphans caused by AIDS.

Today, as with so much of African society, times are changing, and in the extended family's treatment of the elderly, radically so. The growing influence of Western-style education, free market economics, and accelerated rural to urban migration has placed Africa's traditional extended family under tremendous strain, and people's ability and in many cases their willingness to care for the elderly in jeopardy. With swelling numbers of young Ghanaians turning to American-style Christian evangelical churches, the worship of the ancestors has lost ground, and thus the intermediaries, the elderly, are no longer very important. Their knowledge of traditional culture has little place in a world where the ability to earn fast money has become the only skill worth cultivating.

Part of the blame for the elderly's deteriorating condition lies with Africa's gradual integration into the world economy. What centuries of the slave trade and the dislocation caused by colonial rule had failed to do—to break the backbone of African society and its central tenet of the primacy of the community over that of the individual—is being accomplished in a matter of years by the onset of full-fledged capitalist consumerism. The resulting economic strains of competing in a market economy have forced nuclear families to look after themselves first, and to think about their extended families second, if at all.

"I think it has been gradual, but it has been intensified within the past two decades," says Apt. "The trend worldwide, the end of the old world order as far as economics is concerned, has been difficult. Anti-inflation measures have affected those of us in the developing countries even more. And with it of course come problems of sustenance, because if one is not able to look after oneself, it is not also possible for people to extend care to their parents. The salaries they are getting do not keep them going, neither themselves nor their own immediate family. Now, it becomes easier for children to say, 'Look, I can't help the elderly,' because they themselves cannot even cope. They cannot even look after themselves with their so-called new modern salary. It's not like before, when you just went to the farm and picked whatever you needed. Now, it's the money economy, and what is important is the individual, not the greater community."

High birth rates and short life expectancies have meant that the elderly still constitute a small proportion of Africa's population, and the vast majority of them reside in the countryside. But with population growth rates slowing and medical care improving, the percentage of old people in Africa is expected to rise rapidly in the first quarter of the twenty-first century, at the time when increasingly neither the African family nor society is equipped to deal with them. In countries particularly hard hit by the AIDS epidemic, the elderly have had to turn back the years and reassume their role as head of households, as their sons and daughters have fallen to the virus and left their children as orphans. Even in countries where AIDS has not yet reached epidemic proportions, however, the proportion of elderly is on the rise. In Ghana, the percentage of people over sixty years was 4.2 percent in 1960 and is expected to reach 4.5 percent in the year 2000. By 2025, however, it should increase to 6.4 percent, with females consistently outnumbering males.

The tragedy of the elderly is on display just a few miles from Apt's home in Achimota, a suburb of Accra. Akuoko Dokwi and her fraternal twin sister Akwele stand unsteadily outside their rickety wooden shanty, taking a moment from their morning to gaze at the nonstop commotion of the Ghanaian capital, Accra, as if they are from another age. The scene to them is a bewildering one: gangs of youthful street hawkers wearing basketball shoes and baseball caps selling everything from cold drinks to toilet paper; battered buses jammed full of passengers careening around one corner; a massive traffic jam spewing out exhaust fumes at another.

"Modern world," Akwele sniffs, shaking her head and shuffling back toward the shack, which sits amid a dusty patch of barren land. In another place and another time, Akuoko and Akwele would be two gray-haired old ladies, for the most part enjoying the sunset of their lives, looked after by more youthful relatives and imparting the wisdom of their years to a new generation. Their fortunes have led them to a different reality, however. Their only signs of wealth are their sole companions, a few scrawny chickens, and even they are a burden. There is not much to feed them, except scraps from their own meals and from the nearby garbage dump. Because of thieves roaming the neighborhood, the chickens have to stay in a fragrant coop inside the hovel. Prime responsibility for looking after the homestead and their meager worldly possessions falls to Akuoko, who is slightly bigger and healthier than Akwele. In truth there is not much to do, but with their advanced age, it is all they can handle. "When I get up in the morning, I sweep the house and clean the chicken coop," Akuoko says. "Our rooms are full of mosquitos, and we do not have enough money for food. We have no one to help us. A few friends from the neighborhood used to come around with some food, but they have died, so we are alone again."

Life already seems hard enough. Akuoko and Akwele are both seventy years old and are living alone. They are the last in their immediate family line. Akwele had two children, but they died in their infancy, and her husband abandoned her. They cannot return to their village because no one knows them there. The two women have to remain in Accra and face a fast-changing world on their own. With no savings or means of support, Akuoko and Akwele stand delicately on an economic abyss, just a few short steps from homelessness and probable starvation. Caught between urban and rural Africa, ignored by a society in the process of abandoning the traditional value attached to the elderly, Akuoko and Akwele are geriatric orphans when they should have been treated like charming old grannies.

Circumstances conspired against Akuoko and Akwele. Their father, Jato Dokwi, was born in the Upper West region but became an orphan at an early age. Eventually he married, and moved to Accra with his young wife Akua in search of work. While they were still young girls, their mother ran away with a younger man, and her memory remains a bitter one. The mere mention of her name brings a look of disgust to Akuoko's face, and they seem to hold her responsible for their move to Accra, which at best has been a mixed blessing.

As children, their father put them to work on his small farm near the Achimota cemetery and barred them from attending school. "Even when a teacher came to take us to school, he said,

'No. I will let my daughters do farming,'" Akwele says. If they had remained at their village and never come to Accra, today they would surely be living under the care of some younger relatives; and if their father had allowed them to study, perhaps they could have found jobs in the formal sector of the economy so that now they would be eligible for state pensions. But they had the worst of both worlds: no one to care for them and no pension.

"They do not have children or a means of sustenance," says Apt. "It's only those who worked in the formal sector that have pensions, and since most of the elderly worked in the informal sector, they have nothing." To deal with such cases, Apt and a handful of volunteers from the Christian Women's Association decided to take matters into their own hands. "Help Age was formed because a few of us observed that things are not going on as they should. We started to see elderly destitutes in the streets. This never happened before. In the big cities, Accra, Kumasi, you find them, old people begging. My forecast is that if we don't take care, in the next ten years you will find more old people begging in our streets. So we got together to look at this problem and see how we could help. And now what we are doing is thinking ahead. For example, we are discussing setting up day-care centers."

Veronica Ayisi, a youthful sixty-year-old Help Age volunteer, says that more than anything else what she and her colleagues are trying to do is to act as a substitute for the extended family. "We visit the elderly in their homes, we pray for them, we sing for them, we converse with them. Sometimes we sweep their rooms, wash their things, anything to make their lives more comfortable. It's a very difficult task because you have to be patient if they are old. They are a bit troublesome." That is one of the reasons young married couples are no longer prepared to live under one roof with the elderly. Another is that the young, often more culturally in tune with their contemporaries in London or New York, no longer have much time for their elders' traditional rural beliefs.

Add to the changing mentality at the family level the redirection of priorities at the national level: rising external debts and flagging national economies have forced governments to impose "structural adjustment programs" in an effort to please foreign creditors, and to attract investment. As a result, unemployment and prices have soared and basic services for the poor have deteriorated. Few countries in Africa have taken a stiffer dose of free market medicine than Ghana, a country that hoped to revive an economy driven by gold and cocoa, which had collapsed over the first two decades of independence from Britain.

President Jerry Rawlings's government has been held up as an African showcase by the International Monetary Fund (IMF) and the World Bank. But the arrival of the promised land of economic prosperity has been delayed in Ghana, despite international aid flows of some $500 million a year. Rawlings came to power in a military coup in 1981 as a young air force flight lieutenant preaching leftist revolutionary rhetoric. Within two years he shifted sharply rightward and embraced the capitalist economics of the IMF. Since then per capita income has grown at a lackluster 2 percent per year, a rate that would lift the poor above the poverty line in thirty years.[10] And the proportion of Ghana's population below that line is a massive 40 percent.[11] Even the middle classes have been strapped by the austerity measures. "Take-home pay no longer takes you home," Atta Nyamekye, vice president of the Association of Ghana Industries, says, shaking his head in disgust.

To all but a few Western economists, it seems that Ghana's designation as a model of economic reform is a false one. "We need a winner in Africa, and we are all hoping that Ghana is the one," admits one American diplomat in Accra. Such attitudes anger many Ghanaians. "Sometimes I feel that the World Bank needs Ghana more than Ghana needs the World Bank," says Apt. She and many other Africans have come to resent policies which have placed the continent's foreign debt obligations to international banks and governments ahead of the needs of the poor, especially women, children, and the elderly.

Few would argue for a return to the days when state control and rampant corruption and mismanagement brought the once prosperous Ghanaian economy to its knees. But there is general agreement that something is drastically wrong with a situation in which over one-third of the total export earnings depart immediately in the form of foreign debt payments, in essence canceling out the aid flows, and after a decade of structural adjustment, the formal sector of the economy employs just under 200,000 people in a population of 15 million. In a country that suffers from severe neglect in physical infrastructure and human capital, the government is reducing its capital investment.[12] All this in Africa's success story.

"The poor care of elderly people in Ghana is something that has come about as a result of the poor economic situation of the people," says Apt. "Old values are changing because of modernization, specifically education, migration, and industrialization. Because of education, we are getting newer skills and new forms of employment. People are moving as a result of the education they have received to other areas of work, migrating to urban centers, and leaving behind family members."

In her research, Apt finds that many of the elderly derelicts have in fact been rather negligent parents. "You usually find a lot of males falling into this category. They've fathered children, have not looked after them, and in their old age have no money and no one to take care of them. I have an example of an abandoned elderly person who was featured in the newspapers. This person was living in one of the suburbs of Accra, took ill, and was rushed to the hospital. When he was discharged and went home, the landlord did not want him back because he had not paid rent for a long time. And the children and other family members did not want to have anything to do with him because he had not done anything for them."

There was another case in which an elderly man needed a blood transfusion. A doctor tracked down one of his sons, a well-to-do businessman, but the man refused any help. "Who is my father?" he told the doctor. "He never cared for me and my mama, and I don't know him. Let him die." Apt cites these episodes as evidence of a dramatic change in attitudes. "Twenty years ago in a case involving a father who had not looked after his son or a daughter, the general view would be that you must look after your father because he fathered you, irrespective."

The crisis of the elderly in Africa will not go away, Apt believes, and African governments must take immediate action, by using measures such as tax breaks to help the extended family survive, so that the young can afford to fulfill their traditional role of caring for the aged. Simply promising that one day in the future economic deliverance will arrive is not enough.

For volunteers like Ayisi, the solution is to return to basics. "If you have children and look after them, it is a must that they have to look after you," she says. "Parents should bring forth two or three children, and look after them properly. Then in the future they can look after you."

Apt takes a longer view. "The wheels have turned, and there is no turning back," she says. "We can still support family members to look after their elderly, because many people are emotionally attached; people feel guilty that they are not able to look after their elderly. The solution is that young people in countries like ours should begin to look straight into the eye of aging with a sense of planning. Life has changed, and there is no point in saying I am going to have ten children and they are going to look after me. Because most likely the children would have migrated. Education makes you move, either out of the home of your own family, or even out of the country. And caring isn't just money. Sometimes you need someone to be there. So, everybody should prepare right from the onset for their own old age. Put something down because you might have to look after yourself. Plan to have a place to live, plan to invest, do something, but not to rely solely on your children. Because even if the children want to, they can't."

THERE'S NO BETTER symbol of modernizing Africa's past than Sibongile Zungu, a young woman who looks more bewildered than the stout cow being led into the small public square as an offering to her. A great roar erupts from a crowd of three hundred people as the beast saunters by, and Zungu, adorned with beads and amulets, smiles bashfully and bows her head in appreciation. It is not the first time that Zungu has been the center of attention, but she still seems somewhat embarrassed by all the singing, chanting, and dancing in her honor. For a moment she gazes toward the ground and shakes her head in wonder, no doubt pausing to think of her late husband, and then, as if suddenly awakening to her responsibilities, she looks up again and straightens her back with determination.

As her courtiers fan the heat from her face, bring her cool drinks, and listen to her every word while bending down on one knee and averting their eyes, groups of well-wishers compete for the presentation of the most attractive gift, the most inventive dance, the most moving song. One after another, processions of people—often barefoot and obviously dirt poor—bring money, cutlery, colorful clay pots, finely woven woolen shawls, even an electric fan. Women twice Zungu's age, and twice her size, wiggle their bottoms to the amusement of all; decrepit old men offer pumpkins and vegetables with trembling hands; and young men, who had they lived in another community would have been warriors at each other's throats with machetes and AK-47s, shout praises to her courage and intelligence as a peacemaker.

It is late one Saturday afternoon several weeks before South Africa's first all-race elections in April 1994, and local groups of elders, women, schoolgirls and boys have convened the ceremony to express their appreciation for Zungu's efforts to bring peace to their blighted region. Nelson Mandela's African National Congress (ANC) and Mangosuthu Buthelezi's Inkatha Freedom Party (IFP) are in a virtual state of war in the province of Kwazulu, and the killings have reached an astounding rate. But among the seventy thousand people in Madlebe, relative calm reigns, thanks in large part to Zungu. Her subjects are living on an island of relative tranquility, surrounded by very stormy seas indeed, and they know it.

Two years later, Zungu sits in the living room of her modern suburban home, reminiscing about the ceremony. "I was really nervous that day. At that time, I was just finding my way, and everyone expected so much of me." At thirty-four years of age, Zungu is literally a human link between Africa's past and its future. A trained medical doctor, raised in the South African coastal metropolis of Durban, Zungu would not be out of place in one of the city's posh shopping malls, strolling along the Indian Ocean beaches, or perhaps dancing the night away to the throbbing township beat in a fashionable discothèque. Yet here she is, in the rural Zulu community of Gwelezana in the province of Kwazulu-Natal, presiding over the Madlebe clan in traditional style. For Zungu is the rarest of people: physician, mother, and Zulu chief.

Her unusual journey from medical doctor to chief was born in personal tragedy: an automobile accident in 1989 on the road from Durban. Both she and her husband Bhekisizwe Zungu, the chief of the Madlebe clan and a deputy minister in the Kwazulu provincial government, were seriously injured. For days they lay prostrate side by side in the hospital. Bhekisizwe, whose name means "Protector of the Nation," eventually died of his injuries, setting off a bitter three-year succession crisis. A series of meetings among the elders originally settled on two candidates: either Bhekisizwe's half brother, born to his father's second, unofficial wife; or the eldest son of the second ranking royal house among the Madlebe. A long debate among the elders to choose between the two ended in deadlock. Then a compromise choice emerged: Bhekisizwe's wife Sibongile. That idea sparked an uproar of opposition. Sibongile had many strikes against her. First and foremost she was a woman, she was young, she hailed from a commoner family outside the clan, and she was a trained medical doctor, educated in what her detractors regarded as the alien Western system. There was another problem. Sibongile is a Dube, a descendant of the more peaceful farming clan which inhabited the area before the Madlebes, renowned warriors, drove them out in the early nineteenth century. The Dubes still reside about ten miles away along the Indian Ocean coast, and the Madlebe elders, some old enough to have learned of the expulsion directly from the perpetrators, feared that she would return the land to the original owners.

To break the impasse, the Kwazulu provincial government set up a commission of inquiry into the matter, and when it handed down its ruling, Sibongile was the nominee. In April 1992, she was told that she must assume the office of chief of the Madlebe. The irony is that Zungu had no desire to become chief. She knew very little of tribal customs and practices, and until she married Bhekisizwe, her primary school sweetheart, in 1983, the world of Zulu traditions was completely foreign to her. After her father, a schoolteacher, died when she was three, she had been raised mainly by her aunt and uncle and maternal grandparents at the Inanda mission station in Durban where Mandela cast his historic ballot in the 1994 elections.

"We went to church every Sunday, and we were a 'civilized' lot," Zungu says, laughing as she twitches her fingers above her head to indicate what she thinks of the "civilized" label. Her only exposure to traditional Zulu culture occurred on the weekends, when her aunt and uncle would leave the house to attend Christian meetings. "We would be left alone. So we would sneak off and go to the countryside and hear the traditional songs and the stories and everything, see the ceremonies and be given some amulets to wear."

Otherwise, Sibongile remained aloof from Zulu customs as a young girl. From the age of five, her passion was to become a doctor. It all began with the marvel of the radio. Her uncle used to ask her to check the clock and to tell him when it was time for the news bulletins. One afternoon in December 1967, she and her relatives sat down and listened to a report about the world's first heart transplant, carried out by the South Africa surgeon, Dr. Christiann Barnard, in Cape Town. "We heard about this Christiann and that he could take a heart from one person, put it in another, and make that person live. I said, 'How does he do that?' My uncle said, 'Now listen, this person is a doctor and doctors do that.' I had only been to the doctor for dental problems, and I associated doctors with injections and teeth. My uncle said, 'You see, this is a wonderful thing.' I said, 'Can I do it?' He said, 'Yes, you can.' Somehow he picked up on that and he nurtured it. Then each time, he would call me with the latest events about Christiann."

New Roads Taken   *37*

Twenty years later, Sibongile graduated from the Medical University of Southern Africa in Pretoria with a specialization in pediatrics and traveled to Gwelezana to raise a family with Bhekisizwe and work at the local hospital. It was only after she and Bhekisizwe set up their home that she began to enter the traditional world. "I had to remember all those childhood stories and experiences because now I had to practice them." She still maintained her distance, however. Preoccupied with her job at Gwelezana's local hospital, Sibongile left the cultural matters to her husband.

That all changed after the car crash and Bhekisizwe's death. "When I first heard that they wanted me to be chief, I thought that this was one hopeless recommendation. I had no idea what was going on in tribal courts, I had never attended a single meeting of the tribal council, and I just didn't know what to do. And now I was told I was going to lead this big tribe. I thought, this is a mistake. To be honest, when they told me I would have to take over, I thought about going back to Durban. I was the only child at home, the bedroom was still there, and I could work there. But then the other part of me was saying, 'You are letting your husband down, he has never done anything bad to you, and you were on good terms.' I was in the same car in the accident, I had my own injuries too. We spent some time together in hospital. So that part of me was saying, 'No, don't let him down. Try, he will be there, and he will help you.' So I tried."

Zungu did far more than try. She took over at a time when the Madlebe clan and most of the Zulu heartland were in deep crisis, mainly because of the political violence between the ANC and Inkatha, but also because Kwazulu was in the grip of the worst drought the region had seen in years—one that reached into the heart of southern Africa, producing famine conditions in neighboring Mozambique and parts of Zimbabwe and Zambia.

In a way, her position as a woman ready to apply common sense to seemingly intractable problems served the clan well. "What was an advantage was that the whole country was in transition. There was no correct or known formula of doing things. New problems were coming all the time. There was the violence and drought, things that traditional values really could not address. You had to liaise with the army, the police, to ensure security for the people, to find shelter for those whose homes were burnt down. One had to act in time before more people were killed and to raise funds for drought relief. You didn't need traditional knowledge to do that. I think I gained some respect. In the meantime, I was trying to catch up on the traditional culture which I had to know."

The violence that had been building since 1990 reached its peak in the Madlebe area just as Zungu assumed office. ANC and IFP activists were clashing during their respective rallies, and hit squads were on the loose, paying nighttime visits to the homes of their enemies, real or imaginary. Her solution to the problem was a relatively simple and time-honored one: dialogue. After long meetings with both sides, she convinced them to announce the date and time of their rallies and to agree that when one party was in the streets, the other would stay away. The times called for unconventional measures. To douse the flames of political factionalism in one ward, she convinced the army to take representatives of the ANC and IFP up in a helicopter and fly over the community to demonstrate their commitment to peace. When the aircraft zoomed over the ward with flags of both parties flying, people poured into the streets in celebration.

"I wouldn't say it's quite like children, but you know when people fight and they don't know what they are fighting for, I think they are at that stage now," she says. "If I were a politician I would urge these people to unite as Africans, form one party. Single parties do have their own problems, I realize, but I am just looking at the issue of getting Africans to stop fighting each other. Because the violence is not white against black; it's black against black. And it leaves black areas poor. No one wants to invest there; there's no Checkers or Woolworths here. This land is big, it's beautiful, and we could have such shops here and generate the same revenue as the towns. But as long as there is violence, we have no chance."

At times her role has been similar to that of a priest, one who hears the confessions of her people and becomes the repository of community guilt, of the worst secrets and deadly deeds. The murderers exorcised their demons and handed them over to Zungu for safekeeping. "There came a time when they had to tell me in one ward that actually they have killed so many people. That was the ANC people telling me that they killed so-and-so and so-and-so and so-and-so. And that they were looking for these members of the IFP. And the IFP said, 'Well, we knew you were looking for us, and then on this date we hit this house.' They told me the whole story, and then they warned me: 'Don't dare tell the police. We just want our peace now. We are telling these stories because we want to clear our consciences and start a new life. This is for you. You can keep it. But this is not for the police. Okay?' I said, Okay. Now I live with that, and they are happy and free. From that day on, the IFP and the ANC have carried their flags; they do their toy-toying in broad daylight in front of everyone."

And, of course, when times were really tough, she turned to Bhekisizwe. "Sometimes I try to talk to him, and say, 'Well, now, how do you think I am going to get through this? You know this is not my specialty, it is your specialty, and I am doing it for you, and you must help me now.' Most of the time when it is something very difficult, somehow when I don't know how it happens but I get through it, I think he has come to help. I do make some offerings to him to ask for help."

There have been some embarrassing moments. At one Zulu ceremony, while her fellow chiefs dressed in traditional leopard skins and walked with their people to the site of the meeting, she drove up in her car and stepped out wearing a Western-style dress. At another party, an ox was slaughtered and Zungu immediately began eating the tongue—women are forbidden to eat any part of the head. There was a moment of disbelief, but since she was a chief, her colleagues forgave the oversight.

Her education in Zulu customs, laws, and medicines began as she stood in the line of fire. As usual, she has proved to be a capable student, and what she has learned has completely altered the way she looks at Africa and the world. One of her first challenges was to come to terms with the community's traditional healers, who are a critical social force, just as powerful in South Africa as they are in the rest of the continent. An estimated 80 percent of South Africa's black population continue to consult traditional medical practitioners, who are commonly known as *inyangas*. While healers have developed some novel and effective techniques, their main importance rests with their ability to mobilize rural communities in the battle against the major killers of the modern era, from AIDS to malaria.

Zungu's relationship with the *inyangas* was not easy at first, both because of her own prejudices and because the healers saw her as a doctor of "white medicine." "I think we have found a bridge because now they know I understand their background, and our relationship is quite good. I can explain to them that particular remedies can be dangerous, and they can tell me what they have done. Say, for example, a patient has been discharged because we could not do anything to help him at the hospital, and then the patient returns much better. They say, 'Well, I went to my *inyanga* and he gave me something.' I can go to the *inyanga* and ask him what they did. They usually won't tell me exactly what it is, but they say it was this *muti* [cure] and it works."

From her day-to-day experience in Gwelezana, Zungu has learned the lessons that others are discovering in the rest of the continent. "I think we can learn a lot from them, especially over issues like HIV and AIDS, where we still don't know where we are going. I think traditional doctors and medical doctors should be more open with each other." A major handicap is the suspicion *inyangas* feel toward the Western medical world, a result of years of repression by the European colonial authorities and missionaries, and their own business considerations. *Inyangas* have a constant fear that Western doctors and their fellow healers will steal their remedies. "I think it's in the culture of traditional medicine that your *muti* is your secret. But that is true with Western medicine, too. Some companies like to keep their formulas secret."

To describe Zungu's views about the role of traditional healers as unorthodox among practitioners of Western-style medicine in Africa is an understatement. Common wisdom, often expressed by African governments themselves, is that the healers are part of the problem hindering African development and have little or no role in the march toward progress. The same has been said about traditional chiefs, who although they are unelected authorities whose power is based on lineage remain legitimate in the eyes of their followers. Only they provide a link to the political, religious, and cultural systems of Africa's precolonial past.

The issue is particularly stark in South Africa, Africa's most developed and Westernized country, where the ANC, especially its more youthful and left-wing members, has suggested that the institution of chieftaincy is an anachronism that must be phased out. The Council for Traditional Leaders in South Africa, known as Contralesa, was an important supporter of the ANC during the struggle against apartheid, a support the congress welcomed because of the chiefs' obvious influence. But since the 1994 election, Contralesa and the ANC have been at odds. The chiefs, known by the Zulu word *amakhosi*, say the ANC is trying to place too many curbs on their powers.

Chief Buthelezi's Inkatha Freedom Party has been equally guilty of ruining the chiefs' image, using and coercing the *amakhosi* to prosecute its political agenda through often violent means. Zungu explains how it happened. "What some of the chiefs do is to align themselves with party politics, and that compromises the other sections of the population of that area who don't particularly believe in the political party that the chief supports. If the chief supports the IFP, then the ANC people will not have a good stay in the area. And if it is the other way around, then the IFP people will not have a good stay."

Since President Mandela's inauguration, however, the alliance of important traditional leaders has altered quite considerably. The Zulu king, Goodwill Zwelethini, dramatically reversed his hard-line position, dropping his support for Buthelezi, effectively allying himself with Mandela, and urging all the *amakhosi* to adopt a nonpolitical approach. But the king is a weak monarch, and until the central government can enforce its decision to pay all traditional chiefs from national rather than provincial coffers, which in Kwazulu Inkatha controls, Chief Buthelezi will have the *amakhosi* by the purse strings.

So, while the ANC suggests that all local governments must be elected and the chiefs should be relegated to relatively minor roles as advisers, the *amakhosi* remain in a state of limbo. Zungu argues for a compromise that will blend elements of strict democratic procedures with the tradition of succession.

"It is still a mystery issue. Nobody knows exactly what the situation should be in rural areas. If they talk about elections, yes, they can elect the people to help the traditional leader to lead in a way that goes with the times, with the demands of the moment. But the tradition of succession has to be looked at in a different manner. You can't say, no, we'll stop this, and we'll have elections. You have to sit down and look at the law of succession in relation to traditional leaders. There could be adjustments, like for instance on the issue of women. Right now only a firstborn male child becomes the rightful successor, the undisputed successor. The girls, they are just useless, because of course women will go and marry somebody from the outside. In my view, a woman could be the better bearer of the lineage because a child is born through the mother. You can never be sure, when a child is born, who the real father is. But with the mother you are always sure that the person who gave birth to this child is this woman. It's guaranteed."

Disputes over the role of chiefs and traditional beliefs in modern Africa have deep roots. In places such as Freetown, Sierra Leone, and Abeokuta, Nigeria, slaves freed by the Royal Navy off the West

African coast in the nineteenth century were understandably hostile to the old African chiefs who sold them into slavery. Among many of them there was a strong belief that only by adopting Western concepts of constitutional government, Christianity, and commerce could Africa prosper in the modern world. It was a view eagerly nurtured by European colonialism.

By contrast, traditional rulers in the colonial territories, such as among the Ashante in Ghana, believed they and not the young, Western-educated nationalists should receive the mantle of power when the European powers decided to quit Africa. But when independence came, it was as if centuries of African history had never existed, as if the continent had no tradition of government, no culture, no arts. And Marxist revolutionary governments, which took power in countries such as Mozambique and Angola, aggressively repressed chiefs and traditional healers, believing that they had allowed themselves to be used by the Portuguese and that they had no place in the new socialist order.

There also exists a common fallacy—one that was actively promoted by the missionaries from the day they arrived in Africa two hundred years ago—that one can either be a Christian or a Muslim, or an animist, a believer in traditional ancestral worship, but not both. No westerner better summed up the arrogance of ignorance than David Livingstone, the nineteenth-century Scottish missionary turned explorer who banned from communion his one and only convert in Africa, Sechele, chief of the Bakwena people in what today is southern Botswana, after he noticed that one of the chief's lesser wives was pregnant. Livingstone had convinced the chief, over the objections of clan elders, that to be a true Christian, he had to do with one wife, even though at the time the chief's practice of polygamy not only symbolized the virility of the clan but also helped to knit his people together and survive in a hostile environment prone to hunger and drought.

Today, many Africans delve into ancestral worship while at the same time officially adhering to foreign beliefs, such as Christianity or Islam. Zungu is one of them. "I am a Christian who has ancestors, who slaughters beasts for the ancestors, who does everything else for the ancestors, but believes that the human being is the image of God and as such must be treated in that manner and be respected. I believe in both. I have not thrown away what our ancestors were doing. Christianity holds that the human being is made in the image of God, and as such has to be treated and respected and valued in that manner. Because if you harm another human being, it means you are harming your own creator. That is also there in our ancestral beliefs, although it is not structured in the same manner. Your ancestors are human beings who lived before, and you must not harm them. If you do, you have to apologize, although it has to be a symbolic apology, through a slaughter of a cow, or you burn something, and then you talk and make an apology. I believe in such things."

Zungu might have Barry White CDs in her living room and enjoy shopping for nice clothes with her friends, but since she became chief, however much originally against her will, she has gone through something of a metamorphosis. From the vantage point of her relatively small community in Gwelezana, she has had to address questions relevant to the whole of Africa. A highly educated young woman raised in a Christian household, she has come to appreciate Africa's past, to see that without involving it in the present, by driving it underground, the continent will continue to ape a foreign culture, and inevitably it will fail.

"I think our problem is that we have a powerful group, the politicians, who receive their education from mostly Western-based institutions, and in that manner they tend to honor Western values. Then they just look down upon their own systems as inferior. They think it is more progressive to be Western. These people then come back and they have influence over their people because they seem to be much cleverer than the rest. Then they influence policy in their own direction to please themselves. It's just an indication of how much influence the West, Europe, has had on our lives."

In the end, progress in Africa will depend on its ability to innovate its past. "I believe that we do have to take some of the good things that came with our past, mix the two, and come up with something new. Because after all, as in South Africa, this is a new nation made of a people with a past, with a certain experience, a culture. We have to build this new nation on the foundations of the old, rather than on the graveyard of the older one."

A Spirit of Peace

Reaching out with his right arm for balance while crouching down on his haunches in the back of a speeding pickup, Carlos Mhula looked like a surfer riding the whimsical rollers of a twisting country road. His large dark eyes, which just minutes before were twitching nervously from side to side, gradually lowered their guard as a broad smile pried open his square-bearded jaw. "It seems like we are in another country," he shouted with genuine astonishment over the roar of the engine. The vehicle weaved and swerved in the soft, sandy track, sending its four passengers tumbling into each other, as it penetrated deeper into the countryside toward a mysterious remote village called Mungoi. For the first time in an hour, everyone was laughing. Mhula seemed especially gripped by the levity. He had never been to the village before, but for a time it had shattered his world. After Mhula wrote a news story about its people's extraordinary ability to remain virtually untouched by the armed violence swirling around them, the secret police detained him without charge, separating him from his family and calling into question his journalistic integrity. Now he was just moments away from discovering what had made the government so jittery that he had to spend two months behind bars.

That something was remarkably unusual about the village of Mungoi was obvious from how normal, how calm everything appeared to be. Gone from the faces of the villagers were the clear signs of tension, of the utter hopelessness endemic in much of the rest of rural Mozambique, an immense Y-shaped territory in the southeast corner of Africa ravaged by a civil war as old as its fifteen years of independence.

Barefoot children ambled around tidy yards while their parents stretched out on hand-woven reed mats or sat on sturdy wooden stools in the shade of a cluster of mango and cashew trees. In one clearing, a group of jovial young men and women finishing a new home hoisted handfuls of mud onto a skeleton of tree branches fixed into the ground, while in another a toddler was bawling as his mother scrubbed his chubby little body with soap and sprinkled water on his head. Off to the side, an elderly woman smoked a cigarette rural-style, inside out, with the hot coal remarkably and no doubt delicately balanced inside her mouth, while deftly working her bare feet and nimble hands to manipulate an ancient black Singer sewing machine. In the distance, a cassette deck overwhelmed the habitually still village airwaves with the piercing guitar riffs and thumping rhythm of Mozambique's distinctive *Marrabenta* beat. As the pickup skidded by in a cloud of dust, invariably everyone raised a hand in a gesture of welcome. The smiles, the well-kept homesteads, the sight of packs of grazing animals made it seem as if this was an oasis in the middle of a desert of destruction. It was. Mhula shook his head again and chuckled. "Hey man, it's really another world."

The village of Mungoi itself is so small that its very name derives from the family that settled there generations ago and over the years laid down a patchwork of individual farms, or *shambas,* and grazing lands over a realm of several square miles. Almost everyone is either named Mungoi or is related to the Mungoi family through marriage. The landscape is dotted with wattle-and-daub homes common to rural Africa, basic environmentally sound structures of wooden poles, straw, and mud, topped with dense brown thatched roofs that remain cool inside even under the relentless heat of the southern African sun, symbolizing the people's unspoken compact with the land; like their owners, the houses decompose into the soil when their time has come.

In normal times, the residents of southern Mozambique make their living from a mixture of farming, mainly corn and vegetables, husbandry of cattle and goats, and cash sent back from husbands and sons who migrate across the border to work in the mines and commercial farms of South Africa. But these were hardly normal times in the district of Manjacaze, which envelopes Mungoi. The panorama was one of profound upheaval. Hundreds of neighboring hamlets were collapsing, their inhabitants either slain in a wave of unprecedented violence or forced to flee to destitute refugee camps to suffer the indignity of once proud farmers barely living off hand-outs provided by the government and international relief agencies. Families were ripped apart, and thousands of children were made orphans or were dragooned by the warring armies and forced to take up arms as child soldiers. Entire communities were being shredded. Throughout Mozambique, which was known by the first Portuguese explorers in the fifteenth century as the *terra de boa gente*, the land of good people, it was a time of civil war, and the conflict ranked as among the most devastating in Africa's post-independence history.

The war pitted Frelimo—as the ruling Mozambique Liberation Front, which led the country to independence from Portugal in 1975, is known—against a particularly brutal and South African supported rebel movement called the Mozambique Resistance Movement, or Renamo. Their armed dispute for power imposed horrific levels of violence on Mozambique's 14 million people, and transformed the country into a tragic model of the modern conflicts that ravage the developing countries of Africa and Asia.

Women and children, not soldiers, are the targets of this type of low-intensity warfare, especially in countries where living standards are low, the nation-state left by the colonial rulers still weak, and civil societies not fully developed. While by some estimates about 85 percent of war casualties worldwide were soldiers at the beginning of the century, today roughly the same percentage are civilians, mainly women and children. Villages and homesteads, not military installations, are the targets of marauding gunmen whose aim is to pillage for food and to deprive their enemies of sustenance and re-sources. Since destitute armies do not have the luxury of using jet fighters and laser-guided smart bombs, villages are razed, peasant communities are encircled and their residents starved, massacred, or forced to flee. The method is pitiless, designed to humiliate the enemy by attacking its weaker, civilian points, to crush the oppo-nent's spirit, a poor man's version of the type of tactics employed by the Allies when they firebombed Dresden during World War II or by the Americans when they tried to carpet-bomb Vietnam back into the Stone Age.

With the possible exceptions of Rwanda and Angola, nowhere in Africa did war do more damage than in Mozambique. The raw sta-tistics tell only part of the story. At least 1 million dead, $25 billion in damage to the economy, 2,773 primary schools destroyed, some 1,000 rural health clinics obliterated. Of every five infants born, three died before their fifth birthday, slain by automatic rifle fire, machetes, knives and clubs, or struck down by killer illnesses such as diarrhea, measles, malaria, and simple starvation. For children, Mozambique was the most dangerous place on earth. An entire generation grew up knowing nothing but war. Nearly 2 million people, one-seventh of the country's total population, escaped across the borders into refugee camps in countries such as Malawi, South Africa, Tanzania, and Zimbabwe. Three million more abandoned their homes for the relative safety of the cities or the vast unoccupied stretches of beach along the coast. This was, as Mozambicans often say, *a situação,* the situation.

Even at the height of the war, however, the people of Mungoi village kept the *situação* at bay. Their spirit never cracked. Against all the odds, the hamlet survived intact, and the story of how it did so attests to the dynamic vitality of its people's religious beliefs. They discovered the secret that the only way to withstand the worst the twentieth century could throw at them was to rely on their cultural past, to adapt it to the needs of the present and solve the greatest crisis the village ever faced. By doing so, they reaffirmed the great strength of religion in Africa: its capacity for constant change and transformation to deal with the practical problems of the day, a characteristic that some scholars believe is, in fact, the most accurate definition of African "tradition."[1]

For months, rumors traveled down National Highway No. 1 to Maputo, the modern capital of wide Portuguese-style avenues nestled on the shore of the Indian Ocean at the far southern tip of the country, about something incredible occurring in a previously unheard-of village. Its people were so desperate that they sought relief, not from the government authorities or the Christian churches which had made deep inroads since the start of Portuguese colonial rule nearly five centuries ago, nor by taking up arms or forming civilian defense militias. Instead, they turned to their ancestors, the common denominator in the multitude of indigenous religions that remain a vibrant force throughout Africa, despite the best-laid plans to obliterate them by the colonial powers, the independent governments that succeeded them, and the Muslim and Christian missionaries. As the British historian Michael Crowder has written of West Africa, "In those areas which were touched intimately by Europe— whether through the presence of a school, a trading post or administrative center, what is surprising is not that traditional society fell apart but that it had held together so effectively; that traditional

moral obligations to one's family triumphed over Western individualism; that traditional religious beliefs survived alongside and per-
meated Christianity and Islam. . . ."[2]

The legend went that the spirit of a local headman who died
thirty years before returned as a sort of guardian angel armed with
magical powers to protect his people from the war. It soon became
apparent that what was occurring in Mungoi had more to do with
faith than magic. The entire village entered into the psychological
realm, conspiring to refashion its religious beliefs into a weapon far
more potent than guns and grenades. And the ancestor to whom
they turned to save them was a former chief named Augusto Sidawanhane Mungoi.

The original source of the news about Mungoi to the outside
world was Carlos Mhula, who was working as a freelance journalist
in the nearby city of Xai Xai. But since his arrest and subsequent release the year before, a veil of silence had fallen over the village. Despite the dangers, he decided to embark on a quest to discover the
truth behind the legend. With him were Gil Lauriciano, one of Mozambique's premier war correspondents and a good friend, and Carlos Tchlene, a government representative who agreed to come along
to make sure that someone in authority would be there to make
sure nothing went wrong. The odds were that something would.
The journey to the village was a hair-raising one along a tarmac road
littered with burnt-out skeletons of vehicles ambushed by highway
gunmen, several of the kills so fresh that the bitter smell of their
melted rubber tires still hung thickly in the air. The pickup, bucking
like a wild beast over an imaginative array of craters and corruga-
tions, slowed down only for the numerous military checkpoints of
the type that have become common in dozens of countries where
the rule of law and order has broken down.

Here in Mozambique or further afield in other lands stricken by
civil war, such as Angola, Liberia, and Sierra Leone, checkpoints are
a major form of employment, of indirect taxation, so to speak.
Drivers and passengers are united by a single challenge—to get
through paying as small a bribe as possible, and above all, to engage
in no arguments. Highway justice, dispensed by ill-fed and ill-
clothed soldiers of whatever political persuasion, can be lethal.

Those forced by circumstances of family or business to travel National Highway No. 1 developed their own informal intelligence system by flashing a thumbs-up sign to passing vehicles to indicate that
all was clear ahead, or at least it was when they passed. Everyone

was aware that the highwaymen could strike at any moment. Almost without exception, too, each building along the way was in ruins—no roof, no doors, no windows, emptied of everything except charred earthen pots and scores of bullet holes.

But in the few minutes since the pickup turned off the main highway and started up the final stretch to the village, the scars of conflict quickly gave way to reassuring signs of composed rural life. The road itself dissolved into a dirt track filled with people and goats and, occasionally, a massive stubborn cow that looked over its shoulder with disdain and took its good time moving out of the way. The pickup slid into the center of the village to find a dozen children and their mothers milling around quietly, remaining as still as they could in the midday heat. Black pots of corn porridge stewed on a pile of glittering red coals. Several women sat in a circle sewing strips of brightly colored African cloth, called *capulanas,* while the air tinkled with the giggles of youngsters watching a robust white cock aggressively try to seduce a pack of uproarious hens. Everyone climbed down from the truck clearly in the mood to savor the rare tranquility. While Mhula and Lauriciano strolled around stretching their legs, Tchlene immediately perched himself on a thick log under a giant mango tree, slipped off his black leather shoes, and massaged his feet in the dry earth. The scene reminded him, he said, of growing up in the rural areas fifty years ago.

In Africa, there is nothing more cherished than the serenity of village life, though during the war village life was anything but serene. For a few minutes, Tchlene reminisced about his boyhood days hunting small game with a slingshot and walking for hours herding the family cattle and goats. In years long past, everyone in Mozambique, even the most committed urban dwellers, used to make a pilgrimage to their villages at least once a year to visit relatives and to celebrate the holidays. But the war changed all that. Tchlene rarely even left the town where he worked about ten miles east of Mungoi's village, and every time he did, there was a chance he would not see home again. His town, Chidenguele, was routinely encircled by rebel gunmen, and describing it as under the control of the government required a broad leap of faith. Only the very old hilltop center, about the size of a football field, was securely in the army's grasp. The border between safety and danger was defined by a ring of deep trenches from which the soldiers defended the hamlet after dark. The more contemporary buildings at the base of the hill, mainly shops, bars, and restaurants, were abandoned hovels pockmarked by bullet holes and gutted by fire. The fields and forests beyond were in Mozambican lexicon "one hundred percent," meaning anyone who strayed into them was prey to the gunmen. The countryside was a place of terror, to be avoided at almost any cost. For miles around, only in the village of Mungoi did the rural idyllic refuge still approach reality.

Tossing pebbles into the sand one by one and shrugging his shoulders at the contrast between the terror of Chidenguele and the tranquility of Mungoi's village, Tchlene laughed. "Facts are facts." Both the government army and the rebels could pass through the area, he said, "but nothing can happen in Mungoi. The bandits can come here, eat and leave, and Frelimo troops can come, eat and leave. But if they meet here, they just pass each other by." Tchlene rolled his eyes and ran a hand over his hair, venturing cautiously, "You see, the spirit has banned weapons here." He too found it all hard to understand. "The question isn't what I think, but what they believe," he said, extending his right hand toward the villagers gathered around the fire.

A tall, lithe, elderly man with an aristocratic air suddenly stepped forward and introduced himself as Armando Mungoi, a village elder and the nephew of the late Augusto Sidawanhane Mungoi. After a few moments of discussion, he said the village consented to call the spirit of his uncle. A brief word from Armando sent a young barefoot boy in cutoff shorts sprinting down a path through the trees. Half an hour later, he returned, followed by a thin, middle-aged woman, dressed smartly in a bright red *capulana* wrap and a yellow scarf. She strode confidently into the central clearing and casually greeted everyone sitting around the fire. No one paid her much attention, except Tchlene, who could not keep his eyes off her. "She's a traditional healer," he whispered, leaning over. "The spirit of Mungoi speaks through her." Christine Chamane, once a typical rural traditional healer, now was the medium of the spirit of Augusto Sidawanhane Mungoi, her grandfather.

Mungoi's village is living proof that ancestral worship, a theological system that sees life and death as one organic process, remains central to religious beliefs throughout much of Africa to this day. This is what, for example, the pyramids of ancient Egypt represent. The Pharaohs buried there were considered immortal. As Professor Mazrui has written, "The culture of the pyramids recognized no fundamental break between living and dying."[3] It is the same in the village of Mungoi. In the center of the main homestead stands a white cement building, its doorway covered by a giant white sheet with a blue cross that looks like a flag. "Mungoi's tomb," Tchlene said matter-of-factly.

When the relationship works well, the living and the dead interact in a symbiosis. The living must care for the dead, pay respect to them by honoring them in ceremonies filled with elaborate dances, praise songs, the slaughter of a prize domestic animal, and brewing beer. In return, the dead provide guidance through spirit mediums like Christine on everything from what is needed to guarantee a good harvest, to produce healthy children, to ensure adequate rain, or to pick the wisest chief. Only very rarely do they actually intervene as in Mungoi.

In this case, neither the village nor the spirit had much choice. The matter at hand was the threat of annihilation. Manjacaze district was arguably one of the most violent places anywhere. In August 1987, ninety-two civilians were massacred there, and in the months and years after that, killings of fifteen and twenty people were frequent. The village of Mungoi was on the verge of being sucked into that vortex of slaughter until its residents decided that it was time for the spirit of Augusto Sidawanhane Mungoi to return from the dead. And he did—or at least in their minds he did—with telling effect.

Christine and Armando spoke quietly for a few minutes, while the other villagers bounded about silently, sweeping the ground, placing reed mats and chairs under another mango tree adorned with the skulls of various animals, mainly deer, goats, and field rats, used in village religious ceremonies. Three men lugged a huge wooden armchair draped in a white sheet and placed it in the center of the clearing. With the preparations well under way, Christine, Armando, and two other middle-aged women disappeared into a thatched roof hut. Within minutes the sound of low chanting rose from the dwelling. "She's entering a trance to call the spirit," Tchlene said. "Mungoi is coming."

A gentle, reflective man, with sad drooping eyes and and gray-flecked hair, Tchlene considered the words he had just spoken and chuckled to himself at the awkwardness of his own position. As a representative of the Frelimo government, he was obliged to regard beliefs in healers and ancestral spirits as primitive mumbo-jumbo, or, as in the memorable description propagated by the party's European-trained Marxist ideologues, *obscurantismo*. That single word, which ironically was once bandied about with equal gusto by the

Portuguese colonizers and Church missionaries, summed up the government's contempt for the religious practices of its people as it set about its own civilizing mission to transform Mozambique into a modern African state. Christianity and Islam were tolerated, though barely, but ancestral worship was to be confined to the dust heap of *obscurantismo*. This was the official policy. Unofficially, many Frelimo members, particularly sensitive ones like Tchlene who worked in the rural areas far removed from the center of power in Maputo, continued to respect their constituents' faith in traditional forms of government, land tenure, and religions.

That Frelimo would launch its modernization drive along socialist rather than capitalist lines was determined, at least in part, by Portugal's armed denial of African aspirations to freedom, whether in Mozambique or its other colonies, such as Angola, Guinea Bissau, São Tomè and Princípe, and Cape Verde, and by the collusion in Lisbon's colonial enterprise by the other major Western powers. When Frelimo mobilized its guerrilla army in the early 1960s to drive the Portuguese out of Mozambique by force, the only foreign countries offering military assistance were socialist. The Frelimo leadership, after much internal debate and faction fighting, adopted Marxism as its creed, and welcomed support in the form of weapons and training from Cuba, the Soviet Union, Eastern Europe, and China. Portugal's other colonies followed a similar path, as did by necessity the independence movements in Zimbabwe and South Africa.

Guerrilla armies fighting for independence in Mozambique, Angola, and Guinea Bissau were heavily outgunned, but their sheer determination proved more than a match for the colonial army. In 1974, with the morale and endurance of the Portuguese armed forces flagging, young officers in Lisbon overthrew the Fascist government in what became known as the Revolution of the Carnations. Like manna from heaven, freedom came to the colonies almost overnight, quenching their thirst for independence. In Mozambique, Frelimo assumed power and quickly won enthusiastic support, not only due to its lead role in driving out the Portuguese, but also because mass literacy and health campaigns rapidly improved the lot of millions. It created enemies too, however. Western governments locked in their cold war mentality saw in Frelimo and other fledgling socialist-minded administrations, such as the MPLA movement which took power in Angola, Mozambique's sister Portuguese colony on the west coast of Africa, the thin wedge of Communist subversion in southern Africa. The last bastions of white rule in Africa, Rhodesia and South Africa, were still firmly entrenched and militantly hostile to any attempts to promote African rights and nonracial government.

Committed to socialist revolution and facing violent neighbors, Frelimo declared Mozambique a one-party state and itself a Marxist-Leninist party whose "historic mission is to lead, organize, orientate, and educate the masses, thus transforming the popular mass movement into a powerful instrument for the destruction of capitalism and the construction of socialism."[4] Political opponents were jailed or sent off, together with unemployed city dwellers, single women deemed to be "prostitutes," and other undesirables, to reeducation camps in the remote interior. Scarce resources went not to the needy peasant sector but to huge, state-owned, heavily mechanized farms on the Soviet model, which seemed to hold the key to rapid development. The names of the founding fathers of international socialism, Karl Marx, Frederick Engels, Vladimir Lenin, Mao Tse-tung, and even lesser figures such as Kim Il Sung, adorned the streets and avenues of the major cities. In true Stalinist style, the press too succumbed to rigid state control. The tone was set in 1978 by the founding statutes of the National Organization of Journalists, which said in part: "The ONJ is led by Frelimo, is guided by its political line, bases its activity on the party program, organizes its members to resolutely support the revolutionary tasks defined by the party and by the state for all of Mozambican society and, in particular, to integrally carry out tasks defined by [Frelimo's department of] Information."[5]

However admirable their intention to modernize one of Africa's most underdeveloped countries, Frelimo's radical reforms ignited smoldering opposition, especially in the countryside. Following the well-worn path of the newly independent African governments, there was no role for the precolonial political and religious structures, such as the institution of chiefs, ancestral worship, and traditional healers, known as *curandeiros*. All these were to be sacrificed on the altar of modernization. Government officials viewed the culture of their country cousins with contempt. Their attitude was summed up by a senior disaster relief official, Manuel Nogueira, who once said: "These people have lived dispersed for five hundred years and where has it gotten them?"

A central plank of the transformation was the program of "villagization," a bold but ultimately coercive drive to move thousands of peasants into *aldeas comunais*, or communal villages, where they would have easy access to basic infrastructure, such as medical clinics, schools, clean water supplies, and state-run shops. It was similar to the *ujamaa* system introduced by President Julius Nyerere in Tanzania, which borders Mozambique to the north and where Frelimo was based during the independence war against Portugal.

What on the surface seemed like a progressive idea provoked disastrous consequences, since the basis of the peasants' religious beliefs required them to live on the land of their forefathers. Forced villagization was in effect heresy. Moving away from the sacred burial grounds would sever the divine link between the people and their ancestors. Nyerere later described his decision to collectivize Tanzania's village farms, the *shambas,* as one of his greatest errors. "You can socialize what is not traditional," he said. "The *shamba* can't be socialized." In Mozambique, Frelimo further alienated villagers by substituting loyal party secretaries for traditional chiefs as the top local political authorities. During local assembly elections in 1977, chiefs were either discouraged or barred outright from standing as candidates. In at least one case, the voters retaliated against the bans by electing the village idiots.[6]

Frelimo justified its attitude toward the chiefs by arguing that they had been used as pawns by the Portuguese to administer colonial rule and that they represented feudal obstacles to its ambitious development plans. There was always more to it than that. Frelimo also saw traditional political authorities as a threat to its power, as did, to a lesser extent, its nonsocialist counterparts in other emerging nations. Its solution was to abolish them. In doing so, however, it was guilty of gross miscalculation. J. S. Mbiti, in his book *African Religions and Philosophy,* explains the deep emotional attachment to chiefs in Africa this way: "Where these rulers are found they are not simply political heads, they are mystical and religious heads, the divine symbol of their people's health and welfare . . . their office is the link between human rule and spiritual government. They are therefore divine or sacred rulers, the shadow or reflection of God's rule in the universe."[7]

Not surprisingly, some traditional leaders, especially those in more isolated regions, welcomed Renamo guerrillas as a protective barrier against Frelimo and the encroachment on their authority by the new independent state. In the areas it controlled, Renamo allowed the chiefs to retain titular power on the condition that they provided a constant source of recruits and supplies. Rebel field commanders depended on their *curandeiro* healers and spirit mediums for everything from treating sickness to plotting military strategy. It was routine practice on operations to place at the head of an advancing column of soldiers a diviner who cast cowrie shells to see if the way ahead was clear.

The repression of chiefs, spirit mediums, and traditional healers also played into the hands of Frelimo's primary external enemies, the powerful racist governments in Rhodesia and South Africa. The people of Mozambique were unfortunate victims of geography, repeatedly forced to pay the price of living so near regimes that were prepared to wage war against their neighbors to preserve the systems of white minority rule. The Rhodesian prime minister, Ian Smith, had defied the world in 1964 and declared Rhodesia, then a British colony, an independent republic where the whites would rule for a thousand years. Guerrillas fighting to overthrow the Rhodesians and establish the independent nation of Zimbabwe set up bases across the frontier in Mozambique. Rhodesia retaliated by launching devastating bombing raids, and Smith's intelligence chief, Ken Flower, decided to arm and train a small force of Mozambicans to stop the cross-border guerrilla raids. Renamo was born.

Years after his retirement, Flower sat in the luxurious gardens of his home in the posh suburbs of Harare, capital of the independent Zimbabwe he fought so hard to thwart, and explained in an interview that the inspiration for Renamo came from Portuguese counterinsurgency operations against the Angolan independence movement. "I was impressed with the fact that comparatively the Portuguese in Angola had survived insurgency there mainly through the introduction of what they called *flechas* [arrows]. Pseudo-terrorists you might call them. And this fired the imagination."

At the same time, the Rhodesians recruited former members of Frelimo's own guerrilla army, who were seething with frustration at their failure to obtain the perks and good jobs they believed they deserved once independence was won. They were passed over, they believed, because Frelimo, whose top leadership was dominated by the Shangaan people of the south and the Makondes of the far north, was guilty of ethnic discrimination. Frelimo, which had made strict nonracialism and nontribalism as a hallmark of its program, countercharged the dissidents with being opportunists seeking self-enrichment. The dispute served the Rhodesian interests nicely. Most of the dissidents who joined Renamo were members of the Ndau ethnic group of central Mozambique, which is precisely where the

Zimbabwean guerrillas fighting Rhodesia's white minority regime set up their clandestine bases. "Those who came to us in the first instance were clearly dissatisfied with their handling by the Portuguese or by Frelimo or by both. Some of the best men we had in the earliest days were defectors from Frelimo. It gave them, strangely, a way of life," Flower said. "It seemed to be providing what I would call an African solution to an African problem"—meaning that Rhodesia had found someone to do its bidding.

Unfortunately for the Rhodesians, the tactics did not work according to plan. Ian Smith's expected ten centuries of white rule buckled after just sixteen years, and days before Rhodesia became the independent nation of Zimbabwe in 1980, Flower transferred control of Renamo to South Africa, which had its own reasons for destabilizing Mozambique. The apartheid government used Renamo as a battering ram against Mozambique because of the staunch backing of its first president, Samora Machel, for Nelson Mandela's African National Congress. South Africa did everything from training rebel troops, airlifting arms and supplies into Mozambique, and establishing a sophisticated communications network to providing tailored business suits for Renamo leaders on their diplomatic visits abroad. Since Machel's government was avowedly socialist and Renamo claimed the mantle of anti-Communist "freedom fighters," the rebels also enjoyed fawning support in the United States among some right-wing Republican congressmen.

By the mid-1980s, the war was spreading like a bush fire from its epicenter, the central region of Manica and Sofala, home of the Ndau people who originally provided the backbone of the rebels' support, to the far north and the southern districts around Mungoi's village. As it did so, the Frelimo government, like the Portuguese before them, rounded up peasants in the countryside and settled them in poorly supplied and defended "protected villages," what the Portuguese had called *aldeamentos* when they used the same tactic against Frelimo. The idea was, in Maoist terms, to drain the water, the people, from the fish, Renamo. As Job Chambal, then National Director of Communal Villages, put it, "When it is said that we are forcing people into communal villages, it is true. Because if we don't, then the enemy will use those people to destroy their own future."[8]

The people of Mungoi's village were never forced into an *aldea comunal;* and like millions of Mozambican peasants, they seemed to regard Frelimo as a relatively benign force with little impact on their daily lives and Renamo as an unknown entity. That is, until the war bore down on them.

The chanting in the hut came to an abrupt halt, a sure sign that the ceremony marking the arrival of Mungoi's spirit was about to begin. Six women dressed in white formed a single line at the entrance of the dwelling. Everyone stood solemnly in expectation, the silence broken only by the squawking of a single pied crow squatting on a tree branch above. In a few moments, the women started to sway to and fro and to stomp their bare feet in the dust in a mock forced march. They erupted into a song about their suffering in the war: "When they find us, they beat us, they make us carry their things. What did we do? What did we do? We are crying for you father Mungoi." There was stirring in the hut from where the chanting emanated minutes before. The chorus line of women started a new song: "The family is dying, what are you going to do? We are going to find Mungoi. Mungoi always comes to help."

A collective cry went up when from the hut's dark entrance emerged a stunning sight. Christine, now dressed in a dark pinstripe suit, a homburg hat, with a leopard skin wrapped around her waist, walked with regal calm to the center of the clearing, carrying a stick and a hippopotamus hide whip. "That's him. That's Mungoi," Tchlene whispered urgently, pointedly referring to "him." The singing resounded throughout the village as Mungoi, now apparently on old, unsteady legs, headed for the wooden chair shrouded in a white sheet. Armando and several other village elders took their seats by his side, while the women cloaked in white lowered themselves onto the mats on the ground.

At that very moment, an elderly man riding up the dirt track, upon seeing Mungoi, jumped off his bicycle. He walked gingerly toward the gathering, bent to one knee, bowed his head, and clapped several times in a show of respect. Mungoi returned the gesture, and the man, breaking out into a wide smile of contentment, resumed his journey, proudly peddling away down the road.

Armando introduced Mhula, Lauriciano, Tchlene, and myself. Each time he finished a sentence, Mungoi nodded his ascent and together with the rest of the group snapped his fingers three times in satisfied acknowledgment. Mhula nervously explained in a voice so soft it was barely audible that we had come from Maputo to see for ourselves the situation in the village and to hear from the spirit why he returned to the land of the living. Mungoi nodded gravely. Mhula asked if he could take photographs, and again Mungoi nodded and whispered something to Armando, who chuckled to himself. "Mungoi says he has nothing to fear since he is just a spirit," he said.

In a deep, husky voice that sounded as if it belonged to an elderly man, Mungoi started on a long monologue about his death and resurrection in *Shangaan*, which Mhula and Lauriciano took turns translating into Portuguese, although increasingly the task fell to Lauriciano. Much of the time Mhula was busy snapping photographs, eager to return with proof of what had cost him two months in jail.

Calmly, Christine-turned-Mungoi laid out the story, occasionally jabbing the gnarled walking stick into the dirt to emphasize a point. At the time of his death, Augusto Sidawanhane Mungoi was a member of the village's royal family, serving as the local *cabo de terra*, or land chief, responsible for the villagers' relationship with the surrounding farmlands. Dispensing areas for cultivation, establishing grazing rights for livestock, and ensuring protection of the environment were his main tasks. He was one of a line of local chiefs who represented the villagers' covenant with the universe, in which the land provided their sustenance, while their ancestors buried in the soil saw to their spiritual needs.

When not busy with his chiefly duties, Mungoi's favorite hobby was hunting, and his skill as a marksman was well known in the area. He always kept a single-shot rifle at home. One day, however, his love of the sport proved to be his downfall. Returning from a visit to friends, he surprised a band of monkeys turning his house upside down. "I walked in and caught them making a mess of everything," he said, shaking his head, still angry at the thought of the scene he found. "This was not the first time they were up to such mischief, so I picked up my rifle and gave chase. They fled into the forest. Some climbed high into the trees, and I fired at them. I must have hit a beehive, because while I was reloading, a swarm of bees attacked. They were everywhere. My rifle fell to the ground and I heard an explosion. I felt the bullet in the chest." Mungoi later died of his wound. The year was 1957.

Thirty years after Mungoi's death, and twelve years after Mozambique's independence, the village was deep in crisis. The war hit the area like a violent wave. History and the ethnic makeup of the conflict meant that the Manjacaze area was destined to be one of Renamo's prime targets. Manjacaze was the symbolic capital of the Shangaan people, who provided most of Frelimo's top leadership, including its first three presidents, Eduardo Mondlane, Samora

Machel, and Joaquim Chissano. The Shangaans, originally from South Africa, immigrated to southern Mozambique in the early 1800s to escape the military campaigns of Shaka Zulu to unite the Zulu people. In the intervening years, Manjacaze served as the headquarters of the last Shangaan king, Gungunhana, whom the Portuguese captured in 1895 and exiled to the Azores. Since one of Renamo's justifications for its insurgency was the claim that the Shangaans who dominated Frelimo were practicing tribalism against Mozambique's other major ethnic groups, striking at Manjacaze was the rebels' way of piercing Frelimo's heartland.

The village of Mungoi itself was situated in a veritable no-man's-land, too remote to warrant the armed protection of the Frelimo army, yet also beyond the rebels' control. But on December 22, 1987, a Renamo unit attacked the village in the movement's inimitable style. Huts were looted and women and children kidnapped. Everyone who escaped the onslaught scurried into the forest. It was the violence of the raid and the panic it struck in the hearts of the people, Mungoi said, which awakened his spirit from the dead. From that day on, Christine was transformed from a healer into a spirit medium. "As I wandered through the village, I found my nephew," Mungoi said. Armando, like the rest of the villagers, was packing his belongings in preparation to flee.

"I asked, 'What is happening in the land of Mungoi?' and my nephew told me, 'There is war here now, Father.' I asked him why there was fighting, but Armando said he didn't know. So I told him to call a meeting with the rebels here, to tell them that the spirit of Mungoi wants to speak with them." As Mungoi continued the narration, Armando and the rest of the elders looked on enthralled, repeatedly snapping their fingers and nodding their heads in agreement. The children of the village came to sit a few yards away as if they were students attending an outdoor class.

Armando sent word to the rebels, and within a few days a platoon of twenty-two young gunmen arrived for the meeting. "All of them laid down their weapons and sat down, except their commander. I asked him why he wouldn't sit down, and he said he didn't want to," Mungoi continued with an eyebrow raised. "So I told him, 'You know I am not like you, I am already dead, and a spirit cannot die twice.'" After a few moments of hesitation, the youthful rebel commander lowered his weapon and took a seat alongside the others. "I asked him why there was war. 'I heard you like to burn communal villages,' I said, 'but do you see any communal village here?' The commander said no. 'I heard that you want to attack the government, but is Mungoi part of the government?' Again the answer was no. 'Why do you take away the children, the women and the old people?' I asked. 'Do women and children make war with you in the bush?' His answer was no. I told him that I was physically dead, but that I had the powers to defend this area. The commander asked for forgiveness and said he would tell the others that they should not attack the land of Mungoi."

Despite the spirit's warning, sporadic raids continued over a period of months, and dozens of women and children were kidnapped to serve as porters and providers of food and sometimes sex in the rebel bases. The practice horrified not only the individual families but the entire community, for mothers and children embody the collective future of everyone, and they were gradually being drained away. "My biggest conflict with the rebels is the kidnapping of women and children, the abuse of people who are not part of this war," Mungoi said. "Infants are smashed against trees, and people in the bases have been tortured." Something obviously had to be done to halt the abductions if the villagers were to be persuaded to remain on their land, which as a land chief, albeit a deceased one, was Mungoi's prime responsibility. Mungoi dispatched a messenger to ask the government to send some troops for additional protection, but the authorities scoffed at honoring a request from a spirit. If the Mungoi spirit was so powerful, came their reply, then it should not need any help from the army.

"My dilemma was that I had no weapons to defend the area, so I had to try another method," the spirit explained. Psychological tactics were in order, and Mungoi decided to play upon the faith of the Renamo commanders in their own *curandeiros*. Reliance on magic and religious symbols by soldiers and many others, from farmers to even soccer players, is a common practice. The Mau Mau guerrillas who fought the British so successfully in Kenya in the 1950s engaged in such practices as oath ceremonies. In 1996, a Zairian militia known as the Mai Mai Ingilima believed witchcraft bolstered its attack strength in eastern Zaire. *Mai* is a local variant of the Kiswahili word for baptism, *Maji,* which in turn was taken originally from the Arabic word for water. The Maji Maji war of 1905–07 in Tanganyika was inspired in part by the belief that a Maji baptism would render useless the bullets of the German colonial army.

Before embarking on operations in Mozambique, Renamo commanders typically consulted their traditional healers for luck and to foresee the likely outcome. That is when, Mungoi said, he would strike. "I would appear in one of the *curandeiros* because Mungoi can appear in any person. Every time I go to the rebel bases I ask them why they are fighting, because I only see suffering in this land. They say they are fighting because there is hunger, poverty, high prices, that they are fighting against socialism. I tell them that the solution to their problem is to free the women and children, that it is the only way to ensure their good fortune."

Everything the medium Christine was saying was a metaphor, outlined in rhymes and allusions. Yet however it was happening, everyone agreed that dozens of civilians who were held against their will in the Renamo camps suddenly started to appear in the village. Mungoi's reputation grew, and relatives of kidnap victims descended on the village from the surrounding countryside to place articles of their loved ones' clothing in the trees at the entrance to the homestead so that they could find their way back. Word was out that Mungoi could bring them home, and obviously the message reached inside nearby Renamo bases that it was healthier for the rebels to let the civilians go. The person of Christine had, like a lightning rod, become the focal point for the collective desire of the village to be left alone.

"When Renamo frees the people, they provide a guide to lead them to the land of Mungoi," the spirit said. "They also give offerings, such as money and cigarettes. Here is a guitar they sent." Mungoi lifted up a battered version of the rural guitar, an instrument fashioned out of a piece of wood and a half gallon tin can of oil. Then, to emphasize the point, he asked one of the female assistants to retrieve offerings brought by the rebels, mainly a few wadded up bills of currency tied in pieces of linen and tattered packs of cigarettes.

The spirit's apparent ability to secure the freedom of kidnap victims created a new set of problems from a totally unexpected direction. Certain government officials were convinced that the only way a Mungoi medium could achieve the release of the captured civilians was to become involved in some form of nefarious cooperation with Renamo. Hard-liners in the Frelimo army favored liquidating the spirit, although there was, understandably, genuine confusion about how to kill it. Assassinating Christine, for example, might simply prompt Mungoi to appear in another medium. What irked army officers most was the ban Mungoi announced on the carrying of weapons anywhere in the village area. This was seen as a direct challenge to the government's authority. So concerned did the provincial government become that the governor of Gaza province at the time, Francisco Pateguana, discussed the matter with President Joaquim Chissano. The president advised that the spirit should be left alone. Some in the Frelimo army, however, decided on another course. Mungoi was summoned to the town of Manjacaze, seat of the district capital, for a stormy meeting with the local Frelimo military commander, a notoriously ruthless man who went by the *nom de guerre* of Satan. "Satan said I was working for Renamo and that I must stop my work," Mungoi recalled with exasperation. "I responded by saying that if Frelimo told me to stop, then I would. But he alone could not give me the order." After the meeting, Satan spread the word that he would kill the spirit.

Then something happened which stunned even the most skeptical members of the government, something which temporarily made Mhula's life a nightmare. In June 1989, a message arrived in Xai Xai, capital of Gaza province, that twenty-seven Renamo rebels had decided to hand in their weapons and surrender to the spirit medium in Mungoi. Not surprisingly, officials of the Gaza provincial government were uncertain what to do. Theirs was a world of business contracts, road building, food aid for drought and war victims, and the like. Spirits were somewhat beyond their experience and ran counter to officially accepted ideology. "Most people knew that this Mungoi was powerful. Even senior government officials believed in its powers, but few would admit it publicly," Mhula explained. Well before the war, Mhula knew of the excellent reputation which Christine, the traditional healer of Mungoi's village, enjoyed. "My mother used to travel to the area to seek a cure for her intestinal problems. Other people from around the area would go and give offerings so their cows would grow and their fields produce well."

But until the news of the surrender of the Renamo soldiers, all Mhula knew of the spirit medium's involvement in the war were patchy, unsubstantiated rumors. Initially, the government tried to keep the report under wraps, but it was not long before Mhula heard of it. A quintessential street reporter, who cast his net wide and sifted through his catch of gossip in the hope of landing a story, Mhula was one of the new generation of critical journalists that emerged in post-independence Africa, skeptical of their governments' claims and sympathetic to the plight of their people. Living with his wife and two children in a shanty town on the eastern edge of Xai Xai, Mhula rarely had much money to pay for transportation. So he walked, hitchhiked, and talked his way onto military trucks and helicopters to reach the story. He was something of an institution in Xai Xai, a small, modern town of one- and two-story buildings stretched along a single main street on the banks of the Limpopo River. Everyone knew him, and walking around with Mhula could be a tedious affair, stopping every thirty seconds to greet some acquaintance. Little occurred in Gaza province which Mhula did not know about. He was among the first journalists to reach the sights of massacres on the main National Highway No. 1 south to Maputo, and his photographs of charred bodies and burnt-out vehicles were published in newspapers around the world.

Mhula was quickly on the trail of the story, asking friends around government offices and the local radio what they knew about the Renamo unit and the Mungoi spirit. Just as quickly, local security agents were tracking Mhula. The secret police chief summoned him for a meeting and said that the government had not received "orientations" from their superiors in Maputo on how to deal with publicity about the spirit. Thus, he should refrain from writing anything about it. "The idea was that this was a family matter and should not be publicized outside," Mhula said.

Two days later, when the twenty-seven Renamo fighters arrived from Mungoi's village to appear at the governor's palace, Mhula and other local reporters were invited to witness their surrender. He spoke with the rebel unit commander, a teenager named Joaquim Romão, who told him that he and his men were tired of fighting. While they were in the bush scavenging for food, they just kept walking and decided to turn themselves in. The village of Mungoi was the obvious place to do it because the spirit had banned both sides from fighting in the area. "They knew they could go to Mungoi without fear," Mhula said. At the time, he was working for the government's Social Communication office and was writing freelance stories for the national news agency, AIM. The day of the surrender, Mhula sent a report to Maputo.

When the story was published in the national daily newspaper, *Noticias,* two things about it upset the government. First, the article stated incorrectly that the governor met the medium Christine, which would have meant that Frelimo had given at best a witch doctor and at worst a spirit untold legitimacy. Second, Mhula reported that another sixty rebels were expected to turn themselves in at any moment. That revelation, several officials feared, would prompt an attempt by Renamo to stop the second surrender, which in fact later turned out to be a false rumor. Concerned for his own safety, Mhula hustled over to the governor's home and apologized. "The governor told me not to worry. He said the government made much bigger errors, like when they sent helicopters to strafe a rebel base and bombarded a village by mistake."

Despite the governor's assurance, the secret police service, known by its Portuguese acronym SNASP (National Service for the People's Security), arrested Mhula the next morning as he was leaving his house. Mhula was interrogated, bizarrely, about why he wrote the story, and he responded that the governor had invited him to the palace to witness the surrender. He spoke directly to the rebel unit commander, he explained, and he assumed he had permission to file the news report. A police official named Segredo (Secret) was unmoved and after several hours of questions presented a warrant for Mhula's detention. "They took my shoes, jacket and my watch. I was led to cell number seven. It was tiny, about one meter wide. I was terrorized. Each time someone came to my cell, I had to stand with my hands against the wall." At first he was put in solitary confinement. "They never beat me, but the cold would go right to my bones. I will never forget that. Anything could happen with SNASP. Their agents arrested people just for walking down the street with a young woman whom they wanted. So I was really scared. The agent who questioned me was very smooth, trained in Czechoslovakia."

After a month, Mhula was let out of the cell to sit in the sun and was allowed access to newspapers and the radio. It was, ironically, late July 1989, just as Frelimo was holding its historic Fifth Congress, which moved the party away from socialism and opened the door to multiparty democracy. Mozambique's close relationship with the Eastern bloc was coming to an end; the last contingent of Soviet military advisers was withdrawing from the country. Mhula remembered how surreal it was to listen to the radio broadcasts of the congress's reformist speeches from his jail cell.

The minister of justice finally ordered Mhula's release after Amnesty International contacted him to express concern over the case. His troubles were not over, however. His employer, Social Communication, refused to release his two months' back pay until he could find his way around a bureaucratic catch-22. He had to produce a document signed by SNASP which confirmed that he was now a free man. After several weeks, he did. Psychologically, the scars of the detention took longer to fade. He could not shake the feeling that he had done something wrong, and an arrest by SNASP was not exactly healthy for his reputation among family, friends, and colleagues. More than professional interest, his incarceration fueled his desire to see the Mungoi spirit for himself. It became a personal search for vindication.

Mhula did not know it at the time, but what was happening in Mungoi's village, however rare, was not wholly unique. There were several other zones of peace created by healers and spirit mediums whose followers could no longer withstand the violence. One of the more remarkable cases centered on a *macungeiro*, or soothsayer, named Samatenje, who lived in a hilltop spiritual redoubt in central Mozambique near Renamo's military headquarters in the Gorongosa Mountains. Samatenje's methods, as described in refugee accounts, were certainly unorthodox but nevertheless practical. His adeptness at playing off the warring armies against each other helped to create a refuge for his people. "No bandit chief dared enter the zone to rape women or steal food from the population," one witness said, because "they knew they wouldn't come out well. Samatenje could send lions or swarms of bees to attack them, or he would cause enormous thunderstorms which would fill them all with panic."[9] Superstition perhaps, but there is little doubt of Samatenje's psychological power, particularly over Renamo. Consider the following radio message sent by a Renamo section commander to his headquarters:

I report that I have completed all the works of the spirits in my house and the house of Samatenje with red and black pots. After the work, I dreamed of two lions and also spiritual doves. Meanwhile, I received information that in the enemy area of Monhenha, Samatenje, two lions entered and bit the enemy forces. After that, FPLM (Frelimo) forces ordered the population and Samatenje to leave the village of Muvunduzi. Samatenje refused and went home. I report that those two lions are going around in various zones and if seen should not be fired upon because they are the spirits.[10]

By far the most spectacular movement in Mozambique was led by a traditional healer named Manuel Antonío, who used tactics reminiscent of those employed by Alice Lekwenya's Holy Spirit rebel movement in Uganda. Antonío claimed to have been resurrected from the dead in 1989 and ordered by Jesus Christ to form a militia armed only with spears and knives. His *Naparama* warriors believed that Antonío had the power to vaccinate them against bullets with the ashes of secret bush plant. When he first appeared in the heavily populated central provinces of Zambézia and Nampula in late 1989, the local Frelimo authorities and Catholic missionaries in the area were equally venomous in their dismissal of Antonío as a crazy witch doctor. His mobilization drives featured a curious mixture of Christianity and traditional religions, punctuated by songs of martyrdom, one of which went, "The cross is heavy, the cross is heavy, Jesus has suffered, Jesus has suffered." The climax of his elaborate initiation ceremonies was an astounding reenactment of Christ's resurrection, in which he would bury himself under several feet of earth for up to fifteen minutes and speak to the crowds from a mock grave before rising from the dead. Recruiting among young men living in the massive impoverished refugee camps around government-controlled hamlets with the promise of a means to restore their dignity, his *Naparama* movement exploded from several hundred to twenty thousand. In just two years, the *Naparamas* scored repeated military victories over Renamo and captured almost one-half of Zambézia, Mozambique's wealthiest province, before Manuel Antonío was eventually killed in an ambush.

It was getting late in the afternoon at Mungoi's village, and Tchlene was anxious to leave soon so that he could reach Chidenguele before sunset. As Mhula and Tchlene expressed their desire to depart, Mungoi suddenly became very agitated. "You mean you are not spending the night with us?" No, it was not possible. Mungoi turned to Armando and told him to round up a chicken with white feathers for the visitors. "The white feathers will keep you safe. The road is not safe today."

Mungoi said a small prayer to keep everyone healthy, and the meeting broke up in a song. "The family is dying, what are we going to do? We are going to find Mungoi. Mungoi always comes to help." A spontaneous procession formed behind Mungoi. The women in white, the elders, and groups of children marched slowly toward the white building where the corpse of Mungoi was resting. The residents of the entire homestead formed a line around the building as the chorus reached a crescendo. In the middle of the crowd stood Tchlene, smiling and belting out the words at the top of his lungs. Old Africa reclaimed one of its sons.

Roaring off in the back of the pickup toward a bright red sunset, Tchlene chuckled and said, "The government can do nothing here. It has no alternative but to respect Mungoi." Several vehicles passed by bearing little white flags with blue crosses on their antennas. They were miniature versions of the cross hanging in the doorway to Mungoi's tomb. "Those cars can travel anywhere, and they are never attacked," he shouted over the din of the engine. "They are just for the people who live here, for those who truly believe."

PARTLY BECAUSE OF the extraordinary reassertions and adaptions of traditional beliefs by the Mungoi villagers, Samatenje, and Manuel Antonío, and partly because its own state administration in the countryside was collapsing under pressure from the war, by the early 1990s Frelimo's attitudes toward chiefs and healers underwent a sea-change. The shift was apparent throughout the country in villages such as Mungari, one of a handful of government-held hamlets deep in the mainly Renamo-controlled central province of Manica.

Mungari was surrounded by rebel troops and accessible only by air, and the young administrator, Eduardo Singano, positively bubbled with excitement as he explained how much easier his job became after the government gave him permission to enlist the support of the local chiefs, commonly known in the area as *mambos*. The mood was almost festive late one afternoon as a traditional healer attended a long line of patients in a neighborhood called *A Luta Continua*, or "The Struggle Continues," at the center of the village—something that would have been nearly impossible in the days of *obscurantismo*.

Without the help of the traditional authorities, Singano said, he could not possibly see to the wants of the five thousand people under his control. "When we need the population to help get something done, I have a meeting with the *mambos* to gain their support. For example, they organized the clearing of the airstrip," he said with a giggle. "It was difficult before, because we administrators were always in conflict with the chiefs. We did not recognize their authority. Now the government says we can, and it makes my job much easier. I am happier, and the people are content. They have the feeling that we are respecting their culture."

The government's volte-face, however much the result of desperation, won wide popular approval. The authorities were learning a lesson they should have already known. While the history books often focus almost exclusively on the role of Western-educated nationalists in the fight against colonial rule, the picture they have painted is a highly distorted one. Foreign occupation met with stiff resistance by existing societies all over the continent, whether the Ashante of Ghana and the Dahomey in Benin, the Zulus in South Africa, the Hehe in Tanzania, or countless others. In Zimbabwe, the first uprising against Cecil Rhodes's white settler column in the 1890s was inspired by the almost mythical religious figure of Nehanda, and eighty years later her spirit was invoked by the guerrillas fighting to overthrow Ian Smith's white minority regime. Robert Mugabe, now the president of Zimbabwe, received a Jesuit education and remains a practicing Christian. Yet when he escaped from Rhodesia in the late 1970s to join the Zimbabwean guerrilla armies in Mozambique, it is said that he was assisted by an ancestral spirit of the family that sheltered him.[11]

In Mozambique, chiefs and spirit mediums were in the forefront of resistance to the first Portuguese explorers who penetrated the interior along the Zambezi River in the sixteenth century and made their way to the Munhumutapa state of the Shona people in what is now modern Zimbabwe. The first landmark incursion was undertaken by a Portuguese priest named Dom Gonçalo da Silveira in 1560. His goal was to shine the light of Roman Catholicism on southern Africa and thus pry open the gold reserves of the Munhumutapa for the good of the Portuguese empire. "More or less a one-man army of invasion on behalf of Portugal and Rome," is the way Zimbabwean historian and current foreign minister Stan Mudenge has described him.[12]

The young emperor Negomo Mpupunzagutu believed Father Silveira to be a powerful white diviner, and he was especially enchanted by a statue of the Virgin Mary. Father Silveira duly baptized the emperor, but in so doing upset a number of vested interests, especially the traditional Shona religious leaders, the *mhondoro* spirit mediums, and the healers. They conspired with visiting Swahili gold and ivory traders, who rightly feared the Portuguese as commercial competitors, to convince the Negomo that Father Silveira was a Portuguese spy and wizard who was conniving with the state's enemies. In the end, Emperor Negomo ordered Father Silveira to be killed, and in March 1561, crocodiles in the Musengezi River made a meal of his body.[13]

More than a century later, the militant Munhumutapa emperor Nhacunimbili united with the neighboring Changamire Rovzi state and expelled the Portuguese back to the coast. In the south it was no different, with King Gungunhana's warriors mounting a spirited resistance to the Portuguese until the fall of Manjacaze near Mungoi's village.

The last episode of large-scale resistance by traditional leaders in Mozambique occurred in 1917, when a teenage girl named Mbuya claimed to be the medium of the powerful ancestral spirit of Kabudu Kagoro and helped to mobilize the lesser mediums from the remnants of the Shona Munhumutapa state. She was a key adviser to Barue chief Nongwe-Nongwe, who issued a call to arms in central Mozambique after the Portuguese launched a campaign of forced recruitment of soldiers and porters for the fight against the German army in East Africa. Mbuya provided the Barue fighters with medicines to render European bullets useless. On the verge of defeat, the Portuguese hired twenty thousand Shangaan mercenaries to turn the tide.[14]

Even in the modern nationalist struggle against the Portuguese, traditional chiefs initially played a leading role. The first militant anticolonial movement since the defeat of Mbuya was set up by Lazaro Nkavandame, a conservative who organized Makonde village headmen in the far northern province of Cabo Delgado to protest against high Portuguese taxation on cotton produced by Africans. His Mozambique African Voluntary Cotton Society was behind the demonstrations that eventually culminated in a massacre by Portuguese troops of at least six hundred people in the town of Mueda in June 1960. Like the Sharpeville shootings of sixty-nine pass law protestors three months before in South Africa, the killings at Mueda set Mozambique on an inevitable course of confrontation. Two years later, three small nationalist groups joined to form Frelimo as a single liberation front. The first shot in the independence war was fired in 1964 by Frelimo units crossing from bases in Tanzania.

The movement was far from united, however, with major internal clashes between conservatives like Nkavandame and his village elders who viewed the struggle as one of racial emancipation and more radical, generally European-educated champions of socialist revolution. Frelimo's overall military commander, Samora Machel, assumed the presidency, and Nkavandame and his supporters were eventually expelled from the movement. After independence, President Machel's government arrested several dozen high-profile opponents, including Nkavandame, put them in remote reeducation camps, and in the early 1980s executed them.

Once in power, the leaderships in Mozambique and in most of Africa have maintained a schizophrenic relationship with the religions and chieftaincy structure held dear by their forebearers. Many seem ashamed of them. It is a testament to the depth of colonial penetration into the mind of Africa's post-independence leaders that no present-day head of state or president publicly professes belief in indigenous religion, which has been practiced for thousands of years. Nicephore Soglo, the former president of the small West African state of Benin, was rare in finally acceding to the demands of traditional religious leaders in January 1996 by declaring official state recognition of *vodu*, which is followed by 60 percent of his fellow citizens.

Yet for some, the change in attitude has come slowly. Stories of the enduring power of rural beliefs are often greeted with incredulity among the educated elite, more at home with Christianity and Islam, especially in Maputo, a modern metropolis of 1.5 million people. Perched on a series of bluffs overlooking the turquoise Indian Ocean, bathed in the multiracial warmth of Afro-Latin culture, blessed with wide beaches and some of the best seafood on earth, Maputo seems a world away from the rest of the country, totally alien from villages like Mungoi.

Each morning the streets of Maputo are filled with caravans of vehicles loaded down with men, women, and children from the slum neighborhoods completing their trek to the center of town. Rickety gypsy taxis stop to disgorge and absorb passengers, while muscular young men acting as conductors check the fares and bang the back of the trucks with huge screwdrivers to signal that it is time to move out. Fumes from thick lines of crawling traffic settle down on palm trees, passersby, and shoppers in the semilegal markets, popularly known as *dumba nengue*, or "run for your life" in the Shangaan language, reflecting the periodic and ultimately fruitless attempts by the police to shut them down. Every afternoon customers flock to outdoor cafés, seeking solace from the waves of humidity rolling in from the ocean, for cool beers, or to shops selling the latest fashions and imported televisions and stereo music systems. In the evenings, the pace slows, as people once again pour onto the streets to visit friends and catch up on the latest gossip, while the wealthy patronize beachfront restaurants serving up grilled prawns and lobsters and Portuguese wine. Late into the night, rich and poor share a common passion: the discothèques throbbing to the seductive rhythms of *Marrabenta*, disco, and funk.

Despite its cosmopolitan atmosphere, Maputo too has experienced an upsurge in the popularity of traditional customs from the countryside that continues to this day. Partly it is the result of the thousands of people who hoisted their most precious belongings onto their backs, gathered together their children, and fled their rural homesteads for the relative safety and prosperity of the big city. A human wave has hit Maputo's wide swath of slums, the so-called *cidade do caniço*, or "reed city." It is a phenomenon common to most urban centers in Africa, and much of the developing world, where rising population rates and dwindling farming opportunities have sent millions into the cities. In Mozambique, the inflow was accelerated by the war. With the new migrants have come their languages, their healers, and their religions.

Also heightening the attraction of Maputo's poorer residents to *curandeiro* healers is the worsening condition of the hospitals and health clinics and skyrocketing prices fostered by belt-tightening reforms demanded by Mozambique's foreign creditors, especially the International Monetary Fund and the World Bank. The two Bretton Woods institutions arrived in Mozambique, as they have dozens of other African nations, with a blueprint for downsizing. The goal of the "structural adjustment program" is to cut back government spending, privatize state-owned companies, reduce inflation, devalue the national currency, and spur domestic and foreign investment. But as it has elsewhere in Africa, the immediate impact of the program has been to rip the guts out of the government's social welfare policies, force up the prices of basic foodstuffs, such as corn and rice, deepen unemployment, and worsen poverty.

Scores of professionals formerly in the civil service and the school system now look to the private sector, including the black market, for better-paying jobs, sparking a massive internal brain drain. A high school teacher who earns $70 per month can become a driver for the United Nations at four times his salary. Secretaries at international nongovernment organizations can earn more than cabinet ministers. Every day seems to widen the gap between the harsh economic reality of the new world order and the empty slogans of the past extolling the "worker-peasant alliance" and the "dictatorship of the proletariat" painted in red lettering on walls throughout the country.

In the marketplace of health, relatively low-cost traditional practitioners are more than holding their own. One of Maputo's biggest open-air markets, Xipamanini, has an entire section set aside for traditional remedies, such as roots and herbs and even the ingredients for magic potions that will do everything from increase a person's good luck and ensure fertility to keep thieves at bay. The healers themselves perform a myriad of roles, from medical doctor and psychoanalyst to fortuneteller, and often their prescriptions are incredibly effective, particularly in cases involving mental illness or asthma in the young.

The former U.S. ambassador to Mozambique, Melissa Wells, once consulted a *curandeiro* after doctors in South Africa and the United States had tried but failed over a period of years to cure her shoulder ailment. The healer, a woman from the far north of the country, rapidly diagnosed her problem and applied some herbal medicine with a razor blade supplied by Wells. The remedy brought instant relief. When Wells told her doctors in South Africa about the success of the treatment, they shook their heads and admitted that they still had a lot to learn from traditional healers.

Independent African governments have had little more success than the colonial rulers in pushing traditional beliefs underground in the name of modernization. The lesson is clear. A stable and confident Africa needs to be at ease with its cultural past. As Claude Ake has warned, "African culture has fiercely resisted and threatened every project that fails to come to terms with it, even as it is acted upon and changed."[15] In Mungoi's village, the force of that faith humbled even the power of the AK-47.

For the remainder of the war, the people in Mungoi's village remained relatively unscathed. The worst drought in southern Africa's recent memory and the continuing military stalemate brought Frelimo and Renamo to the bargaining table in negotiations that were mediated by a Catholic lay organization, the Santo Egidio Community, in Rome. On October 4, 1992, Frelimo and Renamo signed a peace accord, and hostilities ceased across the country. The agreement committed both sides to hand in their rifles and take their contest from the battlefield to the ballot box. Over the next twelve months, the United Nations dispatched a 6,400-strong peacekeeping force while the Renamo and Frelimo armies moved to assembly areas for demobilization. Two years after the signature of the peace treaty, Mozambicans celebrated the first democratic elections in their history. The vote passed off peacefully, and while Frelimo emerged as the biggest party, Renamo scored impressive gains, winning the most votes in key central provinces. Elected members of the former warring armies took up their seats in a multiparty national assembly. Nearly 2 million refugees left their sanctuaries in neighboring countries and returned home to their farms and villages to begin the difficult process of rebuilding the nation.

Through it all, the village of Mungoi held together. The confrontation with the hard-liners in Frelimo had long since subsided once the army commander Satan, who had publicly vowed to kill the spirit, was himself gunned down one night in Manjacaze town. He was shot by a single assailant who disappeared into the darkness. So far had Frelimo come in its attitude toward traditional institutions that it authorized the establishment of nationwide associations representing chiefs and healers. The irony of its initial campaign against the chiefs and *obscurantismo* is that capitalism is the ruling party's new creed; socialism has been jettisoned; and the government has desperately sought the support of traditional rulers. During the election campaign, two senior party officials traveled from Maputo to the village of Mungoi to request the spirit's support. Their plea was politely refused. "I told them I was neutral," Mungoi said a few days after the polls. "I made a great appeal to the political parties, whether Renamo or Frelimo, to ensure that the war is finished."

Mungoi has heard about the role of the United Nations and leaders of both Frelimo and Renamo in ending the war, but it is his view that the spirits of the ancestors deserve a lot of the credit too. It was, in fact, the result of a meeting of the spiritual minds. "There was not really a conference of the spirits at the national level," Mungoi said, as his attendants clapped their hands and snapped their fingers three times in unison just as they had four years before. "But the force which there is in this region testifies to the fact that there is a will of the spirits of all Mozambicans to end the war, to make sure it is the past. My children and I know nothing of these conflicts. My children were maltreated and many were killed. Now there seems to be peace, and we are thankful that the politicians have heard the voice of the people."

The Healing Touch

S lamming her fist into the palm of her hand, Merci Manci shouts at the class like a strict schoolmarm: "Only when it's erect!" For a moment, the pupils sit in stunned silence, hardly believing their eyes and ears. As the seconds pass, the bolder ones glance from side to side, sneaking a peek at their colleagues. Then a wave of uncontrolled laughter sweeps over the gathering. Some giggle through clenched teeth, while others stamp their feet in a vain attempt to throttle the merriment. The source of the mirth is a stiff tubelike piece of rubber which Manci, coolly straight-faced, is waving around in front of her as she outlines the demonstration. When she detects that her charges are not paying sufficient attention, she suddenly shifts position so that the piece of rubber sticks out from her waist, and she emphasizes the point by thrusting her hips forward sharply. In her hands is a large dildo. More hilarious still is the sight of Manci's sixty-year-old mother, Mary, passing handfuls of dildos round the room and insisting that everyone practice how to cover them with clear rubber sheaths. From the grown men and women wearing elaborate headdresses of feathers, beads, and amulets, to the younger ones with white chalk on their legs to indicate their apprenticeship as traditional healers, *inyangas*, everyone is trying to fit the condoms.

The meeting has brought thirty-two South African traditional healers and *sangomas*, or diviners, many of whom came by horse and on foot, to Holy Cross Hospital, first established by the Anglican Church in the heart of the Transkei, the birthplace of Nelson Mandela. Their assignment is simple: Attend a two-day workshop to learn ways to prevent infection by the HIV virus which causes AIDS. The course is part of a novel campaign launched by the Traditional Doctors' AIDS Project and a nongovernmental organization, AIDS-COM, to enlist the healers in the war against AIDS. The idea is to train approximately thirty healers each session, and each of them in turn will train another thirty, who will do the same for thirty more. Besides their practice on manipulating condoms, there are sessions on using only new razor blades for incisions, the healers' equivalent of injections, and on educating the community to adjust to the presence of AIDS victims, not ostracize them, and to help them find productive jobs.

When the meeting was originally called, many of the healers voiced serious reservations about traveling to Holy Cross. Because of its association with the Anglican Church, the hospital in their view is a symbol of unwanted Western penetration in the Transkei. Like their counterparts throughout Africa, South Africa's *inyangas* and *sangomas* remain highly defensive toward Western culture, a hostility nurtured over the years when the National Party government professing the apartheid ideology actively suppressed traditional medical practitioners. Yet once the healers arrived at Holy Cross, they received a warm welcome by the local hospital staff. Manci says the choice of location was deliberate. "We have to bring the two sides together. No one can fight this AIDS alone."

The most contentious moment during Manci's lecture occurs when a young man makes a show of shaking his head in disagreement. Like Manci, he is a *sangoma*, a practitioner who specializes in diagnosing illnesses that are manifestations of the spiritual world. Manci asks what is troubling him. He replies that he cannot accept the idea that AIDS is a disease that can be prevented by abstinence or a condom. Half of his patients are suffering with problems related either to sexually transmitted diseases or to AIDS. That is true for all the healers, he says, glancing around the room to find everyone nodding in agreement. As a *sangoma*, he knows, and everyone should know, that venereal diseases do not strictly speaking constitute an illness. They are the result of sleeping with evil spirits.

Manci, a stylish thirty-year-old, flips her plaited hair back and looks at the ceiling as she considers an appropriate response. She, too, has had to come to grips with this very issue. She first realized that her calling was to be a *sangoma* in the mid-1980s when she dreamed of the death of Samora Machel, the charismatic president of Mozambique whose victory over Portuguese colonialism inspired a generation of young South Africans to resist the apartheid regime. Machel died in mysterious circumstances in October 1987 when his presidential plane strayed into South Africa and crashed into a hillside, months after, Manci says, she had dreamed of his demise.

Lowering her gaze back to the classroom awaiting an answer, Manci engages the debate. "It is true that there are many disagreements about how this AIDS started," she says. "But we called this workshop to fight the disease. As a *sangoma* myself, I can confirm that these preventative measures," she points to the dildo covered in a condom, "do stop this thing called AIDS." Her declaration triggers an uproar of arguments between the rows of healers, half supporting Manci's views and the other half sticking by the young *sangoma*. Waving the dildo in her left hand, Manci gradually restores order. Then she delivers the hammer blow. "The choice is simple," she bellows impatiently. "You can tell your people that they can either abstain from sex until marriage and then remain loyal to that one person, or they must learn how to use condoms." The gathering pauses briefly and then sets about the condom calisthenics with renewed vigor.

The session at Holy Cross marks a small but vital step in the building of a formidable, if sometimes uneasy, alliance of researchers, doctors, social workers, and healers who have decided that they must engage the battle for Africa's health at ground zero. They form the front line in a war that potentially dwarfs all the other conflicts in Africa, against enemies such as the big killer diseases of malaria and AIDS, armed with overwhelming firepower. Barring miracle vaccines affordable to the poor in Africa and Asia, not simply to the rich in the West, the fight will have to be all-embracing, targeting body, mind, and spirit, if it is to be won. This is especially critical in the case of AIDS, against which Africa, despite its widespread poverty and deteriorating health services, does have some potent weapons. The extended family and its network of responsibility must be bolstered to care for the sick and orphans left behind; education by community activists on how to prevent infection must be strengthened; traditional healers must be given a high-profile role alongside doctors.

In the past, meetings such as the one at Holy Cross have been extremely rare since healers and practitioners of Western-style medicine inhabit distinct philosophical realms. While a medical doctor is concerned mainly with physical manifestations and scientific causes of illness, in the traditional world sickness touches on the individual's physical and spiritual state, as well as the person's relationship with the greater community, the living and the ancestors. Remedies can involve everything from applying straightforward medicinal plants to holding ceremonies to appease ancestral and angry spirits.[1] To some doctors, healers are little better than "witch doctors" dispensing hocus-pocus, while the traditionalists see Western physicians as proponents of "white man's medicine," alienated from the culture of those they are meant to serve.

Yet, as messengers of the need to change society's behavior, traditional healers, Africa's doctor of choice, enjoy immense advantages over their Western-trained colleagues. An estimated 80 percent of South Africans still frequent the country's two hundred thousand healers, who outnumber medical doctors by about ten to one. In the rest of Africa, the healers enjoy equal if not greater popularity. "It's important to train the traditional healers because the overwhelming majority of the black population comes to us," says Manci. "They believe in the traditional way of healing, and they believe in us because we still have the culture."

Long known as effective in cases of mental illness, healers have also shown themselves skilled in treating diarrhea, asthma in youngsters, and headaches. In other parts of the developing world, such as Brazil and India, traditional medicine has been taken more seriously by governments than in Africa. In India, traditional medicine is offered in the hospitals and university curricula.[2] Research into traditional African medicines has been minimal, suffering equally from prejudice and the widespread reluctance of the healers themselves to reveal their medical secrets.

The sheer gravity of Africa's modern health crisis is forcing both sides of the medical divide to seek compromise of the type outlined in an earlier chapter by Chief Sibongile Zungu of the Madlebe clan. The explosion of AIDS, together with the renewed rampage by a gang of lethal diseases such as pulmonary tuberculosis, meningitis, and new, highly virulent strains of malaria, has pummeled a continent that already had the highest rates of infant mortality and the lowest life expectancy in the world. The gains scored by the vaccination campaigns, launched by many newly independent governments as the colonial powers began their withdrawal in the 1960s, have suffered sharp reversals in just two decades. Rapid population growth, economic decline, rising levels of corruption, and armed conflict have been the main culprits behind dramatic declines in per capita spending on health. By the early 1990s, just as the AIDS epidemic was detonating throughout the continent, African countries spent a ridiculously small amount on health, on average $24 per person each year.

The fact is that most governments are under severe pressure from international lending institutions and Western banks to place a higher priority on keeping up payments on their foreign debts than providing medical care for their people. Uganda, trumpeted as Africa's economic success story by many in the West, spends $3 per person on health for every $17 on the foreign debt. Scores of other countries face similar debt-to-health-care ratios. Cold economic logic has nurtured the building blocks of pestilence: poverty, dependence, and disease. The result is too few hospitals with too few beds and too few resources to purchase essential drugs, to pay doctors decent salaries, and to ensure steady supplies of water and electricity. The dilapidated facilities themselves become breeding grounds for disease.

Before the spread of AIDS was properly understood, transfusions of blood tainted by the HIV virus were common, and hospitals routinely recycled syringes or, in the case of traditional healers, razor blades. Impoverished living conditions, poor hygiene, and massive population displacements caused by drought, war, and political unrest only made things worse. Even diseases other than AIDS that can be treated relatively simply have surged forward for lack of resources, education, and access to the victims. In 1995, meningitis afflicted four hundred thousand Africans and killed at least ten thousand. In the month of July 1994 alone, cholera slaughtered ten thousand Rwandans who had fled in the aftermath of the genocide to camps at Goma, Zaire. Malaria claims the lives of at least 1 million African children every year.

When the AIDS epidemic first struck, the response was at best sluggish from African governments stung by Western suggestions that their countries were to blame for the outbreak of the virus. They refused to publicly address the problem and regularly underrated the extent of the crisis. Ugandan President Yoweri Museveni, whose country was among the first to feel the awesome consequences of the epidemic, is rare among his colleagues in discussing the disease in almost every major speech. In 1992, sub-Saharan Africa spent about $90 million on AIDS prevention programs, just twice as much money as Thailand.

Now Africa is gripped by nothing short of a modern-day plague. The raw statistics gathered by the World Health Organization make for mind-numbing reading: 13 million African adults infected with the HIV virus by mid-1996, a figure expected to rise to 30 million by the turn of the century. Already, the epidemic has overwhelmed Africa's hospitals. From Abidjan, Côte d'Ivoire, and Kampala, Uganda, to Lusaka, Zambia, and Lilongwe, Malawi, the percentage of hospital beds filled by HIV-infected patients ranges from 50 to 80 percent. At the main Parirenyatwa Hospital in the Zimbabwean capital, Harare, AIDS is the number one killer of children. An estimated eight hundred people are newly infected with HIV every day in South Africa.

Because HIV is spread overwhelmingly through heterosexual sex in Africa, most of the deaths occur in the twenty-five- to forty-year-old age range. The victims should be in the prime of their lives—high school and college graduates, experienced workers, and usually parents. The impact on Africa's drive to reverse a generation of economic decline will be devastating as scores of workers, educated civil servants, and young mainly women farmers are lost. The World Bank believes that AIDS could slow Africa's economies by one-third of a percentage point, a huge figure on a continent where growth has remained slow and often stagnant in recent years. That could be a low estimate. A study carried out in Kenya in 1996 says that by the year 2000 the direct and indirect costs of AIDS could represent 15 percent of the gross domestic product.[3]

In a sense, South Africa is at the end of the line in AIDS' sweep through Africa. The HIV virus embarked on its journey in the central African countries of Zaire, Uganda, and Kenya in the mid-1970s and traveled south along the truck routes down through Rwanda, Burundi, Tanzania, Malawi, and Zambia, where former President Kenneth Kaunda lost a son to AIDS. Within a decade, it reached Zimbabwe, to the north of South Africa across the Limpopo River. HIV's first targets were the urban elites who have the money to travel and to pay for sex. Although AIDS shares a reputation with other mass killer diseases of thriving on political and ecological chaos, in reality it much prefers the fruits of economic development. Collapsed infrastructure and poor transport links inhibit its spread. In Zimbabwe, the virus encountered something rare and inviting: an excellent road network. It was able to penetrate the rural heartland by piggy-backing on buses and trucks plying Zimbabwe's nine thousand miles of tarred roads. The thoroughfares were built during the days of Ian Smith's Rhodesia so that the troops of the white minority government could reach the more remote areas to pursue guerrilla units fighting for independence. A decade later, the roads conspired in spreading the pandemic to the heart of southern Africa, the potential economic powerhouse of the continent. Zimbabwe is currently the scene of the worst ravages of the epidemic, losing five hundred people to AIDS each week.[4]

The crisis has undermined the important strides Zimbabwe has made in the health sector since the country won its independence in 1980. Robert Mugabe's incoming government took a number of important steps that brought a dramatic turnaround in health conditions for the black majority, who had suffered glaring neglect as second-class citizens under the Rhodesian regime. The new administration immediately eliminated racial barriers to health services. It joined hands with international aid agencies and villages themselves to improve sanitation and provide clean water in the rural areas. An aggressive immunization campaign covered 80 percent of the country's children against the main killers of Africa's young: measles, tuberculosis, whooping cough, tetanus, diphtheria, and polio. Within nine years of independence, Zimbabwe slashed its infant mortality rate by nearly half. By any reckoning it was a remarkable achievement, one that showed what could be accomplished with the necessary commitment.

It did not last. Overspending on inefficient state-owned companies and a bloated civil service, which served in part as a system of patronage to maintain the popularity of President Mugabe's ruling Zimbabwe African National Union (ZANU), chalked up massive budget deficits and fueled a rise in the foreign debt to nearly $4 billion. An economic adjustment program known as ESAP, imposed at the urging of the World Bank and the International Monetary Fund, made the economy more efficient but has worsened unemployment and sent food prices soaring. It also committed the government to slashing the budget, cutting deeply into medical services. Zimbabwe's health system began sliding toward collapse.

To cover costs, the Ministry of Health introduced charges for prenatal checkups and hospital treatment. The impact was immediate, according to Health Minister Timothy Stamps. The maternal mortality rate rose from 251 per 100,000 in the late 1980s to 350 per 100,000 in 1992. Morale has plummeted as working conditions deteriorate. "We are exporters of human capital, and this tended to accelerate in the health sphere in the last five years with the opening up of South Africa," says Stamps. His ministry's figures show that by 1995 there were 1,500 medical practitioners in Zimbabwe, a rise of only 111 since independence, despite the graduation of 80 to 85 doctors per year. The reason is simple. A doctor with four years' experience could expect to earn 6,000 Zimbabwe dollars a month in 1995, or about $650, often less than the average salary for a private secretary. "On Air Zimbabwe flights, many of the air hostesses are fully qualified nurses. It's the same with bank tellers. They're better paid," Stamps says.

While wealthy Zimbabweans, mainly ZANU party apparatchiks, white farmers and businessmen, and a tiny black middle class can turn to well-equipped private clinics, the public health services for the poor suffer. The rising cost of living means that fewer and fewer patients can afford to travel to the local hospital, and there are not enough beds for them even if they could. "The poor are just getting poorer," says Dr. Monica Glenshaw, the administrator of a mission hospital in the remote central town of Murambinda, with about four thousand inhabitants. "They used to come back for reexamination, but now they cannot afford to. The AIDS epidemic has knocked the stuffing out of the poor."

By January 1996, Zimbabwe's main hospitals ran out of linen, food, and essential medicines after the government slashed the Health Ministry's monthly budget allocation by one-quarter. Just two months before, members of parliament voted pay increases of between 34 and 116 percent for themselves and President Mugabe. Fifteen years after independence from the white minority government of Rhodesia, racial discrimination has been pushed aside by class distinction. The underclass, the vast majority of the population, is being hammered just as Zimbabwe is witnessing, in Stamps's words, a "ripening of the [AIDS] epidemic."

In its wake, the AIDS offensive has left thousands of emaciated corpses which evoke its nicknames, the "slimming disease" and the "wasting syndrome." Surveys suggest that between 25 and 40 percent of Zimbabwe's sexually active population is infected. Anglo-American Corporation, the country's biggest employer, believes one-quarter of its workers are HIV-positive and has begun recruiting two and three people for each post. By the year 2005, 2 million Zimbabweans will probably have died of AIDS and related illnesses, such as pulmonary tuberculosis and pneumonia.

The number of deaths is rising so quickly that one of the country's largest funeral services, Mashfords, seriously suggested burying the dead vertically to save space. The scale of human destruction shocked even the most experienced of observers. Richard Rigby, a British doctor who volunteered to work at a rural hospital in southern Africa in 1995, wrote in the *British Medical Journal:* "When I decided to work in Africa I believed I appreciated how bad the AIDS problem was. Now I do not believe anybody really does."[5]

Catherine Office does. Three years ago, Catherine, a shy, soft-spoken seventy-year-old, was a contented grandmother living in her four-room brick house in Highfields, a tightly packed township of one-story dwellings on the outskirts of Harare, and the queen of a relatively thriving extended family. Life was by no means easy. Prices of food, especially the staple corn meal, soared when the government abolished state subsidies under its free-market economic policies. Armed robbery was an increasing danger. Her home is just around the corner from a particularly rough neighborhood called the Beira Corridor where a number of notorious *tsotsi* criminal gangs lived and, from time to time, died in shootouts. But the family was growing, and there was always enough food. Two of her daughters were married to men with jobs, and between them they had seven children. Her youngest son, Moses, had steady work at Castle Breweries; her eldest daughter, Annah Muzamani, was earning $30 a month as a rice packer; and Catherine's husband Ganizani was a farm worker outside the town of Bindura, about fifty miles north of the city. In a society where on average eight people depend upon a single salaried worker, the family was keeping well above the poverty line.

Then came the plague. The first AIDS casualty in the family was Catherine's second daughter, Lateness, who succumbed to the disease in May 1994, leaving four children. Then in November, her third, Eva, mother of three, expired. Their husbands, who Catherine believes are also infected, ran off. All seven orphaned grandchildren, aged three to twelve, were left in Catherine's care. One of them, seven-year-old James, received treatment at a government tuberculosis clinic before doctors made a firm diagnosis of what everyone suspected: he too is HIV-positive. She could not sue the husbands for child support because she had no money to pay for either the transport to court or the cost of filing the suit. But even with all the additional expenses, Catherine was getting by. Then, in May 1995, her daughter Annah lost her job when the rice-packing factory where she worked went bankrupt.

Now Catherine is desperate. She has taken in a lodger for about $11 a month and convinced her son Moses to contribute another $15 a month for electricity and water fees. Otherwise, there is no money for food, clothes, or blankets for the children, who must sleep on the cement floor. Catherine's husband Ganizani returns home from Bindura when he can take time off, but he does not stay as long as he once did. "He does not like all the children around, so he just says hello, stays awhile, and goes away." The family survives off donations from friends and from the *Mashambanzou* Care Trust, a nearby hospice and holistic care center for AIDS sufferers funded by Norway and Britain. *Mashambanzou*—derived from the Shona words for "to wash" and "elephant," meaning "Dawn of a New Day," referring to the early morning hours when elephants wallow in the river—is administered by Catholic nuns. Catherine, deeply religious herself, found out about *Mashambanzou* at her local church, St. Mary's, where she is a regular worshipper. Aiming to fortify extended families in need, *Mashambanzou* runs a variety of AIDS-related projects, including an eleven-bed unit for terminally ill patients at St. Anne's Hospital, an outpatient crisis center, day care for HIV-positive children, and workshops about the disease at schools, beer halls, and churches.

Without the help the center provides, Catherine says the family would not make it. Each month *Mashambanzou*, if its own funds are adequate, provides a bit of vegetable oil and a bag of corn flour, which forms the basis of *sadza*, the thick white porridge that is the staple of the Zimbabwean diet. "What we eat depends on what friends and the Sisters give us. Where would we be without the center? Preparing meals is hard. If I am short of food, then we go without lunch at all, or maybe some soup. If there is food that day, then I prepare *sadza*, and then in the evening, *sadza* again. The main food we eat is *sadza*. I try to find some vegetables to make relish, but the vegetables are very expensive these days."

But for Catherine, the occasional food donations and the day-care facilities for her grandchildren which *Mashambanzou* offers, however welcome, are not the Trust's only benefit. Just as important to her is the concern shown by *Mashambanzou*'s nuns and volunteer workers, who routinely visit Catherine's home to see how the family is getting along. It lifts her spirits and provides a bit of companionship. "At least I know someone else is thinking of the family," she says. "This AIDS makes old people like me feel alone."

The tragedy of Catherine's family is hardly unique. Shuffling out to the pavement in front of her house, she explains that all along the street young adults are dying. "At the house next door, one of the children is at the [AIDS] center, and they have already lost a daughter. My young cousin was buried on Saturday. She left three children behind. Another family on the street has lost two children, and a third one is sick." Roughly 7 million children in Africa have lost their mothers to AIDS, and the figure is growing exponentially. If current projections are correct, one-third of all Zimbabwean children will be orphans by the year 2010. Kenyan Vice President George Saitoti has said that 1 million Kenyan children could be "AIDS orphans" by the turn of the century.

If Zimbabwe and other countries stricken by AIDS are to have any hope of bringing the epidemic under control, it will take a herculean education campaign to change popular attitudes. As the noted Zimbabwean novelist Chenjerai Hove wrote in his collection of short stories, *Shebeen Tales*, "Harareans dismiss the AIDS virus and the threat it poses with the contempt of new graffiti on bus-stop shelters and other public places: 'AIDS: American Idea for Discouraging Sex.'"[6]

Many traditional healers harbored the same attitudes at the initial stages of the epidemic. They believed AIDS to be another weapon in what they see as the Western world's campaign to further undermine African culture. "Many of our traditional communities thought that AIDS was a Western tactic," says Peter Sibenda, the publicity secretary of the forty thousand–strong Zimbabwe National Traditional Healers Association, or ZINATHA. "But we realized that from whatever direction this disease came, it was a reality we had to deal with."

Thanks to that realization, Zimbabwe serves as an excellent example of how cooperation between the two medical worlds can succeed. Suspicion and hostility remain, but since the scope of the AIDS crisis became apparent, the traditional authorities have become an integral part of the Zimbabwe government's battle plan. "We are working on cultural laws to complement Western laws," Sibenda says with a knowing smile, which betrays a keen sense of pride that the government and the medical world are beginning to take the healers seriously. ZINATHA launched its own AIDS education program in 1988, both to make healers aware of the need to use fresh razor blades when applying medicine and to maintain good hygiene. ZINATHA has also targeted customs that promote HIV infection and that medical doctors simply cannot address.

"The only way to change people's behavior and fight this disease is to involve the people's culture, to involve their lifestyle," Sibenda says firmly. "Anyone who comes in and orders people to change their culture will fail. During colonialism, we managed to stick to our culture, despite Christianity. We survived under the carpet, undisturbed. Only the elite were corrupted. Traditional beliefs are still alive." The point now is to use those traditional beliefs and the influence of the healers to fight HIV contamination.

Take, for example, the common practice of biting patients whom the healers deem are afflicted by spirit possession. Sibenda's ZINATHA is committed to banning this, and its sanction will carry far more weight than a government decree outlawing the practice. Another is the tradition of inheritance, in which a widow and all her belongings are "inherited" by the late husband's brother. The custom was intended originally to ensure that the woman and her children were not abandoned but fell under the care of the extended family. In the new capitalist order, however, inheritance has been perverted into a money-grubbing exercise often completely at odds with its intended purpose of looking after the dead man's family. The heightened risk of spreading HIV is apparent, because the widow effectively becomes the brother's wife even if the husband died of AIDS. The changes Sibenda and other leading traditional healers want to see are the right of women to agree voluntarily to being inherited and the choice of using condoms with her new husband.

Likewise anti-AIDS activists condemn the widespread practice of polygamy as backward and guilty of spreading HIV. Instead of attempting to abolish it altogether and force it underground, ZINATHA has focused its efforts on promoting fidelity within the polygamous marriage. "On polygamy, AIDS education must be free from racism," Sibenda snaps. "It would be unfair to discourage polygamous marriages which are in existence already." In any case, the institution will die in its own time, he believes, since few people can afford it anymore.

The way Sibenda sees it, AIDS is not strictly a medical problem but proof that Africa has abandoned its indigenous culture and the community responsibilities it imposes, a spiritual payback for the decision to embrace Western materialism and individualism, or, in Professor Mazrui's words, it is the curse of the ancestors. In the traditional law of most African cultures, promiscuity and prostitution are extreme forms of antisocial behavior; but in just a few decades they have become widely accepted as part of modern life. Many Western scientists agree with Sibenda's views on the long-term role of the cultural breakdown. They theorize that while the HIV virus has been present in central Africa for decades, it remained relatively benign as long as the social mores of traditional rural life kept it in check. As migration and urbanization shredded the moral strictures of village life, AIDS broke out of the straitjacket and roamed free.[7]

In Zimbabwe, the traditional mores first came under severe pressure a century ago when Cecil Rhodes's Pioneer Column and his *vasina mabvi*—"men without knees," as the people called the white invaders with trousers—rode in from South Africa and expropriated a land that had been settled by the Shona people for one thousand years. Colonial rule, migrant labor, the independence war, and, more recently, Western-style "economic freedom" have been telling blows. Lawrence Vambe, a Harare-based writer and businessman, vividly describes the wrenching impact on village life in his classic work on the history of the Shona, *An Ill-Fated People:* ". . . the majority of the young people were more than willing to be sucked into the materialistic machine of the white man. In fact they hurled themselves into the new order with an enthusiasm that made the bitterness and despair of their elders seem all the more hopeless. They were lured from their tribal environment by the promises of education and economic enterprise, which, with their emphasis on individual fulfilment, were now clearly the main motivating forces. . . . In this way the old bonds of tribal and family cohesion, loyalty, discipline, and other things which had kept the VaShawasha people together in the past were torn asunder."[8]

With the demise of the moral codes of tight-knit villages administered by councils of elders and chiefs, customary restrictions on incest, premarital sex, and adultery have been cast aside for the Western fascination with consumption and immediate gratification. "I find that Africans are living in two worlds," Sibenda says. "At home they are more traditionalist than me, but at work and in public they are Western. This brings confusion to the communities on how they may change their sexual behavior to reduce this high rate of transmission of AIDS."

However lamentable the weakening of the traditional mores, they are breaking down. Vambe recalls the public outrage at the appearance of the first prostitute in the village of Chishawasha on the outskirts of Harare. "As I remember only too well, they were not only horrified by Misi's moral depravity, her obvious lack of shame and her defiance. . . . They were also afraid that Misi would lead astray some of the other women. . . . They had visions of their hitherto clean-living tribal settlement turning into a hot-bed of immorality which they believed was the hallmark of European civilization."[9] Commercial sex is booming for two reasons. Urbanization has attracted legions of single men to the cities and mines; and growing numbers of single women, in an environment of increasing unemployment and rising prices of food, health care, and school fees for their children, have turned to prostitution. AIDS itself has exacerbated the problem, as widows in the rural areas have been left with a stark choice: either farm the family plot or engage in commercial sex to earn enough money to feed their children. "It's a simple question of money," says Nancy Masara, a social worker in Murambinda in central Zimbabwe.

Since she started working as an anti-AIDS activist, the strangest things have been happening to Nancy after she turns out the lights and goes to bed. One Friday after midnight, she and her husband Bannister were awakened by an uproar outside their home. When they peered discreetly out the window, they saw a group of men, clearly intoxicated patrons of the local bar, standing on the road at the edge of her front yard and calling out Nancy's name. "They were in front of my house, shouting, 'You are having sex with your husband, but we can't because we don't have condoms! Please give us some.'" Nancy giggles as she recalls the incident. "You see, the men had run out of condoms over at the beer hall, so they came to my house to look for some. Unfortunately, I only keep them in the office."

Another time Nancy and Bannister woke as usual just after sunrise, shared a cup of tea, and walked out the front door together on their way to work. At the front gate, they nearly tripped over a pile of condoms—used condoms dumped there the night before. Nancy is not one for much self-doubt, but she admits that the sight caused a momentary reflection on the wisdom of her chosen profession. She was curious, too, about who was to blame for the prank, though there was no shortage of suspects. The bar owners were upset with her preaching to their clients, as were the soldiers and the police with her attempts to reform the local prostitutes. But she took it in stride, realizing that whoever carried out the deed, it did have a silver lining. Her months of hard work were paying off. "At least I knew they were using the condoms," she says. "Somebody was getting the message."

Nancy's mission is to preach safe sex. It is not a moral crusade but a practical effort to save lives. At the beginning, her safe sex campaign was a tough sell. The local men suspected that Nancy was a moralistic meddler trying to curb their sex drive. Some of the prostitutes, or "commercial sex workers," as they are commonly known, thought just the opposite. They regarded her admonitions about reducing the number of customers as an angle to steal their business. But with her hard work and seemingly endless enthusiasm, Nancy has gone a long way to winning them over, so much so that they show up at her house at all hours. Throughout Murambinda, Nancy is affectionately known as "the condom lady." "A few still laugh and make jokes, but most people now know what I am trying to do," she says. "Everyone has been affected by AIDS."

The suddenness of the AIDS attack on Murambinda has been breathtaking. Before 1986, the disease did not even merit a mention in the hospital's annual reports. Officially known as a "growth point," Murambinda serves as a gateway for miners in the nearby Dorowa area and tens of thousands of people living in the surrounding villages who pass through the town on their way to the major urban centers of Harare, Masvingo, and Bulawayo to the south. Murambinda itself consists of the mission hospital, founded by the Little Company of Mary Catholic Order in 1969, several general goods retailers, a butchery, two bars, seven liquor stores, a stationery shop, an open-air market, and right next to it, the bus depot. That is the most likely spot where the HIV virus alighted on its first day in Murambinda, probably some time in the early 1980s.

Now AIDS is racing out of control, says Dr. Glenshaw, the hospital administrator. "The truly tragic result is that the epidemic has become a normal part of life; it's almost accepted as just another killer like malaria. All walks of life are affected. Twenty-five percent of my hospital staff is HIV-positive now, and it's difficult to fill their positions. But despite everything, there's still a core of pride in this country. The people feel they are Zimbabwean, and they know the solution has to come from within."

Grassroots activists like Nancy Masara have taken up that challenge in Murambinda and in many parts of Africa. What they lack in resources, they more than make up in sheer energy and ingenuity. Nancy first saw the impact of AIDS when she was a social worker at Harare's Parirenyatwa Hospital, where seemingly overnight it fell like a blanket of death on the pediatric wards. In 1992, she moved to Murambinda with Bannister after he accepted a new assignment to manage a general goods store. Nancy did not know what to do with herself in such a tiny town. "I just didn't want to stay at home. I have no children, and sitting in that house all alone, I knew I would start thinking too much and go crazy or something." Bannister laughs in agreement. "She has too much energy to sit at home. Nancy has to have something to do, to keep busy, or she's unhappy."

Bored and increasingly frustrated, she decided to visit the mission hospital to see if they needed any volunteer help. A local project called *Dananai,* a word meaning "unconditional love" in Shona, the language of Zimbabwe's biggest ethnic group, was taking off at the time. Nancy joined immediately. She worked on a new program called "home-based care," which entailed traveling to the villages outside Murambinda to visit AIDS patients who have been discharged from the hospital to live out their days with their families. While she came to understand how hard AIDS was hitting even remote rural areas, she knew that without a change in people's attitudes, the spread of the disease would simply accelerate. *Dananai* decided to start a parallel project called "peer education," and Nancy, a born organizer, snapped up the chance to lead the effort.

A tall, broad-shouldered thirty-year-old with a boisterous laugh and infectious smile, Nancy emanates a sense of physical and spiritual determination that impresses everyone around her. Her work day begins at 7:30 A.M. at the Catholic Mission Hospital in the two cramped offices which have been set aside for the *Dananai* project. Sitting at a wooden table and warming her hands by caressing a hot mug of sweet milky tea, she plans the day's activities like a commander of a civilian militia with her unlikely shock troops—prostitutes.

For her campaign to be effective, she has had to infiltrate HIV's favorite breeding ground: the popular rowdy "beer halls," which typically consist of huge airy rooms serving as half bars and half discothèques where massive stereo speakers blare the twangy guitar rhythms of Zimbabwe's internationally renowned Jit Jive and Chimurenga music. Success depends on reaching Murambinda's three hundred prostitutes. So the first thing she did was to recruit two "commercial sex workers." "I try to pick the very naughty ones, because they are the best at motivating the others. I like to get smokers, even those who take *mbanje* [marijuana]. I have to go to the pub dressed like a prostitute. Anyone who wears makeup, earrings, and has their hair done, and goes to the pubs is considered a prostitute in our culture. Then I try to make friends, discussing social and work problems, acting as if I am one of them. At first they were very suspicious, thinking that I was trying to steal their men or wanted to take them to the police. But after a while, when I won their confidence, I encouraged them to have fewer partners and always, always use condoms."

Someone is obviously listening. Murambinda is literally over-flowing with condoms. There is not a bar or liquor store in town where you cannot find boxes of condoms, and when the owners run out, they come to Nancy to replenish their stocks, lest a random spot check by "the condom lady" result in another of her patented tongue-lashings. In one October alone, Nancy and her assistants distributed 55,613. The high demand, she explains with her usual sense of humor, is due to "bonus fever" for the annual holiday salary bonus awarded in November. That month, however, the figure was even higher. "Bonus time!" she shouts in a booming voice. Distribution peaked in December at 68,000, or 17 condoms for every man, woman, and child in Murambinda. "New Year spirit." She laughs. Even in January, the figure of 58,000 is astounding by any measure. "Single sisters looking for school fees," Nancy says, clearly contented by her clinical analysis of the condom market.

Rather than mount a frontal and inevitably vain assault on prostitution, the philosophy behind peer education is to develop a snow-ball effect by convincing a small group of prostitutes to join the anti-AIDS campaign and then allow them to carry the message forward. "Single sister associations" are set up to discuss safe sex and the need to seek immediate treatment for sexually transmitted diseases such as gonorrhea and syphilis, both of which are very common and dramatically increase a woman's risk of catching the HIV virus. The World Health Organization estimates that the chance of an infected man passing the virus to a woman in a single act of unprotected sex is one in one hundred, but if the woman already has a sexual disease, the odds rise to one in twenty-five. In fact, clinical research in both Zimbabwe and Tanzania has shown that one of the best ways to halt the spread of the virus is to treat sexually transmitted diseases.

"Our message is, 'No condom, no sex,'" Nancy says. A simple concept, perhaps, but one that many women do not have the lux-ury to follow, especially at a time when high prices and scarce jobs have left single women with few alternatives to selling their bodies to survive. "Most of them don't want to be prostitutes, but they have no other means of income," Nancy explains. "Some have been divorced because they could not have children, and in other cases, their husbands have died." The going rate for sleeping with a man is ten Zimbabwe dollars, or about $1.25, so the average prostitute in Murambinda needs seven clients to buy one forty-five-pound bag of corn meal.

One of Nancy's peer educators, Cathryne, says she resorted to part-time prostitution after her husband Davious died in 1993. She was left with three boys—nine-year-old twins and a seven-year-old. "I had nothing to do," she says. "No income." She moved in with her mother to save on expenses, but she had to earn money. "For single sisters like me, what is the choice? There are no jobs, and I have to look after the children and bring in some money for my mother. The other single sisters have the same problem." Eventually she met Nancy, who offered her work as a peer educator. "A lot of my friends and relatives had died, and I got a job with the AIDS counselors here. They helped me with some money so I didn't have to work so much. My mother supports my work at *Dananai* because she thinks it helps me behave better. The other commercial sex workers used to tell me I was talking nonsense, but now they come to my home when they need condoms."

The peer education work of Cathryne and others like her has made for some strange bedfellows in trying to clean up the sex trade. They convinced the police, for example, to impose a fifty Zimbabwean dollar fine, just over $5, on any man they found in the bushes with a woman. In return, when wanted criminals flee Harare or Masvingo to lie low in Murambinda, the prostitutes tip off the cops. Nancy also holds "peer education workshops" with the police, a critical target because like the soldiers they earn steady salaries and can pay for sex, and an estimated 50 percent of them in Zimbabwe are HIV-positive.

The involvement of prostitutes landed Nancy in trouble with the local representatives of the powerful Roman Catholic Church. The nuns at the mission were none too keen about the presence of prostitutes on hospital grounds to work out of the *Dananai* office, and the Vatican opposes the use of condoms as a means of birth control. The breakthrough came when the local priest announced that "we are all sinners in the eyes of the Lord" and offered the chapel as a meeting place for Nancy's "single sister associations."

Nancy believes that the depth of the AIDS crisis requires sometimes unorthodox methods. In Murambinda, there are regular meetings under a tree or on a large rock in open view of the main street during which a dozen sex workers prove how quickly they can slip a condom over a plastic penis with their eyes closed. There have also been discussions with schoolgirls about the dangers of allowing themselves to be seduced by their potentially virus-carrying teachers and rich "sugardaddies." On one occasion, Nancy asked several prostitutes to hold a group session with miners' wives to reveal their tricks of ensuring male sexual satisfaction so that the married men would not stray from home so much. That took some convincing, especially since some of the sex workers could see the potential threat to their commerce. Nancy appealed to female solidarity. "This AIDS disease affects all the sisters, because women in Zimbabwe have no control over their lives."

The heavy toll on young women carries additional disastrous consequences, such as undermining food production. The World Bank estimates that 60 percent of Africa's total agricultural output is produced by women. They are the backbone of the rural economy. They keep the family together by taking care of children, the sick, and the elderly while the men are away working on plantations, in the mines, or in the cities. The vast majority of African women infected with HIV are, however, neither prostitutes nor promiscuous. Eighty percent of them are monogamous, the wives of husbands who sleep around or of miners and casual laborers who might return home only once or twice a year, infecting their wives with whatever sexual diseases they have picked up along the way.

The issue is one of power. Most men have it; most women do not. Wives who refuse sex or demand that their husbands use condoms can expect a severe tongue-lashing or a beating. "Men always have their way," says Nancy, shrugging her ample shoulders. "But now it has become a question of survival, and relations are changing. Maybe if something positive emerges from this AIDS crisis, it will be that women have a greater voice." The problem of women whose vulnerability is intimately linked with their subservience is one that Peter Sibenda and his traditional healers' association also acknowledge. "Women who are married must be able to use condoms if they feel the risk is too great," Sibenda says. "There have to be changes within the marriage." For prostitutes, it is a far more difficult matter. Economic realities leave the sex workers with few alternatives but to compromise on the strict condom policy. Such demands on their clients, or their "husbands," as they call them, often cost them business. "The soldiers are especially difficult," says Cathryne. "If you ask them to use a condom, they refuse."

The only answer, says Nancy, is that "the commercial sex workers need another way of living." So, as they gather on a rock behind the liquor store for their weekly meeting, Murambinda's single sister associations have added an item with a twist to their usual agenda topics of sex and condoms: They talk about new business ventures, or "income-generating projects." For them, the best hope for escape from the life of prostitution and the threat of AIDS seems to be in selling sweaters and bedspreads, and setting up a cooperative vegetable stall at the central market. "If we can substitute one form of income generation for another, then we are halfway there," Nancy says. "The problem is that most of these girls are probably already infected by this virus, but if we can save just one or two, then my work is justified."

It is a sentiment that Dr. Glenshaw echoes as she walks down the strangely hollow cement corridors of the hospital at the end of another ten-hour working day. "The worst part is that no matter what the anti-AIDS campaign accomplishes now, it's too late to save all those people who are already infected," she says. "I just tell myself that my patients are not going to live as long as they used to, but I still have to care for them."

The commitment to caring for those who have already contracted the disease is the central plank of scores of initiatives that fall under the rubric of "home-based care." They have enjoyed wide success, particularly in Zimbabwe and in Zambia, its western neighbor, which are cleaved by the great Zambezi River as it roars down from central Africa to the balmy embrace of the Indian Ocean. Home-based care accomplishes three things. It relieves the pressure on overworked hospitals; it puts patients in family surroundings; and it strengthens that highly developed, though increasingly embattled social safety net that has served Africa well for generations: the extended family system. Its advocates are a core of nurses and doctors who, armed with a few medicines and loads of compassion, believe that placing AIDS patients back in their homes promotes family solidarity and understanding of a disease that has traumatized communities.

"People want to help their relatives, but they are afraid or don't know what to do," says Surudzai Rwafa, whom everyone calls "Sister" Rwafa because she is a nurse at the mission hospital in Murambinda. "It's my task to teach them that these patients are not to blame for their condition and they must be cared for." Surudzai's job is to travel to villages and homesteads within a 50-mile radius of Murambinda each day to visit a few of the 180 patients who have been seen at the hospital and sent home to make the best of their remaining time. Because there are so many patients, Surudzai can only see them once every several months unless she receives an emergency message from relatives. Her tasks involve everything from bathing AIDS sufferers and prescribing painkillers and antibiotics to holding meetings with families and neighbors to explain that the virus is nothing to be ashamed of and that the victims must be made comfortable.

The sun is an orange fireball sliding down a dull blue western sky by the end of this typical day's work of home-based care. Surudzai walks briskly along a dirt path through a corn field and approaches a cluster of wattle-and-daub huts. "One of my patients lives here," she says over her shoulder, explaining her mission. At the center of the homestead, an infant in a tattered blue dress is lying in the shade on a reed mat a few feet from an immense sleeping pig. Surudzai kneels in the dust and gently pulls two-year-old Tsitsi to her breast. Tsitsi hardly responds. She is lethargic. "This little one misses her mother," Surudzai says, hugging the child and rocking back and forth. "She too is infected and will probably die soon." Shooing away a horde of pesky flies, Surudzai brushes the gray dust from the toddler's hair. She lowers her face to the child's ear and hums a tune in her light, high-pitched voice. Try as she might, though, she cannot erase the dull look of bewilderment etched across Tsitsi's face. "It's pitiful," she whispers with a depressed air. "She has forgotten how to laugh."

Tsitsi's grandfather emerges from the main hut. The little girl has been sick for the past week, he says. It seems to be an infection. Everyone around the area is ill these days. Even the rotund pink pig is feeling poorly. Is Tsitsi eating? No, she will not take in anything. Surudzai reaches into a bulging white bag she brought from her hospital pickup truck and scoops out a handful of corn meal. She quickly mixes up a little mound of porridge on a plastic red plate. Hoisting Tsitsi back onto her lap, she coaxes the child into accepting a few spoonfuls. "This little one lost her parents and her brother—he was only four—last year," Surudzai says. "Now she has to stay with her grandparents." Tsitsi suddenly belches, momentarily lifting the cloud of doom hanging over the compound. It is proof that she is eating. "She may last two more years like this, maybe four. But out here in the rural areas, especially with the drought, there's very little food, and children with AIDS don't resist very long."

Surudzai sits with Tsitsi a few minutes before handing some antibiotic pills to the grandfather and explaining the dosage. Make sure she has clean water, she insists. Tsitsi represents a routine case, suffering from the double curse of being an orphan and born HIV-positive in a continent where each day nine hundred children are infected by their mothers, often through breastfeeding, according to the World Health Organization.

Surudzai stands and smacks the dust from her blue jeans before turning dejectedly to walk back down the path toward the truck. As the pickup speeds along the track leaving clouds of dust, she gazes out the window at the passing homesteads. "Look at all those tombstones, fresh and new. All over this area, one out of three or four homes has a new tomb in the garden. So many people are dying now that there are funerals all the time," she says in her singsong voice, as if she is about to burst into tears. "Every day some of the patients I go to visit are already dead."

The journey from realizing her childhood dream of becoming a nurse to dealing with the day-to-day realities of AIDS in modern Africa has been a painful education for Surudzai. After completing her degree at Parirenyatwa Hospital, she was assigned to Murambinda, which because of its tiny size and limited cultural life was a depressing first posting. Initially Surudzai simply went through the motions, hoping to complete a two-year assignment in Murambinda before she could return to Harare. She reported for work on time and left. "I was just going to work to get my salary. But AIDS was starting to make a big impact on the community," she says, lowering her voice. "Then Charles died." Charles was Surudzai's elder brother, who was a bus conductor in Harare, an occupation that carries an extremely high HIV-infection rate. "I told him to be careful. I told him about AIDS. Bus drivers and conductors are at high risk because they travel a lot and sleep around."

Charles's death brought home the tragedy of AIDS in a way that her work at the hospital had never done. "When I was directly affected by AIDS, that's when I could actually understand how the patients felt, how their families felt, what it really means to be touched by this virus. I thought it was my job to put these people in the picture, to give them some hope. Somehow when I visit a family, I feel like I am caring for my brother."

The memory of Charles has equipped Surudzai with great emotional resilience and personal understanding of what families of AIDS victims are experiencing. She needed both when she visited the home of Sylek, a twenty-five-year-old woman she had not seen for months. She had been making regular stops in Sylek's village of Vhiriri, however, because of its abnormally high infection rate. "For some reason Vhiriri has been hit more than other villages around here," Surudzai said as she reached the edge of the village, raising her voice over the roar of a passing truck. "It's probably because it's on the bus and truck route. Many of the young people move to Harare to look for work, and when they return, they bring the disease with them."

Along the main road that slices Vhiriri in two, Surudzai pulled into the driveway. She knew immediately that this would be her last call. Smoke rose from the front yard. Half a dozen women in bright blue and pink sweaters sat around the fire stirring huge black iron pots of *sadza*. More smoke billowed out of the small doorway of a mud hut. "Oh no. I think we're too late," Surudzai said, her soft voice barely audible. "They're in mourning. Someone has died." She approached the gathering shyly, as if she felt that somehow the family might hold her responsible. Sylek died three days before, they told her, and the aunts were preparing *sadza* for relatives who were still streaming in from outlying areas to grieve for her loss. AIDS not only steals the youngest and strongest, it can actually bankrupt a family. The communal mourning and funerals force the average household to dig deep into their savings or go into debt.

As Surudzai entered the homestead, a woman disappeared into one of the houses to retrieve a plastic mat which the hospital lent the family for Sylek to lie on. "We don't need this anymore," she said, folding it neatly. A five-year-old girl in a pink dress named Annah wandered back and forth from her elders in the smoky hut to those gathered around the cooking pot confused about the ceremony. No one, it seemed, was able to explain to her that her mother had gone. When Surudzai reached the outdoor kitchen, the elderly women clapped halfheartedly in unison to welcome her. It was clear at that moment that they did not blame her. Suddenly one of the aunts shouted that she did not understand what was happening. She turned to Surudzai and asked, "Why are all our children dying? Why is it that the young ones are dying and leaving us older people with their orphans?" Surudzai stared at the ground. There was nothing she could say.

The search for answers to such questions often creates new problems. The parents of one of Surudzai's patients, a man of thirty-five who looks fifty, have abandoned their house because a traditional healer said the son's illness was the work of an *ngozi*, an evil spirit, occupying the home. A chief living just outside Murambinda has told his followers that AIDS is caused by a malicious wind brought on by the government's decision to take away the powers of the traditional leaders over judicial matters and land. Strange explanations are not the sole domain of Africa. In 1986, two British astronomers seriously argued that the HIV virus came from outer space.[10]

One of the most frustrating practices to combat has been the propensity of healers, known in Zimbabwe as *inyangas,* to announce miracle cures for AIDS. Some healers see the "wasting syndrome" as a potential moneymaker, and for patients who believe they are infected, news of a magical antidote has obvious attractions. But *inyangas* are not alone in wanting to make money out of fake remedies. In March 1996, Arthur Obel, a leading Kenyan doctor and self-declared chief scientific adviser to President Daniel arap Moi, unveiled a treatment called Pearl Omega which he claimed could both reverse AIDS symptoms and rid the body of the HIV infection. The price tag of the treatment, which was slightly intoxicating, was a whopping $600. Sixty thousand people took the drug, Obel said, until the government banned it in February 1997. Obel claimed the treatment was based on an indigenous herb, and since Kenyan law permits the use of traditional medicines, he was allowed initially to administer it.

In Zimbabwe, Health Minister Stamps publicly chided soldiers, 50 percent of whom medical experts believe to be HIV-positive, for spreading AIDS among teenage girls in a mistaken belief promoted by several traditional healers that sex with a virgin would render them immune to the virus. One doctor in the posh Harare suburb of Mount Pleasant says that he knows of two cases in which young girls were gang-raped by soldiers who were seeking such a cure.

Sibenda's ZINATHA and Stamps worked out a clever scheme to deal with the problem of miracle cures. They appealed to the healers' suspicion of foreign doctors by warning them that if they announced their remedies, the Western medical world would swoop down and steal them. If the healers agreed to keep quiet about the antidotes, the government would forward them to Harare's prestigious Blair Research Laboratory for stringent analysis. Should a treatment be proven effective, the healer who pioneered it would certainly become a wealthy person. So far, while no breakthroughs have been discovered, there have been far fewer announcements of quick fixes. If nothing else, such cooperation has a chance of restoring the balance of pride and coaxing traditional healers to work with the rest of the anti-AIDS program.

Perhaps an equally valuable result of the cooperation is the access the Blair Laboratory now has to the hundreds of herbs and medicinal plants provided by the healers. Africa is home to literally millions of plants, and it is almost certain that among them are to be found the sources of therapeutic drugs. Discovering these will depend on repeating the new partnership between healers and researchers in Zimbabwe across Africa and the rest of the Third World, and doing so quickly. The world's botanical map is shrinking. Tropical forests are under attack on many fronts, from war refugees and loggers in central and West Africa to cattle ranchers and gold miners in Brazil.

Already, herbal-based medicines are the main weapons in the rearguard action doctors of all stripes are waging against malaria, Africa's number one killer. Quinine, historically the most reliable drug, was extracted from the bark of the cinchona tree, and the most promising of the new treatments is a traditional Chinese medicine called *qinghaosu*, derived from the sweet wormwood plant, that herbalists have been using for two thousand years.[11]

AN EXTRAORDINARY PARTNERSHIP between the two medical worlds can be found just a mile or so from the banks of the Niger River, next to what appears to be an abandoned military installation on a towering hill above the dusty capital of one of the poorest countries in the world. At first glance, there is little in Bamako, Mali, to suggest anything other than poverty and underdevelopment. The main road into the city from the north is filled with potholes and traffic jams of creaking minibuses and cars and goats, and streams of people who walk the slow but steady pace dictated by the sun of the Sahel, that dry swath of scrub and savannah which shields the moist West African coast from the furnace of the Sahara Desert. Only a couple of buildings in the entire city stand at over two stories, and most of the streets in the suburbs turn from tarmac to dust less than a mile from downtown Bamako.

The journey up a long, winding road at the back of the city to the National School of Medicine takes about fifteen minutes, but a visit to the Malaria Research and Training Center inside the campus involves a surreal psychological crossing from an underdeveloped Third World nation, with all the attendant problems of unemployment, poverty, and pollution, to the cutting edge of world-class research. Cross the street from the taxi rank and the bustling roadside market, walk through the university entrance, and take an immediate left, two flights up to the Department of Epidemiology and Parasitic Infections, and there is the latest equipment: computers, microscopes, scanners, and a host of other machines with jaw-breaking names, such as the Programmable Thermal Controller, which analyzes the malaria parasite's DNA. Outside, market women haggle over prices of fruit and vegetables in the hope of earning a few dollars a day. Inside, a group of top-flight scientists who are among the best in their field pore over blood samples in pristine laboratories, conduct research on the MedLine database on CD-ROM, and communicate with the outside world by e-mail.

Unlike other major research centers in Africa, the scientists in Bamako are Africans, mostly Malian, but with a sprinkling of researchers from neighboring African countries. This is not a case of Europeans or Americans taking a mobile First World lab and setting it up in the African bush. Rather, it is a center of scientific excellence, which is administered by Malians, where the research is conducted by Malians, and where the most immediate benefits fall to Malians, though the ramifications are invaluable to Africa and the entire world.

The stakes could not be higher. Malaria is the biggest killer in Africa today, more ruthless than cholera, yellow fever, measles, far outdistancing the latest more highly publicized crazes, such as the *Ebola* virus, and even, at least for the time being, overshadowing AIDS. No one in Hollywood ever made a movie about malaria, but in Africa it claims the lives of nearly 1 million children each year. Ninety percent of the 300 million to 500 million clinical cases that occur each year are in Africa. In some parts of Mali, especially in the rice-growing areas on the banks of the Niger River, one out of five children die before the age of five, most of them from malaria.[12]

What sets the center off most from other such bodies is its work in the villages and its close relationship with traditional leaders and healers. Ogobara Doumbo, head of the Department of Epidemiology and Parasitic Infections at the School of Medicine in Bamako, believes that not only must the research be relevant to the lives of ordinary Malians but modern science has much to learn from them. "Traditionally in Africa, Western researchers come for a while, secure the information they require, and then they are off. I wanted to create the link between the research and the communities which need health development. It is a philosophy of establishing field doctors in collaboration with the local communities. That is a dynamic that we have created here."

Altruistic as Doumbo's views may seem, they reflect the cold calculation that village communities have as much to teach scientific researchers as the researchers have to teach the villagers. In effect, the center is attempting to do what so many universities, governments, and professional organizations have failed to do: build a bridge between the so-called traditional and modern faces of Africa. Only in-depth fieldwork can address some of the key questions that must be answered before there is real understanding of the malaria parasite and the mosquito. From the point of view of pure research, the villages furnish the center with a constant supply of blood samples from the hottest malarial battlefronts, which allow the scientists to track how the parasite is mutating. By working with community elders, traditional healers, and especially important target groups, such as women, Doumbo's field workers are able both to help people save their children's lives and to set up an unparalleled observation post from which they can view the enemy.

"Before we begin our research, I send in an anthropological team to find out how the community works, and what its members need and want. In that way, you avoid any conflict," Doumbo says. "We learn what we can do and what we cannot do. And we always work with traditional healers. They are a social power in the society. It is not fair for us to come in and ignore them. On all our visits, we first go to the chief. When we come, we have a community meeting. We talk and they give us feedback." When the scientists listen to the traditional healers, the traditional leaders return the favor. The same is true with midwives, mothers, village chiefs, and rural teachers. The spinoff has been that Doumbo and the center have convinced some of the healers to carry chloroquine in their bags for those areas where it is still effective against malaria.

Rural Mali has provided more than a testing ground, however. Traditional healers have developed their own medicines, and unlike many Western and African scientists, Doumbo and his colleagues are humble enough to admit that the healers often are way ahead of them. With medicines such as chloroquine losing the battle against malaria, a drug called Fansidar is one of a dwindling number of stronger treatments forming the last line of defense. Even the most promising new treatments, such as *qinghaosu*, that to date have proved effective against some resistant strains of *Plasmodium falciparum*, have limitations. French researchers treating a Frenchman who came down with *Plasmodium falciparum* malaria after a trip to Mali found resistance to *qinghaosu* derivatives.[13]

The Mali center has discovered another traditional remedy. Malaria 5 is a combination of three herbal medicines used for years by Malian healers. Together with the Ministry of Health, the center has tested Malaria 5 and proved that it too has effectively battled malaria strains which chloroquine can no longer fight. This discovery Doumbo cites as an example of cooperation between Western and African medicine. "The reason it works in Mali is that we have a department of traditional medicine which has organized the work of traditional healers very well since 1976. We have scientists who are working with them and they study which of the medicines work. And there is now no doubt about it. Malaria 5 works! We have proved it scientifically. Some of the treatments these traditional healers are using have been handed down from generation to generation. They have been tested in the community, and just like the ingredients in Malaria 5, they would not be using them unless they had some impact. These people know what they are doing."

To strengthen the villages' own health systems, the malaria center also supports a program to train community health workers and to build drug dispensaries, using local materials and labor. Through the multitude of local radio stations created since Mali returned to democratic government in 1992, the antimalaria message is getting out on the airwaves. Teachers are being enlisted to educate their students. "It works in Mali because of the democratic system," Doumbo says. "People now must rely on their own initiative. If you have your own health organization in your community, you can do it. In my experience, the system began to work with democracy. It gave the people initiative."

Like AIDS, malaria's toll on the population goes far beyond the sheer death rate. It accelerates poverty and underdevelopment by undermining the health and work capacity of hundreds of millions of people. Anyone who has survived a bout with the dreaded *Plasmodium falciparum* strain knows it to be no laughing matter. Unless it is treated, *Plasmodium falciparum* can kill its victim in less than five days. As it becomes increasingly resistant to standard treatments such as chloroquine, the death toll is rising. From South Africa in the south to Mauritania in the north, the legions of malaria are on the march, and with each passing rainy season, as the parasite absorbs the blows of the latest medicines developed by the world's scientific community, it adapts, to emerge ever stronger. It can do so, Doumbo says, because "the parasite is very, very clever." He should know. In his native Dogon region near the Niger River town of Mopti, more children die of malaria than any other disease. The parasite is so clever, in fact, that while most African adults are immune to malaria if they remain in their home area, should they travel outside the region, they encounter a slightly different parasite and their immunity is useless. Doumbo cites another example. Most infants remain safe from malaria as long as they are breastfeeding, because their mother's immunity has been passed along. But as soon as they stop, the children become vulnerable.

The driving forces behind the Mali center are Doumbo and his entomologist colleague Yéya Touré. Both were trained by Philippe Ranque, a French scientist based at the World Health Organization (WHO) in Geneva, who set up the Department of Epidemiology in 1973. There is also close collaboration with the universities of Maryland, Marseilles, Rome, and Tulane; the last regularly sends a graduate student to Bamako. "We have succeeded in creating a culture of scientific research here," Doumbo says. The fact that a Saturday was the only time he was free to hold an interview already says much about the center's work ethic. "Weekends, weekdays, there is no difference for us. Maybe, in fact, we accomplish more on weekends because it is quieter. During the week, we have so many visitors and meetings about grants that there is not much time for anything else."

The visitors and grants are critical to the center's survival, however. The government of Mali, rated as the third poorest country on earth, is only able to provide the institute with space at the university and to guarantee water and electricity. While it is true that the center relies on foreign funds, principally from the U.S. Agency for International Development (USAID), the U.S. National Institutes of Health (NIH), and the WHO, unlike most aid programs in Africa, it must compete for its funds. USAID provides some core funding, but only enough to secure jobs for four of the thirty full-time staff and the twenty students from Mali's medical school and neighboring countries. Funds for the rest have to come from grants.

The fact that the center has succeeded in attracting the money for the past four years is testimony to the quality of work by Doumbo, Touré, and others. "I have sat in on their presentations when they come over to the States, and it's astounding," says Richard Sakai, a Hawaiian-born resident scientist of the NIH. "Frankly, when some of my colleagues in the United States hear that some African scientists are around looking for money, they have the preconception that their presentations will be second-rate. But after

Doumbo or Touré is through, they are speechless. It's not that their presentations are good relative to other Africans. They are simply as good or superior to anything they have heard anywhere."

The center engages the battle against malaria like a military headquarters planning a pincer movement. Doumbo works with one team of researchers who focus on the parasite itself, testing its DNA to see how it has mutated from one rainy season to another, and correlating its findings with the drugs needed to treat it. The conclusions, pictured on a map, are relayed to the Ministry of Health so that chloroquine is still used in areas where it is effective, and other drugs, such as Fansidar, are sent to regions where the parasite has passed the resistance threshold. That way drugs are not wasted and resistance to them does not occur before its time.

Touré leads a team of entomologists who study the malaria-carrying mosquito, *Anopheles gambiae,* to understand why sometimes it carries malaria and other times it does not. They have already discovered differences in chromosomes, and they are hoping to figure out how to use the mosquito's natural ability to block the development of the parasite inside its own stomach to create a genetically altered mosquito.

One of the most valuable resources available to the center is the medical school on the same campus. The deans are cooperative, they allow the center to take credit for its own research papers and to administer itself, and most importantly, the school provides an army of students from which Doumbo can choose to strengthen research capabilities in both the laboratory and the field. "It is very important that we can select our own collaborators. They come and say, 'I would like to work with you,' and I say, 'Are you sure?' Okay, I put them in a village, maybe for six months, and see how they do. We pay them about one hundred dollars a month, but it's enough. Without that pool of students, we could not work. They really help us. They love to do it. I don't have to force them."

Energized by such infusions of new blood, Doumbo believes that the bridge between his researchers and the villages represents the optimistic future of medicine in Africa. "I grew up in a village and I know how things work and how to avoid conflict. Nobody can change my mind about that. It takes time. If you know what you need to accomplish, and you take time to listen to the communities, you can create a social contract," Doumbo says. "This is the only way to go if Africa is to have any relevance in the next century."

The Battle for the Mind

Optimism fills the warm morning air as the pure voices of two hundred children resound through the halls of the university campus on the outskirts of the Somali capital, Mogadishu. The youngsters sit deep in concentration side by side in crisp new blue and gray uniforms, chanting the Somali alphabet with their eyes glued to their teacher at the head of each classroom. The open courtyard outside is abuzz with the sounds of motion and building. Young men hammer away at new, freshly cut wooden benches, while venerable university custodians sweep dust and refuse from the sidewalks. Over the area drifts the aroma of woodsmoke, a welcome telltale sign that the cooks have lit the fire for the morning tea. In the ramshackle offices and lecture rooms of what used to be the University of Somalia, hundreds of displaced families look on with surprise and wonder as they contemplate the daybreak with a difference. For the first time in two years, the classrooms are being put to the use for which they were originally built, although the age of admission has fallen dramatically. The campus of the University of Somalia is being transformed into an elementary school.

The school is the brainchild of an independent Somali women's group known as Ida, which decided that it was time, no matter how dim the prospects, to start the laborious process of rebuilding Somalia by educating its children. "We say that since the men have brought the country to such a state, it is now our turn," laughs Amina Haji Abdullahi, a high-spirited former university lecturer who is the head of Ida's education department. "We think one of the best ways to attack the violence, ignorance, and poverty which affect Somalia is by touching the minds of the children. They are our only future."

The student body consists of children of families who took refuge in the university from years of battles between rival faction militias that have torn Somalia apart. Just getting the school up and running has proved an incredible trial. First, there are the mundane matters, such as providing study materials and uniforms for the children, as well as ensuring adequate supplies of firewood and food for the daily meals. All this in the midst of a civil war. Then there are more delicate issues. Most of the other schools operating are managed by Islamic groups whose Koranic classes and feeding centers are funded by foreign governments preaching militant Islam. As a result, Ida has had to deal with demands that children be segregated according to their sex. Such notions do not go down well with the women activists. "Amid all these troubles, imagine that the biggest problem we have to fight is against the idea that girls and boys should be separated in school," says Stirling Arush, the tall, elegant Ida consultant who has been a driving force behind the elementary school. "So we made a compromise to appease everyone. The boys and girls stay in the same class, but the girls whose families wish it will cover their heads in veils."

Somewhat surprisingly, what has not been a problem is finding qualified teachers for the school. They are, in fact, tremendously overqualified. Most of them are former university professors, and their main dilemma is to learn how to return to the basics. "It's very difficult to go from being a university professor to teaching little children," Dahair Ali Mahmud, a graying fifty-six-year-old professor of Arabic, says, chuckling at the irony of his own situation. "There is no university now, and since these children need teachers, we professors must learn to adapt. They are so hungry for education, and it's our responsibility to feed that hunger."

The yearning for education which Professor Ali Mahmud describes and the dedication which he and the Ida members personify are evident all over Africa. People will do almost anything to ensure that their children, especially their sons, have access to it. In Zimbabwe, rural women fashion sweaters, tablecloths, and crafts to sell to tourists to pay for school fees. Nigerian market traders devote part of their sales revenue to purchase scarce textbooks from the cramped, streetside second-hand "bend down bookshops" in Lagos. Ask a prostitute in almost any African city why she is selling her body, and more often than not her response will be "school fees."

For the poor, the biggest barrier to school is the sheer expense. In 1994, when Malawi declared free education and abolished school fees and uniforms, enrollment exploded overnight from 1.9 million to 3.2 million.[1] The reason was simple. Parents struggling to make ends meet could not earlier afford the additional costs of educating their young, even when school was a top priority.

The people of the central Angolan city of Kuito took their scholastic commitment to new heights. Mundane worries such as school fees and uniforms would have been welcome preoccupations. The daily concern of teachers and students alike was making the trip to classroom and returning home alive. In 1993–94, residence in Kuito was almost a death sentence. Eighteen months of mortar duels between the Angolan government and Jonas Savimbi's UNITA rebel movement, and the resulting backwash of famine and disease, claimed the lives of fifty thousand people. Sometimes the shells rained down so quickly it was impossible to count them. And yet, as soon as the bombardments let up, the schools invariably resumed. The residents of Kuito were almost maniacal in their drive for self-improvement. Near the main hospital, students regularly attended driving classes even though there were virtually no private vehicles or fuel.

In the center of town, sitting catty-corner to the governor's office was a sturdy Portuguese-style colonial house whose pastel walls, though gouged by bullets and shrapnel, provided a glimmer of its former affluence. One morning its five rooms were bathed in the silence of concentration as fifty secondary school students sat for their examinations. All heads were down at the test booklets spread across knapsacks or the students' laps. No desks remained intact. The monitor of the exams was Fernando Augusto, a slight, twenty-three-year-old history teacher, who like everyone else in Kuito was living a refugee's existence. His home was bombarded into oblivion, and his only source of food came from international relief agencies. He worked for no pay. So did the five hundred other teachers who saw to it that Kuito's six thousand students continued their education, war or no war. Augusto has been teaching since he was a teenager. After graduating from the local high school, he joined the groups of young *brigadista* activists who spearheaded nationwide literacy campaigns. After that, he became a teacher in the regular school system.

When the civil war reached Kuito in early 1993, the city was literally carved up. The bulk of the town was in the government army's hands, while the rebel forces occupied a smaller slice and encircled the rest. Both sides laid down belts of land mines, the rebels to keep the army entrapped and the government soldiers to maintain the insurgents at bay. There was no alternative but to lob shells at each other. From time to time air force jets dropped bombs behind rebel lines. During the siege, it was virtually impossible to venture beyond the one-square-mile city center. "If we thought about the situation we are in, we would become very frustrated," Fernando said with amazing understatement. "I am working out of good faith. We have to have faith, because if we do not, we would be lost. There are other teachers who would like to work, but they can't because they don't even have clothes or shoes."

Standing next to Augusto was another Fernando, a forty-five-year-old mathematics teacher whose surname, Pequinino, means "tiny" in Portuguese and aptly describes his stature. His more philosophical approach could become a motto for achievement. "You have to work where you live and do the best you can. The situation here is not ideal. Now there is war, but someday it will stop. These children have to be ready when it does, so we can rebuild this country called Angola," he says proudly. "Most of these teachers are working because they love it. Since I was a young boy I always wanted to be a teacher."

At the end of the twentieth century, education stands at a crossroads in Africa. While weakening central governments, ever-tightening budgets, and armed conflict have undermined the ambitious plans for training drawn up after independence, everyone agrees that higher educational standards are a prerequisite to economic growth. All the reform programs and much-sought-after foreign investment will make little difference unless Africa's citizens are armed with the necessary intellectual firepower to capitalize on them. Building modern economies and establishing democratic political systems without an educated citizenry would be comparable to trying to run a computer without software. Investment in primary education, says the World Bank, is the single biggest factor that sets off the phenomenal growth of the Southeast Asian "tiger" economies from those of the rest of the Third World.[2] John Nkoma, a professor of physics and dean of the Faculty of Science at the University of Botswana, believes homegrown technology must also play a role: "Science has been a potent force in driving the technological development of the industrialized countries of the North, and the newly industrialized countries of Asia. Clearly, Africa, and the Third World in general, cannot be an exception."[3] Unfortunately, right now Africa's drive for knowledge is in reverse gear. Spending on research and development is less than half of 1 percent of the world's total. Roughly half of all grade-school-age children are not enrolled. If attendance continues to fall at the current rate, 59 million African children will be out of school by the year 2000.[4] There is only one region in the world where the percentage of children who do not attend school is rising. It is Africa.

By all accounts, something must be done quickly to reverse the trend. Part of the answer lies in governments allocating more funds to education, spending those resources more efficiently, and placing greater emphasis on educating young girls, who right now are twice as likely to drop out of school as boys. State intervention alone is not enough, especially where governments increasingly lack the economic and political power to effect change. In many countries, schools exist simply because parents and villagers will them to. In Uganda, home to the once renowned University of Makerere, the government covers less than 15 percent of the cost of primary education.[5] Communities and families make up the rest, whether it is paying teachers' salaries or contributing building materials and labor to erect the schoolhouse. In Kenya, one study showed that parents contribute directly 34 percent of the cost of primary education. In Mozambique, parents must pay individually for "tutoring" sessions by teachers who cannot survive on their regular salaries.

Community participation has always been the basis for successful education in Africa. In the precolonial days, schooling covered a wide range of subjects—everything from the environment, agriculture, pot- and toolmaking, basket weaving, and house building to training in art, dance, and music. Economics classes, to arm youths with all-important skills in market trading, involved instruction in barter and exchange rates so that businesspeople could deal with the proliferation of currencies, particularly along the West African coast.[6] The Yoruba people of Nigeria, acclaimed for their trading skills and business acumen, could count to 1 million.[7] Folk tales, proverbs, sagas, and poems were the texts of history and the tools for honing linguistic skills. Precolonial education usually culminated in initiation rights, and its main function was to pass cultural practices and community identity from the older to the newer generations. Although learning typically emphasized the rights and duties of men and women and their social roles, history and religion were also passed down through oral testimony. In some African societies, young men and women would spend up to six months in what were in effect bush boarding schools, secluded from the rest of their community to study how to become responsible adults. And once they had matured, they in turn became the teachers to the younger members of the community. Education and culture went hand and hand.

When the messengers of Christianity and Islam arrived in Africa over a thousand years ago, they sparked a new impetus for scholarship. The Ethiopian Christian Church has been credited with establishing one of the first comprehensive educational systems, around A.D. 450, with emphasis on the arts, science, literature, and Ethiopian culture. Muslim teachings too had a great impact on sub-Saharan Africa, especially in the ethics and theology of Islam, but also in the reading and recitation of the Koran and the study of Arabic grammar. Elite centers existed, such as Timbuktu in modern-day Mali, where Muslim scholars of international standing studied and taught at the university mosque of Sankore.[8] Throughout the Sahelian region, African Muslims produced works on law, theology, history, and medicine. Sir Frederick Lugard found a sophisticated Muslim system of schools when he led British troops in the conquest of the Sokoto Caliphate in northern Nigeria at the turn of the century. The British Empire, he said, should support them. By 1945, one estimate put the number of students in Muslim schools in French West Africa at over eighty thousand.[9]

With the onset of colonial rule, Western education enjoyed the staunch backing of church and state. It was a useful tool for missionaries seeking converts and colonial officers needing clerks and technicians to run their administrations smoothly. The schools were replicas of European institutions and offered scant African content. The French were particularly enamored with the idea of inculcating Africans with French culture, in effect creating among the elite black Frenchmen and among the rural students servants to the colonial cause. History scholars might have been well versed in the European Middle Ages, but they knew precious little about the development of distant regions in their own countries, much less about the rest of the continent. Beyond the primary school level, the teaching positions were in the hands of expatriates.

Africa's increasing integration into the world economy set off a stampede for Western-style education as parents sought to improve the prospects of their children. Education began to replace traditional status as the benchmark for achievement in the colonial world, and those who earned degrees were automatically pushed to the forefront.[10] Future nationalist leaders, such as Eduardo Mondlane of Mozambique and the Nigerian leader Nnamdi Azikiwe, were among the first of their countrymen to obtain postgraduate degrees and to teach at American universities.

Opportunities for study remained scarce under colonial rule, especially in the French colonies of West Africa. Illiteracy rates of over 90 percent were common among newly independent nations, including Senegal, the Gambia, Côte d'Ivoire in West Africa, and Tanzania and Mozambique in East and southern Africa. By 1960, only 36 percent of Africa's school-age children were enrolled in primary schools, and just 3 percent at the secondary school level, compared to 14 percent in Latin America and 21 percent in Asia.[11] University education was even more restricted. Some countries began independence with fewer than one hundred university graduates. In Sierra Leone there were seventy-two and in Malawi twenty-nine. There were sixteen graduates in Congo—a country the size of the eastern United States—and Burundi had none.[12] When the former Portuguese colony of Mozambique won independence in 1975 after a protracted guerrilla war, it boasted just ten lawyers.[13]

A wave of educational zeal swept independent Africa, producing spectacular gains. Sixty-three million Africans enrolled in school between 1960 and 1983, and in the decade of the 1970s, enrollments increased 9 percent per year, twice as fast as in Asia and triple the rate in Latin America.[14] By the late 1980s, the curriculum in most primary schools had been Africanized so that texts referred to local customs and history, and in at least twenty-one countries part of the instruction was in African languages. But the revolutionary fires of education began to die out in the mid-1980s with the onset of prolonged economic crisis and political stagnation. Living standards fell and the specter of "structural adjustment" programs hung over budgetary outlays. Embattled governments, whether Zimbabwe's democracy or Nigeria's dictatorship, suspiciously viewed secondary schools and university campuses as hives of discontent. Spending on education over the decade plunged by between one-third and one-half. Over the same period, spending in Asia doubled.

Dwindling resources for rising populations mean more children entering the informal labor market to help their families find the basic necessities. Millions have hit the streets to do odd jobs—hawking cheap goods in traffic jams, helping out at the family market stall, and standing watch over makeshift parking lots. "Students don't have time to study. They sell things full time, and at examination time they pay the teachers for good marks," says Mike Miku, a thirty-seven-year-old teacher who works in the *la cité* slums of Kinshasa, the capital of Congo. "This is the way people live. Values that should build the country have been destroyed."

One of the primary reasons for this loss of values has been the failure of political leadership. Just as the continent needs to invest in human capital so that its people can develop the skills to compete against the rest of the world, Africa's rulers are divesting, shifting money intended for education to their own private use or to purchase arms to keep them in power and, through a combination of neglect and repression, forcing those with the degrees to seek work abroad. This brain drain is a tragic signpost on Africa's road to underdevelopment. Some seventy thousand African graduates who studied in Europe have stayed there, and there are an estimated ten thousand Nigerians working in skilled jobs in the United States alone.[15] In general, the quality if not quantity of Africa's schools is deteriorating, and overall intellectual standards are falling.

A severe lack of resources is usually targeted as the culprit. It is only a partial excuse, one that teachers, parents, and schoolchildren are no longer willing to accept. A typical example occurred one sunny afternoon in downtown Harare, the Zimbabwean capital. Waves of tear gas rolled across the commercial center, sending shoppers scurrying for cover while riot police wielding batons chased groups of schoolchildren toy-toying through the streets and chanting, "It's our money! Give it to the teachers." The usually spry midday traffic quickly succumbed to gridlock at the bizarre sight of police running up and down the wide avenues in pursuit of striking high school teachers who were demanding salary increases from a government which said that, under pressure from its foreign creditors, it could not afford them. Surprised by the violent response of the security forces, a crowd of demonstrators and bystanders attempted to beat a hasty retreat through Africa Unity Square as the police opened fire with tear-gas canisters, which trailed tails of stinging mist into the trees and the picturesque park fountain.

The strike, by then in its second week, was declared illegal by President Robert Mugabe's government. Emergency powers, still on the statute books from the colonial days, were invoked. The state's tough tactics backfired, however, rallying support for the teachers and their pay demands among government mechanics, gas station attendants, tax workers, and, of course, the students. The clashes in Africa Unity Square, though one-sided, marked another rip in the relations between the government and the educational sector. Parliament had already passed a constitutional amendment to bring the national university under tight control after a series of university student demonstrations against corruption beginning in the late 1980s. The events in Zimbabwe have been played out before and repeated again in nearly every African country since independence as budget cuts and increasing political unrest put schools and universities on a collision course with authorities. In neighboring Zambia, the democratically elected government of President Frederick Chiluba once closed down the national university and sacked all lecturers because they joined a one-day pay strike. Under the authoritarian regime of President Daniel arap Moi in Kenya, the office of the president must screen all research on national security grounds.[16] In Nigeria, the government has repeatedly sealed off the universities to prevent student demonstrations or to clamp down on strikes called by the staff union.

The confrontation in Unity Square showed something else. The children valued their education so much that they were prepared to face baton-wielding police to demand it. What makes the Zimbabwe case special is that within three years of toppling white-ruled Rhodesia and winning independence in 1980, it achieved what few developing nations have been able to: universal primary education. The formula for success revolves around community involvement, adequate state spending, and committed education workers. A central tenet of the program is that no child should have to walk more than five kilometers to school. Another is that students achieve literacy first in their mother tongue, Shona or Ndebele, and then learn Zimbabwe's official international language, English. "We went around asking the communities which ones wanted a school," says Faye Chung, the minister of education at the time. "Almost all of the villages wanted their own school, and the problem was that we had too many candidates." In 1979, the year before President Robert Mugabe took office, Rhodesia spent $150 million on an education system that was heavily weighted in favor of the tiny white minority. Just over a decade later, state outlays totaled $425 million, and university attendance quintupled. In 1992 a new National University of Science and Technology opened in the southern city of Bulawayo, and a third church-funded Africa University is planned in the eastern city of Mutare.

Severe challenges remain. Budget constraints have forced the government to impose user fees for urban primary and secondary

schools, and low salaries have spurred teachers and university lecturers to seek more lucrative posts in neighboring Botswana and
South Africa. The gap is widening between the elite, still heavily
white schools in the major cities of Harare and Bulawayo, and those
in the townships and countryside.

In general, as the children in Harare were so vocal in pointing
out, the money is there to improve basic educational standards. The
problem is how governments choose to use it. Africa received $10
billion in international aid in 1991, for example, but governments
spent the equivalent of nearly three-quarters of it, or about $8 bil-
lion, on their military establishments. The figure is just below what
the U.N. World Summit for Children had estimated the year before
was needed to reach the minimum targets for improving health, education, water, and sanitation for Africa's women.[17] Foreign debt
payments of some $10–$13 billion only worsen the problem. This
drain on resources has dramatic consequences even in countries
that are lauded for their governments' efficient economic management. There is no chance that Uganda will be able to maintain its
current pace-setting record of economic growth if it must continue
to spend more on repaying its foreign debt than on health and education combined.

However onerous the financial constraints, many Africans believe their countries can do much better with the resources and talent they possess. Professor Nkoma, lamenting the poor progress in
African scientific development, asks, "How many times have our
teachers failed to design experiments with the excuse that there is
no foreign currency? With some imagination, several experiments
can be designed using local materials. How many times have we
seen expensive equipment fail for lack of maintenance and parts?"[18]
That view is shared by African ministers and specialists who attended a mid-decade review meeting in February 1996 in Yaounde,
Cameroon. They agreed that despite all of the continent's problems,
with good management and low construction and recurrent costs,
universal primary education could be reached in most countries
without additional foreign aid.[19]

As the Ida activists in Mogadishu and the Angolan teachers in
Kuito demonstrated, determination and commitment can make all
the difference, and it is not a question of aping European or American or Asian philosophies. "Africans must be participants in the creation of knowledge as a human heritage," Professor Nkoma argues.
"In the end, it is a matter of conscience, and we should be seen to

contribute to scientific knowledge. There are many relatively new areas of research, such as biotechnology, molecular biology, and new materials, where Africans can exercise their minds and contribute to a better understanding of the universe."[20]

That hope infused Africa's elite institutions such as the University of Makerere, which shone as a symbol of national freedom when Uganda gained independence from Britain in 1962. Often called "the Harvard of Africa," its image still adorns Uganda's 500-shilling note. Makerere, along with Nigeria's University of Ibadan, were considered Africa's premier institutions, the intellectual jewels of East and West Africa. But war, government neglect, and outright repression have taken their toll. Makerere's demise can be traced to 1971, when Idi Amin seized power and destroyed the university as a center of learning. Administrators were killed, and up to one hundred university students were massacred in 1976. Campus facilities were left to deteriorate, books became outdated, and student dormitories took on the look of slums.

The university has been making a gradual comeback since President Yoweri Museveni's rise to power in 1986. Professors are returning from exile, although with salaries of just $300 a month, many must take part-time jobs as market traders, consultants, even taxi drivers, to make ends meet. The Museveni government, generally regarded as one of the most competent and honest in Africa, has increased its grant to the university by 200 percent. There is a $400,000 fund to promote independent research, and postgraduate courses are available in each of the science faculty's seven departments.

The heart of Africa's university system has traditionally been Nigeria, and there the signs of a turnaround are vague at best. Nowhere is the belief in the benefits of education greater than in Nigeria, where the University of Ibadan is preparing to celebrate its golden jubilee. The founding of the first full-fledged university at Ibadan in 1948 was followed by thirty-six more, about one-third of all those in sub-Saharan Africa, plus a bunch of agricultural, technical, and teaching colleges. From 1,400 university students at independence, enrollment today stands at 350,000.

Ibadan was formed after the Asquith Commission recommended to the British colonial authorities the establishment of three universities in the colonies: Makerere in Uganda, the West Indies in the Caribbean, and Ibadan in West Africa. Two years after independence, four more universities were founded—at Ifè, Ahmadu

Bello, Nsukka, and Lagos—in an effort to reflect the geographical diversity of the federation. The University of Benin became the sixth during the 1967–70 Biafra civil war. It was the beginning of "an epidemic of universities," in the words of Dr. O. O. Akinkugbe, the former dean of the medical school at Ibadan. Seven more were unveiled by the military government of General Murtala Mohammed, four of them in the north and two more in the east. "Even at that time one could argue that thirteen universities was not really too many for a country the size of Nigeria," Dr. Akinkugbe says. "In the UK, they had at the time forty-something universities with a population of forty million." By the early 1980s, Nigeria went on a university creation spree. "So we now have a total of thirty-seven universities, out of which a total of twenty-four are federal universities. If you ask whether we really needed that many universities, the answer is no. Now the University of California system alone has more students than the whole of Nigeria. So our problem is not that we have too many undergraduates, but that we have too many universities. It is not cost-effective."

For that reason, some Western analysts have argued that Nigeria and Africa as a whole should cut back on university education and should apply little "structural adjustment" programs to institutions of higher learning in order to make the necessary savings. In some of Africa's poorer countries, where governments simply cannot afford huge universities, such proposals make sense; but in Nigeria, with its massive $10 billion in annual oil export revenues, the problem is the lack of efficient spending. "People say the country cannot really sustain that kind of tertiary-level manpower, but I don't agree with that," says Dr. Akinkugbe. "If our resources were properly husbanded and distributed fairly, education should get a much larger share than what it is getting today." The state of higher education in Nigeria today is summed up in a frank World Bank report of 1994: "For the most part, students no longer learn, faculty no longer teach, and research activity is largely non-existent." Dr. Akinkugbe considers what has gone wrong and shakes his head. "It was like [the title of Chinua] Achebe's book. 'Things just fell apart.'"

THE REALITY OF that summation is on display one afternoon as Seye Kehinde pays a visit to his old university. "The first thing you notice," he says, looking over his shoulder and rolling his eyes, "is the stench." He is right about the odor, although it is hard to tell if the smell comes from the wide pools of filthy water behind the block of lecturers' offices or if it is partially a psychological sensation, emanating from the obvious rot of the university itself. It has been seven years since Kehinde, a journalist who works for two muckraking Nigerian weekly magazines, *The News* and *Tempo*, graduated from the Obafemi Awolowo University. Even though the signs of decay were apparent then, he is clearly depressed at the pitiful state into which his alma mater has fallen.

The university, named after the nationalist leader Chief Obafemi Awolowo, is located in the southwestern city of Ifè, regarded by most Yoruba as the spiritual birthplace of their people. According to their Ifá religion, Ifè was the first inhabited place on earth. *Olódù-marè*, the Yoruba High God, had dispatched the *òrìsa*, the benevolent four hundred supernatural powers from heaven down to earth to turn the molten primordial muck into dry land, and the first place they landed was a mountaintop in Ifè. Unfortunately, as the story goes, they discovered palm trees, tapped them for palm wine, and the leader of the group, *Obàtálá*, drank so much that he passed out. It was left to his younger brother *Odùduwà* to use some dry sand brought from heaven, a hen with five toes, and a chameleon to create solid earth.[21] It made sense that a university was built in Ifè, since Ifá contained the Yorubas' most impressive piece of literature, consisting of over 200,000 poems divided into 256 chapters.

In the modern era, hundreds of years after the Ifá poems were first composed, it is clear that the level of rigor in academic life at Ifè has diminished considerably. The university looks as if it is dying, soon to be swallowed by the dense, humid forest that surrounds it. A few students mill with little enthusiasm around shabby classrooms which have not seen a paintbrush in a very long time. Seye strolls through the open air corridors, peeking into several rooms before he finds one of his old history professors, Olusola Akinrinade, sitting behind his desk in a tight office. He is apparently one of the few professors, as Nigerians like to say, "on seat." Several students enter the room one by one to ask Professor Akinrinade if they may borrow some books that are unavailable in the library and the bookstore. He looks at his pupils warily before reluctantly agreeing to the loans. "There are no books around, and most of mine have been stolen," he says by way of explanation. "I have to lend my books out to my students because without them they cannot complete their course work." If not for Professor Akinrinade's generosity, the students would have to resort to the black market or travel to Lagos

and pay extravagant amounts of money in the city's infamous sec-
ondhand bookstores, the "bend down bookshops," to fill their required syllabus.

"When we professors go to conferences, we are completely out-
of-date, because we have not been exposed to current thinking,"
Professor Akinrinade says. "The only way I receive books is from
personal contacts abroad or complimentary copies of journals I
write for." Here is a man who completed his Ph.D. at the London
School of Economics and went on to do postdoctoral work at the
University of Maryland, and he has to worry about students stealing
his books. Professor Akinrinade's salary and housing benefits total
the equivalent of $100 a month, which is about one-third of what
his counterpart at Makerere might earn, and he has to consult for a
private company to buy food and clothes. Other professors and lecturers are even worse off. He knows of one who sells vegetables in
the street market to maintain his family. Others engage in peddling
Xerox copies of their texts. "Our computer building sits empty; we
have no computers. We don't even have enough chalk," he says.
"We are trying to maintain the standards under difficult circumstances, in spite of the government, in spite of society."

When Professor Akinrinade first came to Ifè in 1982, the university still enjoyed an international reputation as one of Nigeria's
best institutes of higher learning, and in those days that was saying
something. Ifè and the nearby University of Ibadan once attracted
students from Britain, the United States, and the rest of Africa. A
stint at Ibadan was almost required for researchers into tropical diseases, for example. Ifè was generally considered a step down from
Ibadan, but if so, it was a tiny step. Signs of the demise were already
evident by the early 1980s, however. One professor at the University of Ibadan wrote in 1983, "For several months now we have
been expected to run a physics laboratory without electricity, perform biology and zoology experiments without water and get accurate readings from microscopes blinded by use and age. Chemicals
are unimaginably short. The result of all this is a chemistry laboratory that cannot produce distilled water and hundreds of 'science
graduates' lacking the benefits of practical demonstrations."[22]

The downfall of Nigeria's university system dates to the dramatic
fall in world oil prices at the end of the 1970s, although state funding did not start to dry up seriously until military officers overthrew
the elected government of President Shehu Shagari in 1983. In Akinrinade's first year at Ifè, the history department had a staff of

twenty-six people, including three graduate assistants and twenty-three lecturers. Now there are eight. In the English department, the number has dropped from twenty-seven to six. One of his colleagues has gone to the University of Missouri, one to Texas, and another to the University of California. Others took up posts in the southern African nations of Lesotho, Botswana, Swaziland, and South Africa. Ifè is a living example of the destructive powers of the brain drain. "We are talking about mass desertion," he says. "The most outstanding ones are those we have lost, especially in the humanities. We still have some excellent lecturers, but they cannot reach their potential. What we have here is the enthronement of mediocrity."

The meager salaries are partly to blame for the exodus, but they are not the only reason. Low morale, repeated student strikes, and the general attitude of neglect by the government have convinced many professors that they have no alternative but to abandon their country. "People think you are insane if you have an opportunity to remain abroad and don't. I should have stayed in the United States, but I still believed in the system." Of Nigeria's twenty-four federal universities, only the core three—Ibadan, Ifè, and Ahmadu Bello University (ABU) in the northern city of Zaria—hold reputations, albeit fading, in the international academic world. "At one American university, the application form says if you are Nigerian and have not graduated from Ifè, Ibadan, or ABU, don't bother applying," Professor Akinrinade says.

"The problem is that those who have the power, the influence to make an impact on the political system, to argue for changes to improve the universities, send their children abroad. Their attitude is that if the universities are run-down, then they will send their children abroad. These are the people damaging the system. How can we have a head of state, a general, who did not even pass his exams at the staff college?" he asks, in reference to press reports about the poor academic record of General Sani Abacha, Nigeria's current military strongman.

The military's accounting methods also leave something to be desired. A commission appointed by General Abacha said it could not trace $12 billion earned in oil exports under his longtime colleague and predecessor, General Ibrahim Babangida. After completing the report, the commission chairman immediately fled the country for fear of retribution. "It is very disheartening when we watch the nation's money being squandered," says Professor Akinrinade. "If they had given just one billion of the twelve billion dollars that disappeared, we could make great improvements in all the universities." The federal university system's budget increase in 1994 was 5 percent, while inflation was put conservatively at 60 percent. "We are approaching a situation where either the whole system collapses, or we rebuild. But how can we do that unless we address the problems of the larger society?"

The larger society, as Professor Akinrinade calls it, has a myriad of problems to address. But even if Nigeria can make a peaceful transition from military to civilian rule, it will take years to reverse the decline in education to train the engineers, economists, civil servants, accountants, and medical doctors who are going to be needed if there is any chance that the economy, and the larger society, will experience a significant turnaround. Any radical change could endanger vested interests. The very types of professionals Nigeria needs are seen by the military as threats to its continued monopoly on power. Since the 1983 coup, the military has systematically attacked and undermined nearly all professional bodies, such as the lawyers' and medical associations, women's groups, and the student movements, primarily because they dare to suggest that civilians might be able to run the country better than soldiers.

Conservatism runs deep in northern Nigeria, where Muslim leaders, known as emirs, still wield great influence over the Hausa-speaking Islamic faithful in alliance with the military government. "When people are educated, they ask questions. Why are we in this situation? Why are the emirs doing all the things they do? So the emirs have consistently opposed the spread of education," says Abdullah Mahadi, a history professor at Ahmadu Bello University in Zaria. "Members of the elite who are close to the emirs are also opposed because they can afford to send their children abroad, even if Ahmadu Bello University collapses. When they return, they are cream of the society, who will be able to lord it over the children of the common people, the *talakawa*. It is a kind of class struggle. They think that education will literally open the people's eyes. They will start to challenge their condition."

Professor Mahadi diagnoses a common situation in Africa, in which the political leaders actually seek to undermine their own educational institutions in an effort to head off opposition to their rule. He recalls driving to the university campus in Zaria one morning when he spotted one of his old professors walking along the road. He pulled over to offer him a lift. "Imagine that. He has been a professor for the past thirty years, long before I went to university. And

I had to give him a lift because he was walking. It was embarrassing, but it's typical. Professors cannot give their children decent education. They cannot give themselves what in popular Nigerian parlance is known as three square meals a day. I don't think they can give one good square meal," says Mahadi. "When it comes to teaching in the sciences, the chemicals are not there. Journals are maybe twenty or twenty-five years behind. It is not that money is not voted for education. Large sums of money in the budget go to education, but it never really goes to education. It goes into people's pockets. This is the state of our great university of the north."

The woeful working conditions of Ahmadu Bello University belie a rich history of formal education and intellectual discourse in northern Nigeria. Islam reached the commercial center of Kano by marching south from North Africa along the trans-Saharan trade routes. In the fourteenth century the ruler of the Kano emirate, the Sarkin Kano, Ali Yaji b Tsamia, was one of the first rulers converted to Islam. But his was largely a palace religion, leaving untouched the great mass of the Hausa people, even those living inside the city walls, twelve miles of thick earthen embankments thirty to fifty feet high. Evangelist teachers linked to the Islamic institutes in Timbuktu and Gao to the west spent years in Kano instructing the elite in Islamic literature, philosophy, medicine, and law. By the closing decades of the fifteenth century, all the major rulers in the Sahelian belt were Muslims. For the next several hundred years, Islamic institutes throughout the region produced a large number of books to carry the message of Allah.[23]

One young radical Fulani intellectual, Usman dan Fodiyo, was coming to the conclusion by the late 1700s that the message had not been taken to heart by the Hausa ruling houses in what is today northern Nigeria. Bolstered by the fierce calvary of the Futa people of Senegal and local Hausa commoners, the *talakawa*, who were alienated by heavy taxation, dan Fodiyo launched an Islamic *jihad* which rolled through the north with such ferocity that it has been likened to the sweep of the Prophet Mohammed through the Hijaz. Ultimately dan Fodiyo set up a powerful state, the Caliphate in Sokoto, which spanned five hundred miles. In the final battle dan Fodiyo lost two thousand men, two hundred of whom knew the Koran by heart.[24] Dan Fodiyo himself was highly educated, having studied grammar, law, exegesis, theology, and rhetoric under the famous scholar of the day, Mallam Jibril of Agades.[25] The fruits of Islamic education sprang up in surprising places. In the early part of the nineteenth century, an increasing number of slaves brought by the Portuguese to the northeastern Brazilian region of Bahia were Muslims. While many of their Portuguese plantation masters were illiterate, some of the slaves themselves were literate in Arabic, and they took leading positions in the slave revolts that rocked Bahia at the time.[26]

During the nineteenth century, when they were not launching new *jihads* to spread the Islamic state's borders and to round up pagan slaves, the leaders of the Caliphate produced an impressive number of books on everything from religious practice and history to poetry in Arabic, Fulani, and Hausa printed on Italian paper imported across the Sahara.[27] British colonial troops conquered Sokoto in 1902, easily overcoming the Caliphate, which was already harassed by wars against Yoruba generals to the south, troublesome animist groups to the east, and unrest among the Hausa peasantry.

In colonial times, Western-style education in northern Nigeria got off to a very slow start, as it did throughout the Sahelian region in French-occupied West Africa. "In Nigeria, the British were not interested in educating the north, partly because they had experienced the results of colonial education in India, in Egypt, in Sudan. They knew what education could do," Professor Mahadi says, laughing. "They were constantly harassed in Lagos and the coastal areas by educated people. So they did not want to repeat the mistake they made in India by giving the people secondary education. Up to the time of independence, there was only one full secondary school in northern Nigeria, Bayero College in Kano."

The northern elite today is deeply conservative and stagnant, living off the largesse of the military government in the form of large subsidies from oil revenues, and resistant to change. "The military undertook not only to give them fat salaries, they built very beautiful palaces for them, gave them big contracts, and they keep on dishing out large amounts of money to them," says Professor Mahadi. Among the *talakawa*, the sense of frustration with the lack of educational and job opportunities has reached at times critical stages, breaking out in sporadic upsurges in religious and ethnic violence. Kano, historically the dominant emirate in the north, has been the scene of some of the most explosive unrest in post-independent Nigeria. Widespread killings of Igbo immigrants from the east helped to spark the Biafra War, and ten thousand people were killed in the intra-Muslim riots led by a radical preacher named Maitatsine in 1980. A new round of violence killed up to a thousand people in October 1991 after young Muslims went on the rampage to protest the visit by a German Christian evangelical preacher, Reinhard Bonkke. A new militant group known as the Muslim Brothers contains many former students from Ahmadu Bello University who are loyal to the pro-Iranian preacher Ibrahim Zakzakhy.

The appearance of such groups has spread fear not only among the Igbos and Christians in Kano but through ranks of conservative Muslims as well. "If we do not nip this thing in the bud now, we may end up with a revolution which is just not religious, but may be political, social, and economic," says former presidential candidate Maitama Sule, a prominent spokesman for the northern elite. "Symptoms of revolt loom large on the horizon today. It is a group of disgruntled elements who are out to vent their anger who are joined by some irresponsible, undesirable waste products of humanity." Disgruntled elements surely, but if they are "waste products," as Sule asserts, the society which has produced them is distinctly that of northern Nigeria. "Whenever you find people not properly employed, not properly educated, there is no other way to express yourself, because you have the police, and the emirs and their agents looking for troublemakers," says Professor Mahadi. "So the most important thing is to express this in Islam."

Education could and should provide an alternative road, says Matthew Kukah, a Catholic priest from the north and author of *Religion, Politics and Power in Northern Nigeria*. Outspoken in his criticism of the military government and the northern elite, his views on education and politics have earned him a certain audience among young northerners, including his religious adversaries. In 1995 he was bestowed a rare honor for a Catholic priest, an invitation by the International Federation of Islamic Students to speak at a packed auditorium in the northern city of Kaduna. "I said, this is the end of the twentieth century, and we are going into the twenty-first century. If you want to be relevant in Nigeria, you must make up your mind. It is wonderful to read Arabic, but don't hope to work in NNPC [the state oil company]. You have to become interested in engineering, architecture. Now you are going to have to show your MBA or whatever. It is no longer a question of I am the son of so-and-so. All these privileges are on their way out."

For the most part, Father Kukah's arguments are making little headway. With most of their options closed, hundreds if not thousands of young northerners have turned inward, toward Islamic sects that have distinctly xenophobic tendencies. They are angry at the world around them, and much of their time is consumed with seeking out villains, imaginary or otherwise. The charismatic preacher Zakzakhy is simply one of the more radical of those voices that seek to woo the ranks of the frustrated young. From his house just a few blocks from the palace of the emir of Zaria, Zakzakhy has won adherents by arguing that Christianity and the unchecked creeping of Western culture threaten the Islamic purity of the north. Zakzakhy draws sustenance from the deterioration of Ahmadu Bello University and from the predominance among the university's professors of mainly Christian Yorubas and Igbos filling positions left by northerners who abandoned education as a profession in favor of jobs in the civil service.

"The Zakzakhy phenomenon has to do with the Iranian revolution. Zakzakhy thought he could do in Nigeria what Khomeini did in Iran. Ibrahim is trying to change society," says Professor Mahadi, who in the early days used to chair some of Zakzakhy's lectures. "He did a lot of things in the university and secondary schools to recruit young people. Zakzakhy is not really learned in the Islamic sciences. He is a political Islamicist really. He is more interested in the power that Islam can give him than the intricacies of Islamic law, sciences, and traditions."

Rather than constituting threats to the state, many observers see behind these radical movements the nefarious hand of the military and the northern elite. "The military have always played this card very well," says Father Joseph Bagobiri of the Roman Catholic Kano Independent Mission, "because the whole thing started during the [General Ibrahim] Babangida regime. That was when the religious divide became very strong." Father Kukah puts the blame squarely on the conservative northern elders. "Let's be clear, there are Nigerians who have invested heavily in violence, in ignorance, in poverty, in turbulence."

The result is that northern Nigeria enters the twenty-first century dominated by a near-feudal aristocracy in the pay of the military regime, its young people stymied by inferior education and scarce job opportunities, at times grasping at extremist religious politics for salvation, and falling ever further behind their southern compatriots in the quest for skills to prepare them to compete in the world economy. "It suits the elite better this way," Professor Mahadi says emphatically. "The very little segment of the society that has been able to get an education, they work very closely with the southerners, in government, in boardrooms of companies, in banking, in virtually all the institutions. So there are only a handful of people in the north who can work, and when there is any benefit from the federal government it is to this small group of society. The same elite says the north must fear the domination of the south, but only when they feel they are losing out in the sharing of the so-called national cake. When things are really going fine, they don't care. It's quite a system, and for them it works beautifully."

A CURSORY GLANCE at the hospital and its rectangular whitewashed buildings, the neat parking lot with a uniformed attendant, and the young students in their crisp white lab coats taking a break in the morning sun, all give the impression of a well-run medical school in the tropics. But the idyllic image is shattered by the knowledge that the water supply has just been reestablished after a cutoff of several months. How a medical school and hospital can function without running water and with frequent power cuts is difficult to imagine. But the University College Hospital at Ibadan does work, albeit with difficulty sometimes. The reason it does is the human factor.

Tall and graying, Dr. Akinkugbe is a warm and charming man who cuts a professorial figure in his white lab coat. He has seen the rise of Africa's top institutions of higher learning and witnessed their subsequent dramatic fall. Yet he is still around, and he still has hope that something can be done. Dr. Akinkugbe's credentials are impeccable. He has studied and taught at Harvard and Oxford, has worked at the World Health Organization in Geneva, and if he wished, he could remain abroad earning a good salary lecturing and in private practice. But home for Dr. Akinkugbe is Nigeria, and despite everything that has happened, despite the political chaos of the 1960s and 1970s and the onset of near-permanent military rule in the 1980s and 1990s, of government by generals with one-fiftieth of his education hiding behind sunglasses and ostentatious uniforms, he believes that somehow he and his colleagues can turn everything around. "One cannot but hope, because we are really in the trough, so the only direction we can go is up," he says with an ironic grin. "I have never given any thought to working outside my country. I can only go for a year or two. My obligation is to my country. Because if we all left, we would have no Nigeria to build. I don't think I ought to go live somewhere else while my country here is underserviced. That may be a kind of altruistic or missionary view, but I think many of us feel strongly about it."

The challenge is how to escape from the vicious circle in which Africa's school systems find themselves locked. The experience of the past decade has proven in Nigeria that schools will not receive their fair share of the national income as long as the government is intent on stealing the money instead of investing in the country's human capital. The international community has attempted to step in with a helping hand, but as is so often the case, Dr. Akinkugbe fears, it might simply be compounding the problem. A $120 million World Bank loan to Nigeria's university system is a perfect example. The official title of the credit is the Federal Universities Development Sector Adjustment Operation Credit Facilities, and the operative word is "adjustment." In theory, funds are intended to help restructure and rehabilitate the universities, employing a combination of retrenchments and training, as well as to restock the libraries of federal and state universities. What upset many professors was its acceptance by the same military government which could not account for the missing $12 billion in state revenues. They feel the loan is a ruse to cover the tracks of government corruption. Dr. Akinkugbe is one of them. "Initially, I thought the idea was a good one. But when it came time for retrenchment of staff, people immediately put their backs up. What business have they to determine whether you retrench the X number? By accepting it, the government is shirking its responsibilities. There are certain things that I regard as primary, innate responsibilities. We might as well not have universities if we expect some group to come and give us funds to have books, which are really the lifeblood of the university system. Even if we did not have to repay the loan, it is wrong. It's wrong for another institution to be doing the government's work for it. If you get too dependent, you abdicate your own responsibilities."

Responsibility, Dr. Akinkugbe believes, is the key. He feels that if Nigeria's system of higher education is to be rebuilt, parents and communities must take responsibility for it, just as the Ida women's group in Somalia with their elementary school, the Angolan teachers in Kuito, and the Zimbabwean government did so admirably after independence. In face of government neglect and dwindling resources, the way ahead, Dr. Akinkugbe believes, is to establish small private universities, run autonomously from state control and with the power to hire and fire lecturers according to their performance. The idea is to put as much distance as possible between the universities and the state. "Many who you will talk to will say that education should be free at all levels. It is a populist view. I am afraid

I don't belong to that persuasion," he says. "I believe this country owes every Nigerian citizen free education at the primary and the junior secondary level; that is, nine years of formal education. Because at the end of that exercise, every Nigerian will be literate and numerate, and can form an opinion. After that, parents should be prepared to contribute to their children's education. I say that because there are many in the university system today, many students, who have no business to be there. They just regard it as a meal ticket, the possession of a university degree."

As it is, competition for places is stiff. The hunger for education is undoubtedly there. Approximately a half million students take the JAMB entrance exam each year for between thirty to forty thousand places. So, many Nigerians have reverted to a time-honored tradition in securing a place for their children: connections. As he chats in his office at the medical school, Dr. Akinkugbe takes a telephone call. It is obviously a friend. The discussion centers on the caller's daughter, something about her need to find a place in school. Dr. Akinkugbe says he will do what he can and rings off. "These are the kinds of pressures that we have every year," he says wearily. Despite the fierce competition, the standards have fallen, a not surprising development in an environment in which books are hard to find, chemistry students graduate without having undertaken lab work, and the country's premier medical school goes for weeks without running water. "If the highest score ten years ago was three hundred out of four hundred, today it may be two hundred and forty or two hundred and fifty, so that if we still have to get X number into the medical school, we are just lowering the cutoff points," says Dr. Akinkugbe. "We are seeing that the quality of students we had ten to fifteen years ago is no longer what we have now, although there is still a *crème de la crème.*"

The lowering of standards and the breakdown of the traditions of quality and academic achievement started to grip the system in the late 1970s, when universities were created willy-nilly and the military administration of General Olusegun Obasanjo responded to student protests by putting the universities under more direct government control. University administrators became dependent on the presidency and less accountable to their community. The vice chancellors were transformed into what one World Bank report called "scholar-politicians." In such an atmosphere, the mission of the university has been lost. Frustration of student life and the repression of student politics in Nigeria has prompted the mutation of social clubs into secret cults, which have often turned to violence, as well as the militant Islamic Zakzakhy movement in northern Nigeria.

Central to rebuilding the university system is to attract the thousands of lecturers who have left for better-paid jobs elsewhere to return home, as the University of Makerere has done with some success in Uganda. "I suppose everyone is looking for an outlet now, but I am an optimist," says Dr. Akinkugbe. "I have a feeling that once the situation improves drastically in the country, a number will come back. Nigerians on the whole are not the type who want to stay away too long. At this point in time, if university teachers find that they cannot buy a car, cannot own a house, and there are no prospects of their doing this in the next ten years, that is the kind of thing that makes them decide to leave for awhile. In this building now, we have lots who have gone to Saudi Arabia for a couple of years. But I think some day they will be back."

The Universal Soldier

As a platoon of army troopers mill about inspecting a motley collection of straw huts that constitute the rebel base they overran the day before, a pair of boys with rifles slung over their shoulders start throwing rocks at each other. The commander of the unit barks a sharply worded reprimand at them and with a violent thrust of his right arm directs everyone to march over the next ridge. A rusting armored car leads the way as the unit emerges from a grove of shady palm trees and into a wide clearing the size of three football fields. Straggling along lethargically, the soldiers pause from time to time to digest the numbing impact of the open sun and the unfamiliar music of the grasslands—a metallic chorus of jumbo-size grasshoppers, frighteningly hulky wasps, and pitiless ticks waiting for their next meal to pass by.

Suddenly a collective shiver runs through the assembly. Heads turn with nervous agility. On the outer margin of the insect harmony, there is an alien noise. The first reports of automatic gunfire burst from a dense wood two hundred yards forward, sending bullets hissing angrily overhead. Everyone falls to the ground. Only Lieutenant Tendai João Goma remains standing, rocking slightly from an afternoon of too much sun and too much of the local firewater, *kachasu*. He stiffens with a gust of adrenaline and orders his soldiers back to their feet. More gunfire explodes from another thicket to the right, at about two o'clock, and a third series of blasts comes from the direction of three o'clock.

A firing line fans out as if in slow motion in front of the figure of Lieutenant Goma—an irascible character with a quick wit and an intense pride in his winning military record. Normally informal and good-natured, with a knack for slapstick humor, Lieutenant Goma is an altogether different proposition when someone starts shooting at him. He motions to the initial source of attack. The young men, despite their oversized uniforms and unorthodox footwear—mainly tattered tennis shoes and rubber flip-flops—fly across the field, dropping down on their bellies and thrusting their AK-47s in front of them. On their commander's roar, they loose off rounds at random toward the trees, sometimes high up into the air, sometimes into the dirt a few yards ahead, but always fulfilling the prime objective: maximum noise. Lieutenant Goma decides to pump up the volume. "Mortarman," he hollers. "Front and center!"

A tiny trooper runs forward with the ears of his Russian winter hat flapping in the ninety-degree heat. "Kill that shit over there," the officer shouts, confident in an inevitable decisive blow. The boy struggles to wrestle the launcher off his back; it is nearly as big as he is. "Fire, damn it, fire!" The youngster slips a shell down the pipe, and with a sharp sucking sound it arcs high into the trees, tumbling softly, harmlessly through the branches. There is no explosion. The soldiers turn to look at each other with faces betraying growing concern. Incoming fire is intensifying from all three directions. By now the armored car, which has no functioning machine gun, is spinning in circles in the middle of the field, the driver apparently having lost control. "Again!" the officer demands from the soldier with the mortar. Another round hurls toward the enemy. The passing seconds confirm its equally feeble impact. The troops look back at their leader with alarm in their eyes.

"Mortarman!" Lieutenant Goma bellows. "Let me see that thing." After he inspects the weapon, he rolls his head in disgust and shouts, "You left the safety on! Now fire and eliminate that shit over there." Up the mortar goes, and its landing sends a muffled tremor through the earth. The little boy turns with a satisfied smile and says with genuine wonder, "It went off, Commander!" Lieutenant Goma is beside himself. "Fire it again, damn it!" The boy looks at the ground in disappointment. "But, Commander, that was my last shell." Nearly surrounded, with just one route of escape, Lieutenant Goma bows to the inevitable and orders everyone to retrace their steps back up the ridge and into the tree cover. As quickly as it started, the firefight has ended.

The platoon marches double time back to a makeshift base for the night. The camp is defended by one hundred fighters, officially government soldiers, but in reality mostly youngsters in their early teens, some still awaiting the onset of puberty. One pocket warrior who cannot be ten years old serves as the lieutenant's personal aide. When the camp awakes the next morning, the fickleness of youth is revealed. Thirty-two of the defenders, the entire northern flank, have picked up their weapons and the platoon's sole donkey and deserted. The lieutenant climbs aboard his truck and after several hours tracks them down in their home village. He threatens to execute them for desertion.

Two days later in the same area, a far more aggressive sort of platoon mounts an open-bed truck for deployment into the interior. The youngsters, most of whom wear good-luck charms, sing war songs and blow whistles as they depart, as if they were a gang of fans heading off to a local football match. At the first village, they surround a homestead and ready their rifles. Only then do they realize that their intended targets are members of their own unit who are cornering a stray cow for supper. They stop again at a roofless brick house to inspect the decomposing bodies of two women and an old man. The rebels did it, the soldiers say. "They leave the bodies to scare us, to say they have power," says one. Farther along the dirt track they spot two civilians walking in a field. One youngster coolly levels his weapon and begs his commander for permission to shoot them. They are probably rebel *mujibas* (spies), he says. When the commander refuses, he shapes his right hand into an imaginary gun and whistles in short, sharp bursts, flicking his trigger finger. "Next time," he whispers.

These scenes occurred in the southern Mozambican province of Inhambane during the country's eighteen-year civil war between the government and the Renamo rebel movement. They continue to happen almost every day in any of a dozen countries where young troopers have come to represent the modern-day universal soldier: a pint-sized, tireless baby Rambo who spends his or her tender years roaming the battlefields of Africa's civil wars. A visit to any war front in the Third World these days is bound to involve a meeting with a little boy carrying a weapon as long as he is tall, wearing anything from an American basketball T-shirt to the shreds of a military uniform, and sporting a grimacing face that can strike both horror and pity simultaneously into the hearts of all but the hardened few. "Most of these children wet their beds regularly," says Esther Galuma, a UNICEF project officer who spent four years in the West African nation of Liberia, where child soldiers have inflated the armies of a half dozen warlords.

For thousands of youngsters, circumstances well beyond their control have dramatically altered their view of the world, replacing their parents and grandparents as role models with images of Rambo and gun-toting thugs masquerading as the local "president" and "his excellency." Children all over the continent have willingly or unwillingly exchanged their school pens and pencils for rifles and hand grenades to become the ultimate representatives of a lost generation. Back in the 1970s, the late Mozambican leader Samora Machel used to describe children as "the flowers of the revolution." Twenty years on, his widow, Graça Machel, conducted a United Nations study into how many of the flowers had blossomed into trained killers. Although no one knows when the first child soldier began fighting, their numbers have exploded in recent years, thanks, in part, to modern weaponry. The new, relatively light firearms, primarily the AK-47 Kalashnikov assault rifle, are easy for children to handle. So armed, they are model soldiers: blessed with great endurance, the ability to survive on relatively little food and water, and acceptance of orders with far fewer questions than their more mature counterparts. "Boy soldiers are ideal," says Dr. Edward Nahim, a psychiatrist in the West African nation of Sierra Leone who is the chairman of a local nongovernmental organization known as Children Associated with War, which helps former child soldiers return to civilian life. "They are good at taking orders, they do not have many outside responsibilities, and for many of them war becomes a game which they enjoy."

The state of children is a bellwether of any society; there is no more poignant symbol of the willingness of military strongmen to mortgage their societies' futures to the immediate needs of the present. Any hope of saving the children requires forcing army officers and rebel warlords first to admit to using and then to releasing their child soldiers. Sierra Leonean social workers were told by a commander of a pro-government militia that if they wanted him to free the child soldiers under his command, they would have to bring "brown envelopes" of cash. In neighboring Liberia, President Charles Taylor, whose movement was probably the most systematic in Africa in its use of child soldiers and maintains its own "small boys unit," once adamantly denied in an interview that any children fought for him. When asked about a little boy wearing a bright blue football helmet and carrying an AK-47 who was manning a roadblock on the main north-south highway, Taylor conceded there were some youngsters around who performed functions as army aides. The ones with guns, he said, borrowed them from their commanders to show off. They were, in his considered opinion, simply being "frisky."

Such cynical dismissals of the problem are common. In Mozambique, after the signing of the peace agreement in October 1992, armies from the two sides started moving into assembly areas where UN peacekeepers were to help demobilize the troops and create a new, apolitical, armed force. The issue of child soldiers, however, was a "taboo subject" among Renamo commanders, who hid their conscripted youngsters in well-guarded bases deep in rebel-controlled zones.[1] Like Taylor, they were attempting to deny their existence.

The embarrassing truth emerged in March 1994 at a rebel base at Neves, in Inhambane, where UN officials, journalists, and Renamo's leader, Afonso Dhlakama, gathered for a ceremony to mark the first demobilization of Renamo troops. The young man chosen to be the model Renamo soldier admitted to the assembled guests that he was sixteen years old and had been fighting for the previous eight years. The practice of using child soldiers was so common that the local Renamo commanders did not even see it as a public relations disaster. The controversy sparked by the disclosure haunted Dhlakama and marred a much anticipated visit to Washington. Upon his return to Mozambique, he attempted to bury the issue by describing the use of child soldiers as "a tradition of African liberation movements," a statement which sadly is true, although the practice is also common in Asia and Latin America. After the revelation, Renamo commanders were shamed into cooperating with the United Nations. Reluctantly, they provided a list of 19 bases where 850 children were living. At least two thousand more simply left on their own accord, either walking back to their homes or migrating to the big cities, where they lived by their wits on the streets.

While a relatively small percentage of Africa's children are child soldiers, the militarization of one part of the youth heightens risks for all. There is no point to an army professing respect for international laws which protect women and children in times of war when the next child around the corner might be armed. Everyone is a potential target. The scope of the child soldier problem caught international attention in 1986 when Yoweri Museveni's National Resistance Movement marched into Kampala, Uganda, with dozens of tiny boys, some as young as five years old, carrying weapons.[2] Since then, the incidence of child soldiers in Africa has been well documented in civil wars in Angola, Ethiopia, Liberia, Mozambique,

Rwanda, Sierra Leone, Sudan, Uganda, and among the urban "self-defense units" in South Africa's townships.

By 1988, there were two hundred thousand child soldiers worldwide,[3] although the 1977 Additional Protocols to the Geneva Conventions forbids the recruitment of children under fifteen years old as soldiers, an age which most human rights advocates consider ridiculously young. When the government of Haile Mengistu Mariam in Ethiopia fell in 1991, some 15 percent of the army was said to be under the age of eighteen. They were mainly young men picked off the streets in the army's notorious campaign of press-ganging recruits, known as *Afesa* in Amharic. In Mozambique, the number of children who fought for the Renamo rebels ranges from 2,300 to 10,000. One independent study found that 28 percent of the children abducted by Renamo were trained for combat, and that in the southern provinces their average age was eleven and a half years.[4] Government forces also recruited children, sometimes marching into schools and demanding that headmasters present them with lists of eligible students, or ambushing cinemagoers. In one publicized case in June 1990, the commander and deputy commander of the Mozambican People's Militia in a northern district were relieved of their duties after they fired weapons into the air during International Children's Day celebrations and recruited youths at gunpoint for military duty.[5] Thousands of children in Rwanda were forced by adults, from fathers and uncles to militia leaders and politicians, to participate in the 1994 genocide against the minority Tutsi people. A UN study in 1995 found that in Angola, 36 percent of children had accompanied and supported soldiers, and 7 percent had fired a weapon at someone.[6] One thousand boy soldiers fought with the Angolan government army, while Jonas Savimbi's UNITA rebel movement fielded seven thousand. UNICEF estimates that one-quarter of all fighters in Liberia's civil war, some twenty thousand soldiers, were children.[7] In neighboring Sierra Leone, the best guess of the total was four thousand, half fighting for the government and half for the rebels.

Different paths bring children to the front lines. Some are forcibly drafted by government armies or rebel warlords needing to boost troop strength. Others enlist voluntarily. They might want to escape the boredom of refugee camps or to exact revenge against those who attacked their families and villages. They might simply have nowhere else to go. They might be intoxicated by the power and prestige which a weapon can command, or be searching for a sense of belonging, the sense of a family, which due partly to the armed violence itself they can no longer find in their communities. Saloman Brima, the Sierra Leonean coordinator of the Catholic Relief Services in the southern town of Bo, says the breakdown of traditional culture is to blame. He attributes the use of child soldiers and gruesome atrocities in that area to the gradual collapse of the Mende people's initiation cults, the *Poro* for men and the *Sande* for women. The initiation is the crossover from childhood to assuming adult responsibility and loyalty to the wider community. A *Poro* "devil" symbolically kidnaps boys from their homes, and community elders put them through a rigorous education in cultural norms and traditional arts and crafts.[8] The society took a number of blows: first, the active repression by the British colonial authorities, then independence, urbanization, and the spread of Western-style education; and in recent years, the war. "Desecration of sacred shrines in the countryside, growing promiscuity among young women, and the loss of dignity and influence among community elders are shredding the social fabric," Brima says. The damage to values is palpable. In some communities there are indigent Sierra Leonean families who are actually pleased when their children join the army because they can retrieve looted property from the war front.[9]

Child soldiers were not a problem in Sierra Leone until the civil war started in March 1991. The conflict was instigated by Charles Taylor's armed faction next door in Liberia because of Sierra Leone's support for opposing contenders for power. He was particularly irked when the authorities in Freetown allowed Sierra Leone to be used as a staging post for the West African intervention force, ECOMOG, operations in Liberia. In retaliation, Taylor pursued a policy reminiscent of Rhodesia's actions against Mozambique. He armed and supplied a guerrilla movement to tap into the widespread disillusionment with the tiny elite in Freetown, the ramshackle capital which took its name from the days in the nineteenth century when British gunboats intercepted slave ships headed for the Americas and deposited their human cargo on the shores of Sierra Leone. Within a year, army officers returned from the war front to demand that President Joseph Momoh's glaringly corrupt All People's Congress government pay, feed, and supply them regularly. Momoh fled, and junior officers established the National Provisional Ruling Council to run the country and the war. Captain Valentine Strasser assumed the position of head of state at the tender age of twenty-seven, and pictures of his ridiculously youthful face hanging in civil servants' offices, hotels, and shops all over Freetown made him look like something of a child dictator. Over the next few years, both the military rulers and the rebel movement known as the Revolutionary United Front, or simply the RUF, actively recruited children. As in Mozambique, the war spread out of control, and the toll was devastating. Some ten thousand people died and a half million fled the country.

CHILD SOLDIERS are the harbingers of the "coming anarchy" theory, which has become fashionable among certain influential Western writers. Sierra Leone is said to be a perfect example of what is in store for West Africa and the poorest lands of the developing world.[10] A combination of overpopulation, environmental collapse, armed conflict over dwindling resources, and the spread of killer diseases would inevitably push Sierra Leone and scores of African nations over the precipice into chaos; or so the prediction went. Problems with this thesis are evident in Sierra Leone. It is impossible to speak of overpopulation in a territory as big as Scotland or the state of New York, inhabited by 4.5 million people. The environment shows no sign of collapse, and Sierra Leone is hardly resource-starved; once known as the Land of Iron and Diamonds, it is blessed with substantial deposits of diamonds, iron ore, rutile, bauxite, and gold. Yet it is true that Sierra Leone is now classified as one of the world's most impoverished countries. The wide disparity in wealth distribution is the problem and lies behind the common saying, "Sierra Leone has no reason to be poor."[11]

The fatal flaw of the "coming anarchy" argument, however, is a contemporary echo of the colonial view, which held that before the European powers arrived, Africa was a blank slate; there was no civil society to speak of. Once again, the human factor is missing in the analysis. There are hundreds of dedicated people in Sierra Leone who do not underestimate the country's terrible problems, but who are also trying to lay the groundwork for a better future. They may lose the battle to halt a future of chaos and conflict, but if they do it will not be without a fight. How else is it possible to explain Sierra Leone's democratic elections in March 1996, when despite all predictions to the contrary, voters braved threats, random shootings, and the active hostility both from sections of the government army and the RUF rebels to cast their ballots? When senior politicians held a special meeting just before the poll date to decide if a postponement was needed in the climate of violence, they were met by a boisterous crowd of pro-democracy protesters led by Zainab Bangura, a towering force in the women's movement. The politicians somewhat reluctantly agreed to proceed, and the vote went off with remarkable calm. Weeks later, the military administration handed over power to the elected government of President Tejan Kabbah. The combination of vocal lobbying by women's groups, human rights activists, the press, and a groundswell of support for democracy from local communities proved that Sierra Leone's supposedly mortally wounded civil society still has some life.

On the battlefield, civilian defense militias formed around groups of traditional hunters known as the *kamajors*. They sprang up mainly in southern Sierra Leone after heavy attacks by the RUF rebels or by off-duty government soldiers, the so-called *sobels*, soldiers by day and rebels by night. Armed with the ancient single-barrel rifles they used to hunt small game, the *kamajors* quickly turned a potent rebel weapon, knowledge of secret bush paths, against the RUF. The *kamajors* knew them better. South African–based mercenaries hired by the government may have kept the rebels at bay around the diamond mines, but it was the *kamajors*, paid by local communities and chiefs, who did the most damage near their forest strongholds. In December 1996, President Kabbah and the RUF agreed on peace terms. The accord did not last. In May 1997, Sierra Leone was struck by another *coup d'état*, this time carried out by disgruntled soldiers who made common cause with their erstwhile enemies, the RUF. International condemnation was universal, with Organization of African Unity (OAU) Secretary General Salim Ahmed Salim describing the coup as "a loss for Africa." With the backing of UN Secretary General Kofi Annan, Nigeria dispatched troops to Freetown and demanded that President Kabbah be returned to office.

A critical task in rebuilding the nation is reclaiming the militarized children before the lack of schools, jobs, and, in many cases, families pushes them to direct their martial skills toward a life of crime. Few child soldiers emerge from wealthy families. Typically, they are from poor and working families, living in overcrowded urban slums, isolated rural homesteads in the war zone, or impoverished camps for those displaced by the fighting. A widespread feeling of social exclusion feeds the child soldier phenomenon, and rebel commanders cleverly exploit it. In remote corners of Sierra

Leone and Liberia, they have set up video parlors powered by generators to show violent action films such as *First Blood* to indoctrinate their young fighters. Rambo's experience as an uneducated Vietnam War veteran resorting to his military prowess and cunning to pay back a society that has persecuted him as a vagrant carries a powerful resonance. Rambo's character has been likened to the mythical youth trickster of the Mende tradition in southwestern Sierra Leone named Musa Wo.[12] His daring and disruptive exploits are meant to remind Mende elders not to neglect the young but to use their energy for the good of society.

The modern-day child soldiers bear a similar message for society. They have been traumatized by violence, and the long periods the children spent in the authoritarian regime of military life leave them with a low regard for civilians and an inability to make decisions on their own. "They will not take any orders except from their military officers," says Father Mick Hickey, an Irish priest who works with demobilized child soldiers in Sierra Leone. "They have a total disdain for civilian life." Unless the children can find a place to live, they threaten to end up as delinquents—the boys as armed robbers and the girls as prostitutes—for whom traditional social mores have little meaning and for whom violence has become an acceptable means of communication. "The child must be given a feeling he belongs somewhere, whether it's in the family, in the community, or some other arrangement," according to UNICEF's Esther Galuma. "The recovery of the children will be very slow and very painful." Difficult it is proving to be, but not impossible.

The attempt to rebuild the children's faith in civilian society is at the heart of the Children Associated with War project in Sierra Leone. Dr. Nahim, the psychiatrist, is on its board and Father Hickey administers the program. Starting from humble beginnings, Children Associated with War has become one of the most successful efforts in Africa aimed at the reintegration of child soldiers. Serving as symbolic substitutes for the Mende elders dealing with the troublesome trickster Musa Wo, the young adults who work as the project counselors act as the children's big brothers to keep them focused on rebuilding their lives. They are people like Emmanuel Foyoh, a tall, quiet man, who seems to have a permanent scowl on his face, as if he is suffering from some unspoken pain. Although his coworkers, Ignatius Samuels and Ismael Ibrahim, are somewhat jollier young men, something appears to be gnawing at them, too. Money is short, and some of the teenagers they are counseling have intimated that Emmanuel and his colleagues are stealing funds that were meant for them. The problem stems from their chosen mission: to help guide eighteen trained killers, albeit teenagers, back into their society. "It's very risky," says Emmanuel. "We are dealing with children who took up arms, and when their dreams are not realized, they might decide that we are to blame."

Emmanuel, Ignatius, and Ismael are intelligent, educated, in their late twenties, and surely they can find alternative jobs. So why do they work with the boy soldiers? It is certainly not for the money. Their monthly pay of about $50 does not stretch very far in a city where food supplies are often interrupted for months by highway ambushes; prices in the open-air markets are soaring. Emmanuel begins by saying that, in fact, he was a refugee like most of the estimated three hundred thousand people around the Bo area. He was a counselor for the program for child soldiers in the eastern city of Koidu, in the heart of the Konu diamond-mining region, until the RUF overran the area. Fifty-five child soldiers who had just returned to civilian life simply disappeared, many of them probably forcibly enlisted in the rebel ranks. Emmanuel made his way to Bo, and immediately enlisted as a counselor.

"What we earn is minimal," he says. "There is no traveling allowance, so we must visit the children on foot, which is difficult during the heavy rains. But if someone does not help these children, the country will be full of armed bandits. There will never be peace in Sierra Leone." Ignatius and Ismael nod their agreement. "What is going to happen to these children if they have nothing to do?" asks Ignatius. "There are few jobs, and all they know how to do is fight with weapons." Emmanuel breaks in. "Many of the children have returned to the war because they cannot adjust to this type of civilian life. The real problem will come after the war. Our country is training these children to become bandits, and they could turn out to be worse than the rebels. So we are working in this program for the future of our country. It might not seem like very much, but in a way, it could be the most important thing we will ever do in our lives."

The bulk of the 370 children who initially entered the nationwide demobilization program came from the army loyal to the military government in Freetown. Many were volunteers. Others were picked up in army sweeps of the streets along with petty criminals who were effectively given guns to further their careers in the interior. The army, racked by corruption and incompetence, greedily accepted all. "The children are used as hunting dogs," Emmanuel says bitterly. "Whenever there is a battle, the older soldiers who have wives and children retreat to the back and leave the children at the front." The first contingent of Sierra Leone's child soldiers, the youngest of whom was seven years old, were released from duty in June 1993. The first major job was to find their immediate families, or at least their closest relatives who live in relatively safe areas. After efforts by the International Committee of the Red Cross took too long, Dr. Nahim and Father Hickey set up their own team of Sierra Leoneans to carry out a speedier tracing program. While that work was under way, they housed and fed the youngsters, many of whom were deeply unhappy about their departure from the army. "They were very aggressive, hyper alert, often fighting, and they did not sleep properly for the first several months," says Father Hickey. After six months or so, most of the children started to calm down. The ones who did not ran away to rejoin the army. Until the children's relations were located, Children Associated with War needed to find something constructive for them to do, either to learn a trade or to return to school. But since most of their families were facing their own dire economic problems, the project chipped in with small stipends to encourage the children

The early weeks and months after the children leave the army mark a crucial turning point in any rehabilitation scheme, because it is the window of opportunity for counselors to carefully negotiate a process of "destroying the past" of military life and putting something new in its place. In some countries, such as Mozambique, social workers have turned to traditional cultural figures, such as *curandeiro* healers, to perform purification ceremonies to win community acceptance of the wayward children. In Sierra Leone, Children Associated with War relies on intense counseling by committed young men like Emmanuel to keep the boys and girls busy in school and apprenticeships.

Emmanuel walks around the back of Bo's whitewashed Roman Catholic Pastoral Center to a makeshift carpentry shop where some of the former child soldiers learn to build. Wood shavings fall to the ground in piles as a short, wiry young man named Foday Mustapha, shirtless and wearing cutoff trousers, pushes a plane along a board. The fact that he is enthusiastic about his work and picks up the skills quickly indicates that he is well down the road of "destroying the past." Yet his future remains tenuous. Job opportunities are scarce in Bo, which for long periods was surrounded by the rebels and scores of freelance bandits. After Foday arrived in Bo, he moved in with an elder brother who attends Bible college. But because he earns no money, food is a constant worry. Yet the very destruction brought about by the conflict gives Foday hope that his new trade will be in high demand. "There is always work for a carpenter," Foday says, laughing. "There is so much to build in Sierra Leone." Foday's progress has been so exemplary that Emmanuel and his colleagues appointed him chairman of the group of "resettled children" in the city. This is not to say that Foday is, in Emmanuel's words, "completely right in the head." He giggles a little too much and at awkward times, and he is easily distracted. Still, there is nothing to suggest that he is anything but an ordinary apprentice carpenter—until he points out the scars on his legs from shrapnel wounds he received in battle.

Foday enlisted in the army four years before, just after the RUF rebels launched their war. He was thirteen at the time and was living with his family in the far eastern town of Pendembu, one of the early flashpoints. "I decided to join the army because of what the rebels did to my family. They killed my younger brother, my stepmother, and my uncle," he says. "The rebels entered the region, burnt people's houses, and I don't agree with that." While the remainder of his family moved to a refugee camp, Foday ran away to the main army barracks in the eastern region at Daru and enlisted along with dozens of other boys and girls his age. He recalled those early days as a time of camaraderie and excitement, far removed from the drudgery of rural life and the refugee camp. Soon he was given an AK-47 and was considered a full-fledged fighter. "Discipline was very strict, and you could not disobey orders. As we used to say, 'Obey de las odah.'"

One aspect of military life which he did not expect was the massive intake of drugs, particularly before battles. Drug abuse is rampant among both sides of the Sierra Leonean conflict, as it is in Liberia, and has become a staple in the military world. The child soldiers are pumped full of a variety of drugs, such as alcohol, cocaine, marijuana, and ephedrine, an active ingredient in asthma medication. In what must constitute an arms merchant's dream, the most commonly abused substance is said to be gunpowder. "You either drink it with alcohol or cook it in the food," explains Dr. Nahim. "It makes people very alert and removes their fear. After you consume gunpowder for a while, you are not the same person." Foday concurs. "We were given a lot of drugs to make us strong. Drugs like gunpowder in our food and cocaine. They make your heart strong, to have zeal. The drugs made me feel that I was not afraid of anything." Foday does not know how the officers obtain the drugs, but he remembers that on at least one occasion, his fellow soldiers took some cocaine off the body of a well-known rebel commander named Charles Timba, who was widely known as "Rambo." "The rebels are on drugs all the time," says Dr. Nahim. "They are injected with cocaine, sometimes heroin. It's part of their pay from the diamond smugglers."

From an enthusiastic recruit bent on revenge, Foday was soon transformed into a cynical fourteen-year-old killing machine wired on all kinds of mind-altering substances while watching his friends being struck down on the field of battle. "One time we were in Mobai and were ordered to attack a rebel base near Baiima," he recalls. "We went there, and then the rebels counterattacked. Most of the children were at the front, and many of us were gunned down as we advanced." Another time he and three friends ran into an ambush as they walked from their barracks at Daru to the nearby town of Mobai. A hand grenade killed his friends and left Foday with his shrapnel wounds. Often the enemy is gangs of armed children like themselves. "We could see them face-to-face, and they were small like us. Once there was this girl, she must have been thirteen years old, and she was fighting us very hard. No one could stop her, until finally our commander hit her with a shot."

After nearly two years, the drugs, the blood, and the loss of friends were starting to take their toll. "I was not feeling good about being in the army anymore. Sometimes I was sick." Dr. Nahim says it is a common reaction. "Over time, the drugs make the soldiers delirious, disorientated, and they begin to lose the sense of time and place. Soldiers start refusing to take orders and fire into the air at random. They get out of control." Strasser's military government allowed a UNICEF representative to visit the main barracks around the country and offer the child soldiers a way out. While doing so, however, the official made unrealistic promises that left the children bitter. When he finished his contract and left the country several months later, UNICEF temporarily dropped the project, leaving it to a coalition of Roman Catholic priests and concerned Sierra Leonean citizens to pick up the pieces and form the Children Associated with War. "The man from UNICEF said all of us children were going to be demobilized," Foday says. "We would be able to go to school and learn a trade. We kids were promised money, allowances, bicycles, shoes, and clothes, and because of that we were happy. But those things never happened. I don't even have enough money for my own tools." Emmanuel's scowl hardens. "That is why our work is risky," he says.

The undoubted star of the reintegration program in Bo can be found in a dank cement room at a hostel behind the military hospital. Sayo Kamara initially seems to be painfully shy. He feigns ignorance of English and only a basic knowledge of the Krio (Creole) dialect, the lingua franca of the West African coast, which emerged from a mixture of English, Portuguese, and a host of African languages. Emmanuel intervenes and assures Sayo that he should feel free to express his opinions. It becomes immediately clear that not only does Sayo speak English but his command of the language is excellent, perhaps even better than that of his counselors. He flashes an embarrassed smile when Emmanuel announces proudly that Sayo, a child soldier until two years before, is now, at seventeen, a model student at the top of his class at the Bo Commercial Secondary School. His soft voice, smooth skin, and obvious humility make it difficult to understand how such a gentle boy found his way into one of the continent's dirtiest little wars.

Sayo was living with his family in northern Sierra Leone when the RUF overran his village. Together with his parents and three sisters, he fled the area and ended up in a refugee camp. At the age of fourteen, he decided to enlist. "My purpose in joining the army was to take revenge for what the rebels have done to my people," he says. "They have disrupted my people's way of life. My elder brother Ibrahim was already a corporal, so joining the army seemed the best thing to do. My parents agreed with my decision because they had no money to feed me and my three sisters." With his parents' blessing and Ibrahim's connections, Sayo made his way south to the barracks at Daru, where he joined Foday and a few dozen other children. "I was a normal soldier, and at any time we could be ordered to fight. It was a very tough life, but after a while you get used to it. Having other children around me made it easier."

The soldiers, children and adults alike, receive almost no pay and are given little food. They take what they need from civilians they encounter in the countryside. "We had no money for anything, so during battles we would scavenge for anything we could find in the villages we captured. You had to do anything you could to survive," Sayo says, hanging his head in obvious shame. That partly explains why so many of the highway ambushes and village attacks attributed to the rebels in the Sierra Leone war are actually carried out by government troops. It is the *sobel* factor, and for the high commands of many armies it has become a matter of policy. That way, they do not have to worry about properly feeding and supplying their soldiers. Let them prey off the civilians. "We were given drugs to make us more active to fight," says Sayo. "They make you feel more ready for action, not afraid of anything. But sometimes the drugs made me feel sick. In battle, my heart raced out of control."

It was the extreme levels of brutality and the deaths of many of his young comrades that persuaded Sayo it was time to change careers. Initially, he was skeptical. "A man came to tell us that we were going to be demobilized, and our superiors told us it was a privilege to be able to leave the army and have a chance to study. I was not too convinced about leaving the army. I was used to the life, and having a gun made us feel like big men." But he agreed to go, and ended up at the temporary shelter in Freetown run by the Children Associated with War team. Eventually he decided to move to Bo to live with his uncle so he could attend the well-regarded local secondary school.

Sayo is an excellent student and is so eloquent that Emmanuel, Ismael, and Ignatius asked him to appear on a special radio program to urge other child soldiers to quit soldiering. "I told them that all young soldiers should return to civilian life and go to school, that the army was no place for children," he says. "But after I spoke on the radio, some of the older soldiers around the town were angry with me. They said I was a fool, that I didn't know what I was talking about." Despite the criticism, Sayo is convinced it was the right thing to do. "The war is still going on, and most of my friends are deformed or killed. I met one of my friends, Ibrahim Kaikai, in the hospital here last month. He was shot in the foot. I sat by his bed and told him about my new life. But he said he will never leave the army unless the war is finished. Even if the army did not give him anything, he said he would fight for his people. All of his family has been displaced, and he does not know where his parents are. He says he has no place to go except the army."

STRONG FAMILY support obviously smooths the path back to normal life for the child warriors. This is especially true for the young girls who have emerged from the army ranks. They encounter worse problems, unique to their sex. In Uganda, abducted girls are often "married off" to commanders of the Lord's Resistance Army, which is involved in a guerrilla war in northern Uganda against the government of President Museveni.[13] If and when they return to their towns and villages, they are often considered damaged goods and end up working as prostitutes. The same has occurred in countries like Liberia, Mozambique, and Sierra Leone. "Some of the young girls are 'rations,'" says an outraged Emmanuel, the counselor in Bo. "That is, they satisfy the sexual urges of the officers. Imagine, the Sierra Leonean armed forces has little girls registered as soldiers. It shows what this country has become!"

Angela Tucker does not seem to have been a "ration." Like Foday and Sayo, she volunteered for military service and was later demobilized. Today, she lives in Freetown with her very strict grandfather, Andrew Tucker. Looking at her now, a chubby seventeen-year-old in stretch bicycle shorts and Chicago Bulls T-shirt relaxing in the comfortable living room of a middle-class, two-story house in a Freetown suburb called Kissy, it is hard to imagine Angela carrying an AK-47 in the Sierra Leone bush. She fights back a smile, somewhat ashamed to discuss the issue in front of her grandfather. He is definitely not smiling. "What possesses the children of Sierra Leone to run off and join the army, I will never know," he says, shaking his head. "I just don't understand this generation."

Angela ran away from home in January 1992, when she was fourteen years old. Her brother Moiri, then fifteen, was a corporal at the Daru barracks, and he wrote to her about what a great time he was having in the army. "I was bored in Freetown, with school, and my father was so strict. I wanted to do something exciting," she says. "Moiri told me how to make my way to Daru. One of the my friends, Victoria, had an aunt in the army who also told her how exciting it was, so we ran off together."

Angela and Victoria made their way to Bo, enlisted, and then were posted to Daru. "It was great. I was able to carry an AK-47, I met with a lot of young people my age, and we were never afraid," Angela says. To hear her tell the story, the army was like a big youth camp. The only reason she agreed to demobilize was that most of her friends, including Foday and Sayo, did so too. But she quickly grew restless. When she returned to Freetown, Angela begged her parents to allow her to leave their home in the distant western outskirts of town and to live with her grandfather. Her excuse was that the schools were better in Kissy, but Tucker believed she was trying to escape the discipline of home. "She thought that by living with us and not with her parents she would have more freedom," Tucker says, with one eyebrow cocked at his errant granddaughter. Angela nods her head, admitting the truth. "But she went from the frying pan to the fire."

Grandfather Tucker, it turns out, is no soft touch, and he has banned some of her more rebellious friends from the house. "She was a bit adventurous when she returned from the army, but I didn't punish her because I felt that she had already repented and suffered enough. But I did have to be more strict with her, to force her to mend her ways, because she used to leave the house without permission." Angela enrolled in Richard Allen High School in Kissy, and her grades in Form 4 are average. The first day he sent her off to school, Tucker ordered her not to talk to the other students about her experiences in the army. "I told her to try to fit in like any normal child and just concentrate on her classes."

Tucker's is a tall order. For Angela and other child soldiers, fitting in has proved difficult. In the army, normal rules of civilian life do not apply. Their weapons give them authority well beyond their years, and in any disputes with civilians, all they have to do is point their rifle to ensure a satisfactory outcome. A remarkable number of children appear to come through the experience of violence and atrocities relatively unscathed. For others, it takes months, sometimes years, for them to overcome their trauma.

One who was deeply affected by his war experiences is Ahah Kungbana, but like Angela, his family has helped him through the roughest times. After leaving the army, he suffered from frightening nightmares, especially of his friends dying. Ahah is one of those child soldiers Dr. Nahim talks about who, under the pressure of widespread violence and drug abuse, cracked. He turned his gun on his superior officer, a common occurrence on the front line. At the age of fifteen, Ahah was court-martialed. Ahah grew up in the eastern region of Konu but was driven along with his family into the city of Koidu after the rebels attacked their rural homestead. "The schools were closed, the teachers would not teach, so what was I to do?" He joined the army. After a brief training period, Ahah was handed a rocket-propelled grenade launcher and sent into battle. Like the others, initially, he enjoyed the life. But soon friends started dying, and the drugs started to make him feel sick. Then came the shooting incident involving his superior. Ahah will not talk about it, and his aunt, Nancy Nyandemoh, with whom he lives in Freetown, says it is better that he does not. "Ahah needs to look to the future and forget the past," she says, stroking his shoulder. "The past is over."

When Ahah first arrived, Nancy says, he was in terrible shape, physically and psychologically. Blood would occasionally trickle out of his right ear, which had lost the ability to hear thanks to repeated explosions of the grenade launcher. Ahah used to get into fights a lot. "He gave us a small, small problem," Nancy says in Krio, laughing, "but now he done change." Indeed, Ahah has gone through a virtual metamorphosis, thanks to the care and stable environment provided by Nancy and her husband, Ahah Nyandemoh, and to the counseling of the Children Associated with War workers in Freetown. "Ahah was having all kinds of problems when he first came to the program," says one of the counselors, Antony Koroma. "There was a lot of rage inside. Some of his friends ran back to join the army, and it took him a while to get used to civilian life." Intense counseling sessions and big brother talk were needed to keep him from running away too. "We told him to leave everything behind at the front and to listen to his aunt and uncle," says Leslie Mboka, another member of the Freetown counseling team.

Then Ahah found that he enjoyed school, and he excelled as a student. He is attending St. Edward's Secondary School, and like Sayo in Bo, he is at the top of his class. His ambition eventually is to gain entrance into university and study for a law degree. Ahah has found religion, too, and regularly attends the services of a charismatic Christian preacher called Mammy Dumbuya. He also shares with Sayo the friend named Kaikai, the boy who was shot in the foot but said he would never leave the army. "Kaikai was in the program, but he could not stay here," Ahah says. "He ran away again. He said the schools have nothing for him. He does not want to learn from books. Kaikai said the gun is his teacher."

In Sierra Leone, family ties and the determination of the Children Associated with War counselors have proved to be a remarkably potent mixture in ensuring the success of reclaiming the youth of war. In Mozambique, experts embarked on a different tack. Since the mid-1980s, when the problem of child soldiers used by the Renamo rebels became apparent, psychologists from the United States and Europe flew in to study the phenomenon and provide Western-style psychiatric counseling to some of the youngsters who either were captured by the army or made their way to government-controlled zones. In general, their conclusions, not surprisingly, were that child soldiers had been horribly traumatized by their war experiences and by the rebels' practice of forcing some of the children to witness and participate in atrocities carried out against their own villages. It was part of the rebels' "socialization process" to force the child soldiers to forget their past and cement their allegiance to Renamo.[14]

What the experts did not count on was the steel will of many of the children themselves. Once the children began moving to the transit centers at the end of the war, they presented a totally different picture from what had been expected. "Nobody really knew about the children," says Jean Claude le Grand, UNICEF's emergency coordinator in Mozambique. "There were a lot of rumors—'they have been kidnapped too young; they cannot remember about their background.' But when we started registration, they all knew about their family, and they all defined as a priority to be reunited with their families. I have been impressed by the way I have not seen any visible sign of trauma."

When the children reached the thirteen transit camps set up by UNICEF and the international nongovernmental agencies, they brought their military organization with them. "In the transit centers, the children were very well organized," says le Grand. "There is a hierarchy, but also a democracy. Every time one of the leaders would leave to be taken to his home, the ones left behind in the centers would elect a new *chefe* [chief], and the new *chefe* would immediately appoint someone to monitor the food stocks. Each time there was a change, the children implemented their own network of control." It was the military system they knew, and their loyalty to their erstwhile kidnappers, the Renamo rebels, never wavered. Tiny Renamo flags hung on the tree branches around the camps. As traumatic as life may have been in the rebel army, it had provided the child soldiers with a seductive taste of power.

Returning the children to their families presented its own problems, not least the complex logistics involved in tracking down relatives who had been scattered sometimes hundreds of miles by the war. Once the families were located, however, there was the issue of what to do about the villagers' reluctance to accept the return of children who had killed. The children were not ready either. Mauricio Cumango, an upbeat thirty-five-year-old cook at one of the demobilization camps for the children, remembered what they were like the day they arrived. "They were almost all soldiers," he says. "Frightening, very tough and angry. Some of the neighbors from the surrounding villages occasionally walked by and shouted insults at the children, calling them killers and murderers. That really upset the children, and they shouted back that they were forced to fight, that they never wanted to become soldiers."

At that point, all the international expertise and funding became irrelevant. The only solution was to tap into local village customs. "Systematically a ceremony is performed, basically a purification ceremony, which involves all kinds of symbolic deaths and rebirths of the child," says le Grand. "It is a ceremony to push away the bad spirits that they might have brought back with them. During the ceremony, the child is covered with blood in an imitation of death and birth. They are reborn to the group in a reintegration process."

One of the children who was waiting for such a rebirth was a little boy named Mario Matavele. His friends called him Chivite, or "the angry one" in the Shangaan language. He readily admitted that he had blood on his hands, that he took another human life. He was not ashamed of it. After all, it was his job; he was only following orders. "The angry one" may have fought on the front line of the civil war, but all he wanted to do was see his mommy and daddy. "The angry one" was eleven years old. He spent his days at the Chonguene transit camp in southern Mozambique hanging out in his tent or playing soccer with his bunkmate Martins Buque, a ten-year-old veteran of the war. He was in the second month of waiting for someone to take him to his family's house about fifty miles away. "I want to go home and see my mother, and maybe go to school," he said, and then added almost as an afterthought, which reflected his accelerated rise to adulthood, "I want to find a woman and work."

Most of Mario's friends, the ones who survived, that is, handed in their guns and were escorted home by the government's Social Action Department with the help of nongovernmental organizations such as the Red Cross and Save the Children USA. But it had been difficult to locate Mario's parents, Armando and Helena, so he had to wait. It was possible that they wanted nothing to do with him, that they could not bear the shame, since the rebels were guilty of extraordinary brutality, especially in the south where they were highly unpopular. It was also possible that his parents were dead—victims of starvation caused by the war, or perhaps murdered by little boys just like Mario. He last saw home three years before on an afternoon when his father sent him to the family cornfield to drive off some wildlife looking for a free lunch. "I was chasing monkeys," he said. "They were always trying to eat the corn. Then, a group of soldiers came out of the bush. They said I had to go with them." The

Renamo unit delivered Mario to a base, where he and other children underwent several weeks of basic military training. After that, a few of them were issued AK-47s while the others took up machetes and clubs or just became porters. Mario obviously showed military promise: he received an automatic rifle. He was eight years old. "All the time shooting and running, shooting and running," he said. Typically, the young fighters were subjected to close firing to dull their senses to the natural fear of gunfire. Some were forced to kill cattle and others to murder civilians, sometimes even relatives and neighbors, to prepare them to become seasoned killers.

Initially, Mario missed his parents and his home, and the monotonous diet of beans and corn, with only an occasional piece of bush meat, was difficult to get used to. But after a while, he felt comfortable in his soldier's life. "My unit was my family, and the commander told us everything to do. We just followed orders," he said, echoing Foday Mustapha's favorite saying, "Obey de las odah." Luckily for Mario and his mates, by the time they became operational, the war was winding down. Mario's twenty-five-strong unit engaged in only three military operations, including one that involved a month-long march. For Mario, the first two battles were horrifying. His unit was told that they were attacking military targets, and while they did encounter resistance, Mario remembered seeing women and children being caught in the crossfire. "I was very scared. I tried to run away, but the commanders would push us up to the front. If we ran, they would beat us to make us go back. Some of my friends died, but we had to leave them. When one of our guys died, we usually hid his corpse, took his shoes and gun, and moved on." By the third battle he was ready. "I fired my rifle, and I could see that I hit someone. I felt that bullet enter his body."

When peace was eventually declared, it shattered the child soldiers' world, at least temporarily. Like many of the other children, Mario was particularly bitter that in his view, the rebel leadership abandoned him. "Our commanders left us at the base with no orders. They vanished. We did not know what to do. We were lost." And so he waited. By the time Mozambique held its first elections in October 1994, all but 20 of the original 850 children registered by UNICEF had found a home. Mario was one of the few who had not. But as he bided his time in Chonguene, he remained confident that he would. "The Red Cross is taking care of the others first," he said, stretched out on a huge smooth gray log like an African Huckleberry Finn. "Then they will come to take me home."

THE CASES of Sierra Leone and Mozambique have proved that Africa's lost generation may not be so lost after all, provided the young fighters are given the chance. The transformation of soldiers into children has at times been miraculous. The key to the success has been the ability to restore the warm embrace of the community and to instill a sense of pride in their own accomplishments in school and in work. It is not impossible to think that some of these children will one day become responsible leaders in their own right. Certainly someone like Sayo Kamara, if he sticks to his current course, has a very bright future.

But what of those children who participated in the worst crime of their generation: the genocide in Rwanda? Surely, if they can be saved from the genocidal mind-set, anyone can make it. It is far too soon to reach a conclusion. The tiny central African nation is still grappling with the psychological and physical wounds of those three months in 1994 when at least a half million of the minority Tutsi population was slaughtered by large segments of the majority Hutus. But there are reasons for optimism. In an isolated parcel of land twenty miles southeast of the Rwandan capital sits the Gitagata Re-education and Production Center. Made up of dark damp dormitories filled with rows of bunk beds in an encampment surrounded by a tall wire fence, the center is home to several hundred boys between the ages of seven and eighteen who are being held by the Rwandan government on charges of participating in the genocide.

The camp itself is remarkably relaxed, considering the nature of the crimes allegedly committed by the inmates. Conditions are far better than the adult prisons, where up to ninety thousand accused of genocide are being held in horrific conditions, with everything from water and food to simple space in severely short supply. Since their arrival in June 1995, the children have been attending primary school classes, are involved in carpentry and farming, and are able to play soccer. For the most part, they have a great deal of control over their daily lives. They elect *kapitas*, or captains, to take charge of everything from food and water to washing their clothes and sorting out fights among themselves. They begin their days at 6:00 A.M. with a wash and breakfast, usually porridge, and by eight A.M. they are in school. At 8:00 P.M., they return to their dormitories. Foreign relief agencies look after their major needs, such as food, firewood, and water. Government social workers hold meetings with the children to discuss the horrors of the genocide and to convince them that the majority of Hutu people and the Tutsi can live together in the same society. Most of them stand a chance of doing so. Under Rwandan law, children under the age of fourteen cannot be held responsible for their crimes and cannot be tried in a court of law.

One of the inmates, a little tyke named Kubgirimana, knows he is accused of being a perpetrator of genocide, but he is not sure what the word actually means. He tries to ignore the wire fence and the armed soldiers patrolling it. All he wants to talk about is playing soccer and his dream of one day returning to his home in the nearby region of Gitarama. Kubgirimana is seven years old. He is about three and a half feet tall. In response to questions about the killings or what he was doing during the massacres, Kubgirimana simply grunts. His parents died when he was small, and he was living with his grandmother at the time. He did not see any bodies, he says, and as far as he is concerned everything was normal until some soldiers walked up to his house one day and said he was under arrest.

It is the same story with his buddy, nine-year-old Claude Nzamuranbakaho, who was arrested in Kigali. Claude says his parents are still at home, but they never come to visit him. Social workers at Gitagata suggest that either they died, were arrested, or fled the country. Claims by the social workers at the camp that the children are probably safer there than walking around freely have at least a ring of truth. Many survivors of the genocide demand that the child killers be punished no matter how young.

One survivor who thinks differently is Jean Marie Higiro, a twenty-five-year-old social worker at the camp employed by the Ministry of Justice. His grandparents and several uncles were murdered, but in his manner there is an extraordinary lack of bitterness. "Many people do not understand why we take so much trouble for these children," he says. "It's difficult to work with them because I know they were involved in the killings. But it's important to help change the situation in the country. It's evident that I am sad, that people died simply because of politics, but I am here to help the children understand, to teach them, so that this sort of thing never happens again. We need to create a new reality. We can't do what they did and just kill these people, because if we did, we would just create a vicious circle which would never end. Revenge would solve nothing."

As bleak as the situation seems, Jean Marie, who arrived at the camp a few days before the children did, believes that much can still be done. "It's not really the children's fault because they were brainwashed by their parents. 'Tutsis' are evil, they were told. If a little boy hears his father talking like that and sees his father killing people, it is only natural that he will want to do the same thing. Any one of us would act exactly the same way. It's very easy to teach children bad behavior, but to teach them the good, that is far more difficult. If we can change their mind-set, I think that even the most difficult children could get along in society," Jean Marie says. "It's our only hope."

Heroes of the Apocalypse

A stinging drizzle melts the front lawn of the Namasheke parish church into a bog of amber mud as a lean, middle-aged priest in a black habit turns to the west to behold a panorama of breathtaking beauty. A dark green patchwork quilt of banana trees and corn stalks rests atop a horizon of sharply rising hills and dizzying valleys folded around the rich blue waters of Lake Kivu—a virtual Garden of Eden in the heart of Africa. Behind the bespectacled clergyman, several hundred villagers stand in a giant semicircle outside a maze of wooden poles enveloped by green plastic sheeting to keep out the rain. Under cover are the only people seated in chairs, the invited guests, mostly middle-level governments officials with a sprinkling of European diplomats and human rights monitors sent by the United Nations. High-pitched voices of government representatives and priests boom over a crackly PA system mourning the deaths of eight hundred thousand people murdered by their own countrymen. The impassive faces of the villagers moistened by the rain give no hint that the pleas for peace and penance are making an impression. In front of them, thousands of human skulls, leg bones, and rib cages are piled four feet high along a line of huge, freshly dug pits intended to be a final resting place. Tall young soldiers in crisp khaki uniforms avert their faces, tears in their eyes, as the shifting wind carries a wave of stench so primal that the audience scrambles to press handkerchiefs and any available scraps of cloth over their noses.

The brief ceremony has been repeated dozens of times throughout the tiny central African republic of Rwanda to allow survivors of the one hundred–day genocide in 1994 to pay their last respects to the departed, and perhaps so that people can begin to put the past behind them. Alas, the past proves enduring; the turnout of the local villagers is disappointingly meager. They are members of the majority Hutu people, and in all probability many of them or their relatives had a hand in the butchery. Scores of their neighbors who had the misfortune of being identified as members of the minority Tutsi group are lying in the skeletal piles by the grave. As the voice of the final speaker fades away, the priest, Father Oscar Nkundayezo, removes his glasses and rubs his eyes before striding back toward the crowd. "Hurry, hurry," he shouts while clapping his hands. His parishioners begin the task of reburying the remains, which were exhumed from hundreds of clandestine pits and mass graves found in the general vicinity of Namasheke. "We are all the same in God's eyes," Father Oscar says in urgent tones. "We must send them to the Holy Father with respect." With dread in their eyes and a cacophony of low groans, gangs of men grudgingly obey, lifting the rancid bones in their bare hands as if they were carrying stacked wood, and dumping them in the new collective tomb.

After a few minutes with the work well under way, Father Oscar escorts several dozen special guests through the muck round the back of the church, past a neatly manicured hedge, and up a brick walkway to a sitting room. There, he and the church nuns serve cool drinks and beer, which are only modestly successful at erasing the nagging odor that fills the parish air. These visitors are having nothing to do with the physical interment; the unspoken rule is, let the ones who killed them bury them. By the time the reception is over, the finishing touches are being put to the mass grave. The guests climb into their four-wheel-drive vehicles for the three hundred–mile drive back to Kigali, the capital. The soldiers board trucks to return to their bases. The local residents stream out of the church grounds to their homes, giggling and joking as if nothing out of the ordinary has happened.

It seems unthinkable that this was the scene of a mass murder. Resting in the southeastern prefecture of Cyangugu on the border with the Democratic Republic of Congo, formerly Zaire, Namasheke is an area of spectacular vistas. Its allure even seems to outshine the rest of Rwanda, a country so picturesque, so well ordered, that it has prompted many European visitors to gush about its being a little Switzerland in Africa. Half of the country is a mile above sea level, and in precolonial times, what has become known as "the land of a thousand hills" provided a wall of protection against outside threats, from malaria to Swahili slave raiders from the Indian Ocean coast.

Rwanda's soil is so fertile and its mild and humid climate so healthy that its territory is one of the most densely populated areas in Africa. With almost all of its available land put to productive use, Rwanda resembles one giant, well-manicured garden. The genocide was equally meticulous. Agricultural metaphors such as "clearing the bush" were favored extremist exhortations to murder, and so thorough was the gardening job that in Namasheke, it wiped out 90 percent of the Tutsis. In one two-day spree, some five thousand people were shot, macheted, or bludgeoned to death.[1]

Not all Hutus joined in the killing, and not all of those slain were Tutsis. Even as the slaughter broke out, scores of brave individuals, Hutu and Tutsi alike, risked everything to stop it. Their lives are still in danger, threatened by those with blood on their hands who want to eliminate everyone who witnessed their crimes. But every day that they and others like them survive, so does the hope that Rwanda has a chance, however faint, to heal its wounds, so that Hutu and Tutsi can coexist as they once did, without doubt sometimes uneasily, less than one hundred years ago. Father Oscar is one of those who resisted the genocide when he was in charge of the Cyangugu Cathedral near Kamembe, the main city in the prefecture, about thirty miles south of his current posting in Namasheke. There are countless others who acted with similar courage, from Thérèse Nyirabayovu, an elderly woman who lives in the slums of Kigali, and Jean Nitikina, a shop assistant in the southern city of Butare, to Beatrice Nyiransengimana, a farmer in the central region of Gitarama, whose husband and children were murdered by her own brothers because she married into, as she puts it, "the wrong tribe."

Father Oscar explains what has happened in Rwanda with one word: "egoism." In Rwanda, he says, egoism mutated into the violently asserted primacy of an extreme group of Hutus over the good of the entire society, Tutsis and Hutus included. "Egoism takes a lie and uses it as a weapon," Father Oscar says. "All Rwandans should be honest. We must recognize that whether Hutu or Tutsi, we are of the same category of man. Every day egoism is protecting a lie. In the past in Rwanda, the Hutu and Tutsi lived together and shared everything. Things were not perfect, but they even intermarried without restriction and they lived on the same hill. Then the politicians stirred up the individual's egoism for their own ends. They killed people, eliminated their brothers, created problems in the name of a new authority, of a new conception of money and property. It is without conscience."

Father Oscar's diagnosis of the Rwandan tragedy finds echoes in almost every country on the continent. Ethnic conflict is not the result of spontaneous combustion, as often portrayed in the shorthand of breathless news reports about "tribes" being at each other's throats for centuries. Look behind the veil of any outbreak of ethnic tension and there is sure to be a band of politicians spitting the poison of tribalism as a means to gain power and influence. The Rwandan genocide of 1994 and the rebellion it sparked in eastern Congo three years later signaled the apocalyptic potential of ethnic rivalry in an era of spreading poverty, intense competition for land, and the destabilizing uncertainties of multiparty politics. Not since the Nigerian civil war in the 1960s has the issue of ethnicity been thrust to the forefront of the African agenda as now.

The reason for the concern is simple: ethnic tension has the power to destroy nations, particularly when people are looking for scapegoats to assuage their frustration with economic hardship. Ethnic prejudice takes a variety of forms, sometimes centering on differences of culture and language; but when that is not possible, as in Rwanda, the focus is on appearance, class differences, and collective myths. "Left with shells of a fragile and fallible civil society, the majority have sought ways of defending themselves," Basil Davidson has written. "The principal way they have found of doing this is through 'tribalism,' perhaps more accurately clientelism: a kind of Tammany Hall–style patronage, dependent on personal, family, and similar networks of local interest. Insofar as it is a 'system,' clientelism has become the way politics in Africa largely operates. Its rivalries naturally sow chaos."[2] Yet ethnicity alone cannot explain Rwanda's genocide. Any understanding of the cataclysm must take into account a combination of ethnic rivalry, particularly the intense form which Belgian colonialism did much to foster; rapid economic decline matched by a population explosion; and the breakdown of traditional religion. The mixture is not entirely unique to Rwanda, and its lessons carry a stark warning for the rest of Africa.

For centuries before colonial rule, independent political units usually based on ethnicity did what nations all over the world have done. They engaged each other in diplomacy, trade, and war. As Davidson has pointed out, "In a large historical sense tribalism has been used to express the solidarity and common loyalties of people who share among themselves a country and a culture. In this important sense, tribalism in Africa or anywhere else has 'always' existed and has often been a force for good, a force for creating civil society dependent on laws and the rule of law."[3] This relatively benign sense of ethnic identity was transformed a century ago when the Europeans met in Berlin to carve up Africa. With their pens and straightedges, they grouped dozens of ethnic groups, or hundreds as in the cases of Nigeria and the Congo, into new nation-states. European colonialism mixed as a potentially explosive cocktail in Africa as in parts of Eastern Europe and the former Yugoslavia. The fledgling African state was a source of predominant economic power, and politicians found ethnicity a handy weapon in their battle to seize the controls of government.

In the early independence days, armed secessionist movements arose in Congo's mineral-rich regions of Katanga and Kasai. But Africa first tasted the true destructive power of ethnicity when the Igbo people of eastern Nigeria attempted to secede in the 1967–70 Biafra War. At the same time, Nigeria's wise handling of the war's aftermath—a policy of "no victor, no vanquished"—proved that despite the loss of 1 million lives, coexistence was possible even in a nation with, at latest count, over 350 ethnic groups. Nevertheless, ethnic conflict has continued to claim victims. In Sudan, the Muslim Arab north is fighting the Christian and animist African south. The near-twenty-year civil wars in Mozambique and Angola, in which together almost 2 million people died, were heavily influenced by ethnic rivalry, as was the conflict in Liberia. The biggest crisis ever faced by Zimbabwe was ignited by a heavy-handed military clampdown by President Robert Mugabe's government, which enjoys overwhelming support among the more numerous Shona people, against the Ndebele stronghold of then opposition leader Joshua Nkomo. But like Nigeria, Zimbabwe found a solution. The two rivals merged their parties, and today Nkomo is Mugabe's vice president.

One-party states and personalized authoritarian rule kept the lid on ethnic politics throughout much of the 1970s and 1980s. Countries such as Côte d'Ivoire, Guinea, and Senegal in the west, and Kenya, Tanzania, and Zambia in East and southern Africa appeared to have found a means to cool the passions. Former President Nyerere always maintained that his greatest triumph as Tanzania's leader was the forging of national unity, although recent years have seen the stirrings of separatism on the islands of Zanzibar and Pemba. Most governments considered ethnicity an evil, an unwelcome legacy of the "tribal" past that should be erased from memory if Africa was to enter the modern era. Perhaps if the new African states had fulfilled their people's deep desire for rapid economic development and honest government, the pull of ethnicity would have faded. But they did not. More than at any time in recent memory, there are signs everywhere that ethnicity is again riding high. Africans all over the continent are identifying themselves by their ethnic group first and their official nationality second, whether one is speaking of the Hutu of Rwanda and Burundi, the Baganda of Uganda, the Lozi of Zambia, or the Yoruba of Nigeria. Today, for better or worse, the tea leaves of ethnicity are required reading for a clear understanding of conflict, politics, and economic power in almost every country.

In many ways, Rwanda was different from its neighbors. Unlike most modern African nations, it was not an artificial creation of the colonial mapmakers. Before the arrival of the Europeans—first the Germans, and after World War I the Belgians—Rwanda was an established African state, ruled by a king, the Mwami, whose word was considered divine. Its people were divided roughly between 85 percent subsistence farmers, or Hutus, and 14 percent Tutsi pastoralists, with a tiny population of the Twa pygmies, the original inhabitants of Rwanda. The Hutu and the Tutsi spoke a single language, Kinyarwanda, shared a common religion, and inhabited the same *musozi*, or hills. The genocide, too, differed from its historical predecessors, such as that of the American Indians or the Jewish Holocaust. While the Hutu extremists went about eliminating the Tutsi population, they also targeted opponents among the Hutus themselves. Among the first killed was Agnes Uwilingiyimana, the moderate prime minister who in her previous post as education minister had enraged the champions of "Hutu power" by removing school placement quotas favoring Hutu students.

Words such as "tribe" and "ethnic group" are at best blunt instruments when applied to dissecting the Rwandan tragedy, because ethnicity overlaps with social class and because of the common culture and language. The Tutsi are thought to have been a nomadic people who arrived in the Great Lakes region several hundred years ago from somewhere in the Horn of Africa, probably Oromoland in southern Ethiopia.[4] Tall, lean, with angular facial features, the Tutsi were clearly physically different from the smaller Hutu farmers and the Twa pygmies they found living in Rwanda. And yet, they did not set up their own "Tutsiland." Instead, they assimilated to Hutu society, adopting its language and its religion, a system of ancestral worship known as *Kubandwa*. The kingdom of the Mwami, whose authority was symbolized by the sacred drum, the *kalinga*, included

Tutsi, Hutu, and the relatively scarce Twa. The Mwami represented the trinity of Tutsi, Hutu, and Twa, and all Rwandans were supposed to be descendants of a mythical ancestor, *Gihanda*. The king and those at the very top of society were always Tutsi, and those on the lowest rungs were exclusively Hutu; but in the middle there was great mixture, with rich Hutu families and poor Tutsis. All fourteen major clans in Rwanda were distinctly nonethnic in that they included families of Tutsis, Hutus, and Twas. Whether one was a Hutu or Tutsi depended more on politics, ancestry, and cattle ownership than ethnicity.

Precolonial Rwanda was a feudal society in which everyone had a role and the lines of responsibility were clear. Communities had certain obligations to the Mwami, such as tending royal land and cattle, and providing collective labor for the state. Poorer villages aligned themselves with local lords of the manor by exchanging labor and food, provided collectively, for protection and sometimes cattle. A Hutu family might even climb the social ladder to reach Tutsi status, or *icyihuture* (de-Hutuized), with the cattle presented by a *shebuja*, a patron. Hutu fighters also routinely received gifts of cattle for their performance in battle in the service of the king. Two of the three types of chiefs under the king, in charge of men and grazing lands, were always Tutsis, but the third group, the land chiefs, was almost exclusively Hutus. Wars were fought and discrimination practiced, but the conflicts were never purely between Tutsi and Hutu.

The relationship began to deteriorate in the mid-nineteenth century during the reign of the Tutsi Mwami Rwabugiri. The king was hungry for a grander realm, so he conquered both Hutu and Tutsi lineages, which remained beyond his reach. His state cultivated ethnic discrimination by stressing physical characteristics, favoring those who were tall with thin noses over those who were shorter with flatter nostrils. By the time the Europeans stepped into the mix, positions of social status were slowly hardening into ethnic division. The *abazungu* (whites) accelerated the process by designating the Tutsis racially superior to the Hutus. The British explorer John Hanning Speke is credited with starting the myth about Tutsi ethnic supremacy in his *Journal of the Discovery of the Source of the Nile*, published in 1863. Speke and other Europeans, particularly the influential "White Father" Catholic missionaries, could not accept that black Africans were the architects of the sophisticated political and religious kingdom which they found in Rwanda. There had to be some white blood somewhere. Speke and the Europeans who followed him believed they knew the source. Tutsis were Europeans in black skins, the reasoning went. Some said they originated in Greece or Asia Minor. Speke was probably right when he pinpointed Ethiopia. The problem was that the ethnic superiority viewpoint stuck in the minds of both Europeans and Rwandans. The Tutsis came to believe they were superior, and the Hutus felt inferior, despite the fact that the Tutsis were the ones who embraced Hutu culture and not the other way around.

The racialist theory found practical application under first the Germans, beginning in 1897, and then the Belgians. The Tutsis enjoyed favor and the Hutus discrimination under the new powers in the land, the colonial administration and the Catholic Church. The institution of land chiefs, dominated by Hutus for generations, was abolished. *Kubandwa*, the religious glue of Rwandan society, was driven underground. At the day-to-day controls of the colonial administration were Tutsi administrators who preyed upon the Hutu elite and their own Tutsi rivals. They confiscated Hutu landholdings and transformed traditional community responsibility for voluntary labor into more onerous individual forced labor. Backed by the Europeans, Tutsi royalty was able to fulfill its expansionist dreams by subduing the last remaining tiny independent Hutu principalities in the northwest in the early twentieth century.

Christianity was another source of Tutsi advantage. Until the 1920s, Christianity competed poorly with *Kubandwa*. But its alliance with colonial government and the educational opportunities it provided made conversion a prerequisite for social advancement in the colonial state. Suddenly, Rwandans flocked to the church.[5] Catholic priests flung open the seminary and classroom doors to the Tutsis, but rebuffed Hutus. A decade later, the colonial authorities sealed the ethnic divide once and for all by issuing ethnic identity cards. The last nail in the coffin of traditional culture came in 1931, when the Belgians overthrew the Mwami, King Yuhi V Musinga, who rejected Christianity and championed Rwandan beliefs. He was replaced by the more European-friendly Mutara III Rudahigwa, who converted to Christianity, drove a car, and wore Western clothes. Among Rwandans, his nickname was "the king of the whites."[6] The combination of Tutsi administrative control of jobs and land, privileged access to education, and command of forced labor laid the groundwork for a pan-Hutu feeling of persecution. Hutus began to regard all Tutsis as "feudal exploiters." Even Tutsi women were deemed prettier than their Hutu counterparts.

As the French scholar Gérard Prunier points out in his landmark book *The Rwanda Crisis—History of a Genocide,* "Thus through the actions, both intellectual and material, of the white foreigners, myths had been synthesized into a new reality. And that new reality had become operational, with its heroes, its tillers of the soil and its clowns. Feelings and social actions would henceforth take place in relation to this reconstructed reality because by then it would have become the only one. The time-bomb had been set and it was now only a question of when it would go off."[7]

Relations between the Tutsis and the Belgians deteriorated as agitation for independence swept through the rest of Africa in the 1950s. The Tutsi elite turned up the pressure on their erstwhile benefactors to quit Rwanda. The attitudes of the Belgian clergy were changing too, along tribal lines. The French-speaking aristocratic church leaders of the early colonial period were gradually replaced by lower-class, often Flemish priests, who felt a natural sympathy with the downtrodden Hutu. The combination prompted the Belgians to reverse thirty years of policy and effectively switch sides. On the eve of independence in 1959, Belgian paratroopers helped a new church-educated Hutu leadership to overthrow the Tutsis in the so-called *muyaga*—"strong wind"—and to establish what came to be known as the Hutu Republic. The wind was bloody, and up to ten thousand Tutsis were killed. Hutu chiefs replaced Tutsis, and a quota system limited the number of Tutsis in schools and the civil service. Over a hundred thousand people fled to neighboring countries, including Uganda, where thirty years later the children of the exiles formed the Rwandan Patriotic Front (RPF) to use armed force to return to their parents' homeland.

The battle lines were drawn. "From the time of the Hutu Republic, the population was indoctrinated from birth with the notion that the Tutsis were snakes who wanted to dominate them," says Alexis Birindabagabo, the Anglican bishop of Kigali. "After the formation of the Hutu Republic, Tutsis could not make it in the state administration, and thus had to work extra hard to make it in business. They were very successful, and this created a lot of jealousy among the Hutu."

In the 1980s, the collapse of world prices for coffee, Rwanda's main foreign exchange earner, sent the economy into a downward spiral. President Júvenal Habyarimana's government instituted a "structural adjustment program" at the urging of the International Monetary Fund. The budget was slashed by 40 percent. Competition for land was fierce. Both Hutu and Tutsi regard as theirs the fertile valleys and hills of Rwanda nestled between the dense tropical forests of Congo and the dry savannahs of East Africa. Worried about worsening deforestation, the government restricted the opening of new land. Rapid population growth and a severe shortage of land confronted the peasantry with a collective crisis. Without farming or employment opportunities, young men could not advance and marry. When Habyarimana announced that there was simply not enough room in Rwanda to accommodate the return of Tutsi exiles abroad, he virtually guaranteed that the exiles would take up arms to press for their birthrights.

The children of the Tutsi exiles grew up into troops of the Rwandan Patriotic Front. On October 1, 1990, they crossed the Ugandan border to fight their way back into Rwanda. They were battle-tough, led by men such as Paul Kagame, Rwanda's current vice president and defense minister, who were veterans of Yoweri Museveni's movement in Uganda. Most of them studied in Ugandan schools and spoke English, not the French that predominated in Rwanda. The RPF, though Tutsi at its core, echoed President Museveni's advocacy of nontribal government and made common cause with moderate Hutus such as Pasteur Bizimungu, who later became president.

The RPF invasion sent the Hutu elite in Kigali into crisis mode. They were already shaken by the economic crisis and by President Habyarimana's decision, under pressure from France, to relinquish the one-party status of the National Revolutionary Movement for Development, the MRND, and to sanction a limited multiparty democracy. Hysteria was acute among a clique of top advisers known as the *akazu* or "little house," who were especially close to the president's wife, Agathe Kanziga. Hence their nickname: the *Clan de Madame.*[8] They were the main proponents of "Hutu power," and they enjoyed intimate links to sections of the Catholic Church whose schools educated them. At one point the archbishop of Kigali, Vincent Nsengiyumwa, was a member of the Central Committee of President Habyarimana's ruling MRND. He enjoyed the exalted position of being the official confessor of the president's wife Agathe, whose three brothers-in-law formed the backbone of the extremist *akazu*, the *Clan de Madame*, in which the plans for genocide were hatched.[9]

To its advocates, the dream of eternal "Hutu power" in Rwanda was in jeopardy. Under their orders, the French-trained Presidential

Guard recruited heavily among the unemployed youth to form a Hutu-extremist militia known as the *interahamwe*. Its name, which means "those who stand together," was taken from the Hutu communal work parties of the 1970s and 1980s. The extremists' propaganda machine channeled popular anger over falling living standards into Tutsi-bashing. The constant refrain was that the Hutu *muyaga* revolution of 1959 had let too many Tutsis get away, and now, in the form of the RPF, they were storming back. Any Hutu who advocated dialogue and compromise with the RPF was an *ibyitso*, a traitor to the Hutu cause. As the London-based human rights group, African Rights, has commented, "Hutu extremism manifested a dangerous mix of absolute political power and an abiding sense of being the victims of historical injustice."[10] The RPF was coming for the land, the propaganda insisted, and if the people killed the Tutsis, the Hutus could take their farms and cattle. Successful Tutsi businesses were special targets of *interahamwe*. "People were forced into desperation by the economic conditions," Bishop Birindabagabo says. "Don't forget that Rwanda was a near-totalitarian state, and whatever the president said was gospel. We have an expression dating from the days of the Mwami king, *irivuzumwami*, which means, whatever the kings says cannot be contested."

In this case, the word of the effective king, Habyarimana, was being questioned from many quarters. The international community urged economic and political reforms and peace talks with the RPF. Hutu moderates clamored for democratic change. The extremists demanded the opposite. On the surface, Habyarimana opted for reform. He allowed Hutu opposition parties into a coalition government, and in May 1992 opened peace negotiations with the RPF in Arusha, Tanzania. The following year, the two sides signed a peace agreement which entailed a power-sharing arrangement and the integration of the Rwandan armed forces with the rebel RPF. A ceasefire took hold temporarily, and the United Nations sent a small peacekeeping force. The peace deal never became reality. President Habyarimana faced severe extremist pressure from the *Clan de Madame* to abort the agreement and threats by international donors to cut off aid if he did. Hard-liners inside the government began distributing arms to radical Hutu militias. Hit squads assassinated several prominent Hutu. By early 1994, Rwanda was primed to explode.

The time bomb set decades before during colonial rule went off on the evening of April 6, when the presidential plane was shot down by an antiaircraft missile over Kigali's airport. Both President

Habyarimana and his Burundian counterpart, Cyprien Ntayamira, were killed. The Hutus, not surprisingly, blamed the murder on the RPF guerrillas; but the missile that hit the president's plane was fired from the airport perimeter, which at the time was being patrolled by the Presidential Guard. Subsequent investigations suggested the hand of the extremists gathered in Habyarimana's own wife's *Clan de Madame*.[11] They feared that Habyarimana was going soft on the RPF, and that with a promised multiparty democracy, the true proponents of Hutu power were threatened. The president, and anyone else who advocated a dialogue with the RPF, had to go. The crash was the excuse for the genocide to begin. Within forty-five minutes, the *interahamwe* militia and the *gendarme* police set up roadblocks all over the country and began killing Tutsis and Hutu *ibyitso* traitors.

The international community did not try to stop the slaughter. The small UN peacekeeping force operated under a limited mandate, which restrained it from intervening. Two weeks after the start of the genocide, the Security Council voted to withdraw 90 percent of the UN troops from Rwanda. The United Nations refused for a while to even acknowledge that genocide was under way. The initial view of the U.N. Secretary-General at the time, Boutros Boutros-Ghali, was that it was a case of Hutu and Tutsi killing each other.[12] "As soon as the massacres started in Rwanda, world opinion was not aware of what was really happening, and then the international community withdrew from the country at the first opportunity," Father Oscar says bitterly. "In some cases, the outside world supported the genocide. France distributed arms, it trained the *interahamwe*."

France's role in Rwanda may well go down in history as the darkest of any Western nation in Africa since the slave trade. A strong backer of the Habyarimana government and the *akazu*, primarily because Rwanda was a loyal member of the francophone Africa camp, French military instructors trained and armed the security forces which spearheaded the extermination process. Prunier, an adviser to President François Mitterrand during the crisis, has written, "The *akazu* judged the world according to their standards of their provincial dictatorship, but they probably would not have gone off the deep end if they had been sure that total international isolation would result. Thus France was the unwitting catalyst of ultimate Rwandese descent into the blood bath."[13]

Over the next three months, the extremists led by the *Clan de Madame* organized the slaughter of Rwanda's Tutsis and any moderate Hutus deemed traitors to the cause. The killing was carried out with chilling efficiency by a chain of command stretching from the highest officials in government to the lowest-ranking neighborhood councillors. But even so, like the 1959 *muyaga*, it failed to finish the job. The well-trained and equipped army of the RPF occupied Kigali and eventually drove the Rwandan armed forces and the extremist militias into exile in Congo and Tanzania. With approval from the U.N. Security Council, France launched a military expedition on supposedly humanitarian grounds called Opération Turquoise, which provided a secure corridor for the genocidal army to pass into the Congo. Nearly 2 million Hutu civilians fearing retribution went with them into refugee camps in Burundi, Tanzania, and Congo, where the biggest settlements were. One million Tutsi exiles leading an equal number of cattle poured down in massive columns from Uganda to fill the vacuum.

The international community responded to the crisis by providing millions of dollars for the refugees in Congo, Burundi, and Tanzania. Instead of helping Rwanda to rebuild its shattered economy and to care for the survivors of the holocaust, the international community spent $2.5 billion on the refugees in Congo and Tanzania, compared to $572 million for rehabilitation and reconstruction inside the country in the first two years after the genocide.[14] One study on the international community's response to the Rwandan disaster stated: "It appears to Rwandese who have lived through the horror of genocide that the international community is more concerned about the refugees than the surviving victims of the genocide."[15] Through its support for the refugees, the outside world—wittingly or unwittingly—allowed the forces that perpetrated the massacres to rebuild their army and prepare for an invasion. International aid to the camps in Congo and Tanzania, Father Oscar says, made a mockery of the notion that humanitarian aid is neutral. Many of those in Congo were not refugees but criminals fleeing from justice.

Father Oscar is a mild man, his views understated. The international aid agencies and their humanitarian operations in Congo and Tanzania did more than just feed the murderous militias who fled there. At their worst, nongovernmental organizations and respected UN agencies such as the High Commission for Refugees actually hired people guilty of genocidal crimes. At best, they used the existing power structures, such as the *préfets* (district administrators) and *bourgmestres* (mayors), which transferred virtually intact from Rwanda, to distribute the food and relief items, thus reinforcing the authority of the old government and the militias. Hutus working for the aid agencies in Congo often were forced by the militiamen to pay parts of their salaries to the old government.[16] The camps became arms depots and recruiting grounds for the army, which was being rebuilt for a new violent grab for power and another go at Tutsi extermination. This is not some wild accusation leveled by supporters of the RPF government, but the conclusion of a study funded by the Organization for Economic Cooperation and Development, which is perhaps the most exhaustive independent examination ever conducted into a UN humanitarian operation. Its five-volume report said that the leadership of the old government used murder and torture to prevent the refugees from returning to Rwanda, and fostered intense social pressure that tagged anyone who wanted to go home as a traitor to the Hutu cause. "In the same way that a Hutu identity was created by forcing complicity in the genocide, 'Hutu-ness' is now being defined as loyalty to the former regime," it stated at the time.[17]

A new scenario was established, which lasted for over two years. The *interahamwe* militias, fed, clothed, and, indirectly at least, armed by the international community, continued to infiltrate Rwanda to bomb electricity pylons and mine roads. When they entered the country, they were fed and sheltered by their relatives who remained behind. They assassinated Tutsis who survived the genocide and Hutus who protected them. Their goal was to destabilize and to provoke the RPF army into discrediting itself by carrying out reprisals against innocent Hutu villagers. The tactic worked. The security forces killed at least six hundred unarmed civilians in 1996 alone.

The Rwandan genocide had pitted neighbor against neighbor, priest against priest, brother against sister, and sometimes husband against wife. It also revealed an incredible heroism among those who could have joined their neighbors and their relatives in succumbing to the murderous euphoria, but who decided that no, Rwanda must seek another way.

IN CYANGUGU, one such person is Father Oscar Nkundayezo. Almost everyone who survived in the main town of Kamembe has a story about him and his sometimes unorthodox ways of keeping people alive. One young man, Théodore Nyilinkwaya, remembers how Father Oscar helped him to bribe members of the *interahamwe* militia to ferry him and dozens of others in wooden pirogue canoes across Lake Kivu to Congo and safety. Father Oscar also concealed people in warehouses and even hid a woman under his bed until he could negotiate her safe passage out of the area.

As a mass of Tutsis took refuge first in Cyangugu Cathedral, then in Kamarampaka Stadium, and finally in a camp called Nyarushishi, Father Oscar was there to comfort the escapees. To reach them, he had to pass through numerous roadblocks manned by machete-wielding and gun-toting killers who roughed him up. He was after all an *ibyitso* traitor providing succour for the enemy, the *inyenzi,* "the cockroaches," as the Tutsis were called.

In Cyangugu, the genocide was initiated by the security forces with a scorched-earth campaign to burn all the Tutsi houses they could identify. They went door-to-door looking for "cockroaches." A group of armed men came looking for Kayitera Canisus, a soft-spoken twenty-three-year-old "Hutsi," meaning he had a Tutsi father and Hutu mother. In the genocidal mind, Canisus had the blood of the enemy in his veins; he was a bug to be smashed underfoot. "They asked my mother Agnes where I was. Because she was frightened, she told them that I had already been killed. They didn't harm her because she was a Hutu, but they killed some of our domestic animals and carried them away to eat." Canisus and hundreds of Tutsis from all over Cyangugu fled to a local secondary school. They stayed the night, and the next morning watched in horror as a mob, which included little boys, set upon a well-known primary school teacher with machetes and axes. "When I saw that, I told myself that this is the final day." He and the others ran to the cathedral, where Father Oscar was already coping with scores of refugees. Canisus found his brothers Karianga and Clavier there.

Over the next few days, thousands more Tutsis arrived at the cathedral to hide from the militia gangs combing the area for *inyenzi.* Father Oscar and other priests provided the refugees with bags of rice brought by the Catholic relief agency, Caritas, and attempted to shield them from the killers. On their fourth day at the cathedral, a group of *interahamwe* rode up in a blue truck led by an elderly man named Yusufu Munyakazi whom survivors describe as a particularly brutal killer. As soon as they climbed down, the militiamen opened fire on the refugees and emptied their weapons indiscriminately into the cathedral. Dozens of people were killed; hundreds of others escaped into the nearby forests, where they hid until the militias left. Later in the day, the local *préfet,* or district administrator, Manuel Bagambiki, arrived with a group of soldiers and announced that all the refugees had to move to Kamarampaka Stadium, "to ensure their safety," he said. No one believed that, since Bagambiki had been seen operating with the *interahamwe*, but in the end they went. "From the cathedral to the stadium it was one kilometer, and we walked with the escort of the soldiers," Canisus recalls. "We reached the stadium at four P.M. That same day, Father Oscar brought food."

The refugees huddled in the stadium in a death watch as militiamen arrived each day to march groups of Tutsi men out of the camp. "On the second day, the *préfet* returned with the soldiers, and he had a list of names which he read out. He said, 'You will explain why you are RPF spies, and you are going to explain how you have done it and why you have done it.' Everyone named on the list kept quiet. Then the *préfet* exploded in anger and screamed, 'If you refuse to come along, everyone is going to die because of you! If you agree to go, everyone else will be all right.' After that, many people left with him. They never returned. The next day, the *préfet* was back with the soldiers and another list of names. Fifty more people went with him. Everyone knew that whoever left the stadium was walking to their death."

For the next several weeks, the wait continued. The *préfet* would arrive with a list of names, read them out, and threaten and cajole until the wanted ones left with him. Canisus's eldest brother Charles Gatera was one of them. Canisus never saw him again. One day, the *préfet* threatened to withhold the refugees' food unless they obeyed him. "He said, 'If you don't want to cooperate, I will take the people I want.' All that day, they put the refugees into lines to ask for identity cards which said whether you were Hutu or Tutsi. Those who did not have their ID cards were taken away and killed. That day the situation was incredibly bad. Members of the International Red Cross came to the stadium with some food. They were handing out containers for water and food just as the *préfet* was returning to kill others. A white man who was the chief of the Red Cross told the *préfet* that 'if you are planning to kill all the people in the stadium, there is no point in feeding them.' The *préfet* told him that it was not he who was killing the people, but the soldiers, who were angry because of the death of the president. The *préfet* said he was not involved. From that day there were negotiations between the Red Cross, the *préfet*, and the bishop."

The negotiations led to an agreement that the refugees would move to another camp in Nyarushishi where they might be safer. They boarded buses to make the journey, and as they passed through dozens of roadblocks, soldiers and militiamen shouted at them,

"Bring us those cockroaches, we want to kill them!" Along the way, Tutsi refugees, especially the elderly, were selected at random for execution. Canisus recalled how an old man named Inshokosa, a local veterinarian, perished when the buses reached Nyarushishi. "The soldier said, 'Come with me,' and the old man said, 'I am not coming.' He sat down on the ground and put his hands over his head. The soldier walked up and put a pistol to his head and shot him. The bullet went in the right temple and came out the left side."

Nyarushishi was a death camp. Food, water, and medicines were scarce, and dozens of children died of dysentery. The *gendarmerie* surrounded the enclosure and picked off anyone who attempted to leave in search of food and firewood. The refugees' lifeline was food from the Red Cross and Father Oscar. "Like he did at the Kamarampaka Stadium, he brought us help from the cathedral and celebrated mass. He came every morning and afternoon. I remember that once he brought me some bread and said it was from the Jesuit fathers because I had studied with them. He is a very good man with a good heart. He took many risks. They could kill you for helping Tutsis. I think you could say he saved many people morally rather than physically, because he didn't have the means. He supported people and helped them to find food. And, of course, he prayed."

Looking back one Sunday morning before delivering his main mass at Namasheke parish, Father Oscar takes little credit for his efforts to save Tutsis, saying he was just doing his Christian and patriotic duty. "More than anything it was a moral intervention I was making. Every time I entered the Kamarampaka Stadium, I did not know what I would find. The way I saw it, I was carrying out the work which my Christian beliefs required of me." Not all of the clergymen felt the same way. Father Oscar remembers how one of his colleagues in Cyangugu acquiesced in the murder of another. "We had one priest who, while he did not kill anyone, he also didn't prevent anyone from being killed. He didn't show one bit of compassion. He rode around in the same vehicle with a *gendarme* who had murdered a fellow priest. He was in the very vehicle that the murdered priest used to drive. I saw the vehicle one day with the assassin. The assassin stepped out, and then the priest stepped out. I couldn't believe it."

Father Oscar shakes his head in disgust as if trying to expel the memories from his mind. While the refugees view him as a pillar of strength against the barbarity, he actually felt quite impotent. "I could not really save anybody. I was more exposed than the victims were. I was going to the stadium in the morning, midday, and the afternoon without even having time to lie down for awhile. The *gendarmerie* all along the road would question me aggressively about what I was doing. Sometimes they shoved me; other times, they were satisfied with insulting me. I would hold mass for the people, pray for them, and bring them some food. There was nothing else I could do."

Even now, long after the genocide has supposedly ended, Father Oscar's torment is not over. Many of his parishioners, the vast majority of whom are Hutu, still sympathize with the assassins. "You can see the problem by the low turnout at the reburial ceremony," he says. "Some of the people from this area refused to attend because they feared retribution. I have told them that we have a debt to pay to the families of the people who were murdered unjustly. We must recognize the error of the assassination of these people. Because it was wrong. It is wrong to kill infants just because of their origin."

That is not the way the perpetrators of the genocide saw it. Present and future generations had to be eliminated for the "bush-clearing exercise" to be complete. The number of children slain reached beyond two hundred thousand, fulfilling the edict of one political commentator on the Hutu extremist radio station, Radio Mille Collines, before the start of the genocide: "To kill the big rats, you have to kill the little rats."[18]

Some of the little rats got away, thanks to Father Oscar and other Hutu families. The number of Rwandan children who lost their parents in the massacres runs into the tens of thousands. They are scattered all over the country, and the resources of the government and the international aid agencies are simply far too stretched to care for them all. Some have been absorbed into their extended families; but such was the methodical nature of the killing that in many cases there are not even distant relatives for them to turn to. Others receive limited support from church-funded Rwandan nongovernmental organizations. For all of them, survival requires large doses of self-reliance and solidarity. If they can make it, perhaps Rwanda can too.

That hope can be found among a community of orphans, all Tutsi "little rats," living in a small house in the Gikondo suburb of Kigali. Marie Louise Umutangana is effectively the mother of the other eighteen children, but she is having trouble coming to grips with her new role. When she is introduced as the *responsable* or head of the household, she runs off in tears. It's little wonder. Marie Louise is fifteen years old. The only adult in their midst is the very senile mother of the woman who originally brought them to the house, Donatilla Mukarurangwa, who died in a car crash in Kigali in March 1996. Some of the children do not even know her name; they just call her *mukecuru*, "old woman." The children receive material but mostly moral support from a Catholic nun who lives nearby and from Bishop Alexis Birindabagabo's *Barakabaho* ("Let Them Live") Foundation, which helps with food supplies and looks in on the children from time to time. Other than that, they are on their own. They prepare their own food, fetch their water from a communal tap, care for two two-year-olds, maintain the household, wash their clothes, make sure everyone leaves for school on time, simply everything.

As Marie Louise outlines their daily routine, Benjamin Mayi-turibi, an irresistible two-year-old with massive dark brown eyes, walks in nonchalantly, climbs on her lap, and falls asleep with his head on her chest. He promptly starts snoring. "Everybody takes care of him," Marie Louise says, suddenly laughing. "We all love him." Marie Louise frequently breaks into tears, even when discussing such mundane matters as how much food and water they need. She is obviously deeply traumatized, and for good reason. At the age of thirteen, she alone among her six sisters, two brothers, and her parents survived the genocide; and now circumstances unimaginably beyond her control have placed her in the position of a teenage mother. Although two other young women are seventeen, it was decided that she should remain at home to look after the little ones because she dropped out of school.

What is striking about the household is how well it is run. Any major decisions are taken by an executive committee of the eldest five children, which meets twice a week in a communal room filled with pictures of Jesus and a hand-painted sign, obviously fashioned by a child, which says: *Do you have a problem? Jesus is the answer.* A normal day begins at 6:00 A.M. when they break up into three teams to do the morning chores. One group grabs the plastic jugs and walks to the local well to fill the containers with the twelve gallons of water they need each day, although when they wash their clothes they require triple that amount. A second group builds a fire and prepares tea; it is the task of a third detachment to sweep out the three bedrooms. The teams take turns doing the different jobs. There are few complaints, Marie Louise says. "Everybody understands the situation we are in, so they never refuse their tasks. Sometimes we have problems with the little ones, but nothing serious. All the kids generally play around here so we can keep an eye on each other."

By 7:00 A.M. they sit down for their breakfast, and thirty minutes later the students are off to school. Marie Louise stays at home with the infants and prepares the daily lunch. Because they are so many, she has to begin cooking by ten. Routinely, the ingredients are rice, beans, and oil, provided by the *Barakabaho* Foundation with donations from several international nongovernmental organizations. In theory, they receive a fifty-pound bag of rice every two weeks, but there are times when the delivery is late and the children have to walk into town to remind the foundation. Odette, a Catholic nun who lives close by, supplies potatoes, and if the children want to have a birthday party, they can count on her to find some meat. School fees were paid by Donatilla before she died, but now that she is gone, they are hoping the foundation will fill the gap.

Donatilla was like a mother for the group, and in fact, Marie Louise owes the woman her life. It was while she was visiting Donatilla, who was a friend of her parents, in the eastern province of Kibungo, that the genocide erupted. Back home in Butare, Marie Louise's entire family was wiped out. Donatilla's brother, Ignace Rebero, was the first member of the family to die. He was standing guard outside the house when the *interahamwe* murdered him. That is when Donatilla decided that they should flee to Kigali. "That same night we fled and went into hiding. We hid each day with a new family, most of them Hutus. We couldn't stay long, because they would be killed if we were found in their homes. So we moved at night. We were saved by God."

Josephine Mukandahunga, a small seventeen-year-old with a stylish flat-top haircut, was saved by Hutu priests. She was living in Gitarama district with her parents, her younger sister Alphonsine, and their brother, Cyprien, when the massacres erupted. Her elder sister, Immaculeé, was pregnant and living with her husband. Josephine's family were relatively poor farmers, with only two cows, hardly fitting the image of the Tutsi overlords portrayed by the extremist Hutu propaganda. The militias set fire to their house and to those of their Tutsi neighbors and killed everyone's cattle. "We all ran in different directions. Alphonsine and I made our way to the Kabgayi Mission and sought shelter there. There were thousands of people at the mission, and we knew many of them because they were our neighbors. There were so many people there was nowhere to sleep, so we just laid down where we were. I had no idea where my parents were." In fact, Josephine never learned what happened to her parents, Eustrache Boyi and Patricie Mukaremere, except that they were murdered, as was Immaculeé's husband, she later learned. Cyprien, then ten years old, had been taken in and hidden by a Hutu family.

There were twenty-five thousand people at Kabgayi,[19] and in the face of a total onslaught by the *interahamwe* militias, Josephine says the mission priests did the best they could to feed and protect them. "The priests brought us food from time to time, but it was very little. There were too many people. The *interahamwe* kept coming each day and trying to force their way in, but the priests would attempt to stop them. The militias usually got two or three people a day and killed them." After the genocide subsided, Josephine and Alphonsine returned to the burned-out ruins of their parents' home and found that Cyprien and Immaculeé had miraculously survived. There was nothing for the children to do in Gitarama since most of their relatives had perished.

Josephine learned that Donatilla, her mother's sister, had moved to Kigali, and because she had stayed with her in Kibungo in 1992 while looking for a place in school, she decided to make her way to the capital. With Cyprien and Alphonsine in tow, she found Donatilla after a few days. "What we would have done without Donatilla, I do not know," she says. "She was our saviour." Immaculeé, a widow and a mother, remains in Gitarama trying to make a living farming, and Josephine visits her on holidays. But she has no immediate plans to return home. "Life is very difficult in Gitarama, and Immaculeé has enough problems without us, with her baby and everything. It's not easy here, but we all look after one another, and it's not so bad."

There is no sign of bitterness in the children's home. Their feelings are on display in a sign written on a bedroom door near the entrance of their house. It says: *Awahoro Naganze ku isi hose* (*May peace reign over the world*). There is no talk of revenge against the Hutus, and in fact, both Marie Louise and Josephine recognize the heroics of many. "Most of the families who hid us were Hutu," Marie Louise remembers. "They gave us shelter and food, and they could have been killed at any time. The genocide wasn't really the fault of all the Hutus. It was the politicians who are responsible, and some people who followed them."

Thérèse Nyirabayovu decided that she was not a follower. Thérèse is an unlikely resistance fighter against genocide. She is a slight but energetic sixty-six-year-old Hutu widow whose bantam stature did not prevent her from defying the most systematic killing spree in the history of Africa. For three months, she had the power of life or death over a family of Tutsis, and against all the threats and social pressures her neighbors could bring to bear, she resolutely chose the path of life. Since the death of her husband Marenge Nazard in 1980, Thérèse had lived a relatively quiet life on the western edge of Kigali in a poor shantytown neighborhood called Muhima. When the violence erupted, she was in her mud-brick house with her daughter, Nyiromana Thérèsie. She paid no heed to the gangs of Hutu youths roaming the dirt streets, chanting and handing out racist anti-Tutsi leaflets. She was one of the few who had not been infected by the virus of hatred. She was poor, her Tutsi friends were poor, and in her eyes there was no difference. "I regarded everybody around here as a brother and sister," she says. Thérèse thought the youths and their political propaganda were a lot of nonsense. "I saw all the parties moving around mobilizing people, but I wanted no part of it. I could not even read those papers. I am," she says, roaring with laughter, "just a member of the party of God."

Two days later, the killings became widespread and more systematic. The initial targets of the gangs were the wealthy, whether Hutu or Tutsi. "Whoever was rich was taken as the enemy," she says. The initial pattern was a brief return to the precolonial days when one was a Tutsi not simply because of supposed racial characteristics but because of wealth. Thérèse remained indoors for most of the time, and she did not realize how dire the situation was for the Tutsis until her neighbors, the Serukarare family—the mother, three daughters, and a son—appeared at her door begging for help. She immediately took them in. It was dangerous, she knew, but she felt she had no choice. "They came here because we had been friends for a long time; we had everything in common. I decided to take the risk that even if we would be in trouble, let them come here. I said we would receive them and if they die here, let them die here, because we had never had a quarrel with them. When they arrived, I handed myself over to God. Whatever happened to myself, and the refugees in my house, it happened. I was ready for any eventuality." A few days later another young Tutsi man showed up looking for a hiding place.

Thérèse's earthen home is a modest one, with a small sitting room, two bedrooms, and a tiny kitchen area, and as the violence spread, it filled up with her relatives trying to stay clear of the mayhem in other parts of the city. During the day it was not so bad, because they could sit outside while the Serukarare family hid under the beds. When night fell, the marauding gangs, usually drunk on banana beer, went door-to-door searching for "cockroaches." There was not much sleeping space, so they all piled into the bedroom together and pulled the blankets up tight so anyone looking in could not tell how many people were there.

As Hutus, Thérèse and Nyiromana were able to walk the streets with impunity and to purchase food and fetch water. But they had to be careful. In order not to raise suspicions, they had to disguise the fact that they were cooking dinner for the extra members of the Serukarare family. So they made sure their neighbors saw them preparing meals outside the house for a relatively small number of people, and then took them inside to share among the rest. It became apparent that there was not enough room for everyone. Thérèse decided that the two boys would have to move outside, but they could only do so under cover of darkness. Hiding women and children was one thing; but if the gangs discovered she had given shelter to young Tutsi men, everyone would be slaughtered. So one night, she slipped the boys out of the house and helped them to bury themselves in a pile of bricks at a nearby abandoned lot. Feeding them presented another puzzle. But Thérèse quickly found the answer. "When we returned from the market, we simply dropped some food and water into the pile of bricks for the boys and continued walking so no one would notice. That way they stayed alive," she says with a sly smile, obviously pleased with her ingenuity.

Soon, however, matters became more serious. The *interahamwe* militia targeted Thérèse's house. Obviously some neighbors had informed on her. "They started to come to check regularly, at least five times a day. The *interahamwe* knew that the boys were around, and they said the boys were RPF "cockroaches." Because the militia said we were helping them, then we must be with the *inyenzis* too. Our neighbors were telling them that we were hiding the enemy, especially the boys. But the boys were in the bricks outside, and they never found them. I do not understand how, but they remained hidden. The neighbors kept pestering the militia to dig holes around the bricks to find the boys, but they never did. The neighbors would point and say, 'You check properly, check properly!'"

In frustration, one gang attacked Thérèse, smacking her with a stick, "but not for too long because I was weak," she says, grinning. Elderly, yes, but Thérèse is anything but weak. She stood her ground.

They bashed Nyiromana's face so hard that her teeth are still loose. But both she and her mother refused to betray their friends. "Why would we give up when we had gone through all that?" Thérèse asks. "I was the only one around hiding people. One other neighbor did it, too, but she was killed." By July, the RPF had captured Kigali and forced the Hutu militias to retreat to the south and west. The few Tutsis who survived emerged from their hiding places.

To this day, Thérèse says she does not understand how the genocide occurred. For an explanation, she turns to God. "He who created the heart did not make them equal," she says. "Even those who were killing were wearing the same rosary as I am. God did not do this, for if he did, we would not be around anymore. It was not God, it was Satan." In Rwanda, one person's God is another person's Satan. Thérèse and Nyiromana now live a fairly isolated existence in Muhima. The only Tutsis around are the Serukarare family they saved. As for the Hutus, they have ostracized Thérèse because she helped Tutsis. "The Hutus who participated in this genocide are no longer my friends. We are different. Our only good neighbors are the ones we saved. Everyone else treats us differently now. The Hutus don't accept us. When there is a wedding or a feast, there is no chair for us. So we are a little bit alone. But I don't regret what I did. I am proud."

The sense of isolation and hostility which Thérèse feels from her fellow Hutus is common throughout Rwanda among those who defended the Tutsis. It is written on the nervous face of Jean Nitikina, a forty-four-year-old shop assistant in the southern city of Butare, as he pedals up a street and slides off his bicycle. He is still receiving threats from his Hutu neighbors, and he says he is sure that if his boss discovers he has been talking about the genocide days, he will lose his job. His crime was to have saved his next-door neighbor's children. When asked why he took such a chance to save the family, Nitikina looks down at his powerful, trembling hands and says, "He was my friend."

The southern city of Butare is a quiet, provincial town of one-story buildings just east of the Nungwe national forest and home to Rwanda's national university. Its people were generally liberal on matters of ethnicity, probably because of the high level of intermarriage, says Madeleine Mukarwigema, a Tutsi worker at the Association of Genocide Survivors, who is sitting at the reception desk of the association's tiny cinder-block office in downtown Butare. "Mixed marriages were normal here. After the genocide, an association of widows was established, and two hundred and fifty of the three hundred members were Hutus. Their murdered husbands were Tutsis." Another reason was the popularity of the Parti Social Democrat, the PSD, a significant force of opposition to President Habyarimana's ruling MRND.

Initially, Butare's residents refused to have anything to do with the extermination. So lax were they in their genocidal duties that they earned the nickname of *ntibindeba* (it does not concern me), a heavily loaded word which carries special weight in a society that from time immemorial had been under strict centralized control, first by the Mwami kingdom, then by the Belgian colonial state, and finally by the Hutu-dominated post-independence government. Since all Hutu children were weaned on the propaganda that the Tutsis were feudal overlords plotting for the day to return to oppress the Hutus, being an *ntibindeba* meant being a traitor to the cause. For nearly two weeks after Habyarimana's assassination, the town itself was largely quiet. Then Théodore Sindikuwabo, who became "interim president" after Habyarimana's death, arrived to deliver a series of speeches demanding that the people of Butare stop "sleeping" and carry their weight in the "bush-clearing" exercise.

Nitikina says that because residents of his neighborhood, the Muhoro sector on the north edge of Butare, refused to "work," the *interahamwe* was forced to import people from the nearby Karama sector. "They told them, 'You have to go and work because the people of Muhoro have not done their job.' It's hard to say why the people in Karama were more active, but they used to attend all the political meetings to mobilize everyone for the killings. They were different in my area. People in Muhoro were not so interested." The difference between the two areas, Madeleine says, is that the people of Karama are more educated. "It was the educated ones who took the lead in the genocide because they felt they had more to gain by wiping out the Tutsis. The poorer ones who were involved did so out of fear or because they could steal some cattle or land. But the real killers were the ones with education. They felt that if they could eliminate the Tutsis, they could take their jobs and businesses." The Karama sector, just across Rwanda's main north-south highway from Muhoro, is a particularly notorious place, the scene of some of the worst massacres of the genocide. Estimates of the number of people killed there run up to thirty-five thousand.[20]

Nitikina's next-door neighbor, Jean Simugomwa, a Tutsi pharmacist, disappeared when the slaughter started. One morning the *interahamwe* gang leader, a man named Chiuma, knocked on Nitik-ina's door and asked him to accompany him to the pharmacist's house. Eleven of his children had locked themselves inside. "The children were crying and screaming inside because their parents had not returned home. So Chiuma asked me if I knew the ethnic group of the mother, Murorende. I knew if I told the truth—Tutsi— that the children were dead. I said I didn't know for sure, but I thought she was a Hutu. So Chiuma asked, 'Can you take care of the children and the wife when she returns?' I said yes. I was just telling them lies. Murorende's parents had already been killed, so the militia must have known that she was a Tutsi."

It was a question of money. As Father Oscar discovered, the right payment could buy a stay of execution for individual Tutsis. Nitikina bundled the children into his home, and when Murorende appeared one evening, he gave her shelter too. For the next several weeks, different gangs of *interahamwe* would appear at his house de-manding to know who the children belonged to. Simugomwa had left a sizable amount of cash in the house, and every time the mili-tia started asking questions, Nitikina paid them off. "They were mainly interested in the money. Sometimes they would demand two thousand francs, sometimes three thousand and even six thou-sand. I just kept paying them, and they would go off and buy ba-nana beer and get drunk." Simugomwa's relatives learned that Ni-tikina's home was a safe haven, and within a few days the man's parents and his brother appeared to ask for refuge. In all, he took in twenty-five people. They lived off the food from his garden, mainly beans and potatoes, and they found a supply of salt in the back of Simugomwa's pharmacy. "That was how we were able to keep everyone alive until the RPF arrived."

After the RPF occupation of the area, everyone hiding in Nitik-ina's house returned to their homes, and for a while, Nitikina thought that the worst was over. But like Thérèse, he soon noticed that his Hutu neighbors were ostracizing him from community functions. As the months passed, their cool attitudes turned into open threats. "The Hutu people around tell me openly, that 'should our army the *interahamwe* return, you will be the first to be sorted out because you hid the people and those people are accusing us of responsibility.' They don't like people like me because they feel that as long as there are witnesses around, they are responsible."

The desire to eliminate the witnesses is central to the genocidal mind-set: everyone must participate, and those who refuse must be eliminated. As Nitikina says, "If there are no witnesses, then there is no responsibility." Estephanie Mukarubera was one such witness. Her house is several miles north of Butare about five hundred yards from a highway turnoff marked by a one-room rural shop where villagers from Muhoro and Karama come to purchase small consumer items such as salt and soap and to trade gossip. Just a few feet from the front steps of Estephanie's home is a tiny makeshift grave surrounded by tree branches to keep out animals. It is where she is buried.

A tall young man named Emabre opens the front door to the house to reveal a modest living room, filled with paintings and likenesses of Jesus Christ, the pope, and the Virgin Mary, as well as pictures of the household's father, Antoine Sachinde, who died in 1982 of natural causes. Emabre's elder sister, Bertrude, and his younger brother, Gabriel, step out of a back room. Bertrude's eyes are severely bloodshot; she has been crying. It has been two weeks since Estephanie, their fifty-seven-year-old mother, disappeared late in the day after she walked to the family's cassava field about five hundred yards from the house. The children waited for several hours and then began a search of the area. When Estephanie did not turn up in the evening, they alerted the police, who although ostensibly loyal to the new government are rarely effective.

"We are not sure who killed her, but because it was April, the anniversary of the genocide, we believe it was either those who participated in the genocide or their relatives, because my mother knew the killers," Bertrude says, wiping tears from her eyes. "Perhaps they wanted to get rid of the evidence. After we reported her disappearance to the authorities, they went to the field, but they couldn't find the body. The police asked the neighbors, and three days later, they found part of my mother's body in the field. It wasn't there before. Someone put it there. A few hours later they found her head about one kilometer away, in the Karama sector." Someone apparently from Karama killed the old woman, severed her head, stripped it of hair and teeth, and took it back as part of a routine practice to prove, probably to their superiors, that she was in fact dead, that she could no longer identify the murderers, that another part of the bush clearing was complete, another piece of evidence erased.

Although Estephanie was a Tutsi, the fact that her late husband Antoine was a respected Hutu appeared to have saved her during the genocide, unlike thousands of other Tutsis in mixed "Hutsi" relationships. Perhaps because they were so common in the Butare area, Estephanie's "Hutsi" children were off-limits to the gangs, too. For obvious reasons, they had been raised in an environment free of the prejudice that had begun to pollute Hutu-Tutsi relations in the mid-nineteenth century. There were no inferiority or superiority complexes in Estephanie's home, and in fact during the massacres it became a safe haven for relatives and Tutsi neighbors. For two young men, Emabre Gisa and Serge Rutayisire, the refuge was fleeting. "One day in June, the militias came at two in the morning. Five of the refugees were hiding around our compound. One was in the cow's enclosure, but two of them, the young men, were in this house," Bertrude says.

Emabre, who shared the name of the young man hiding in his house, said he had been walking around the neighborhood that night to monitor what the militias were doing. "I am considered a Hutu, so I did not have any problems moving about. During that time I would venture out to see what was going on and then come back to the house to tell everyone. But on that fateful night there was a big group of people coming here. They wanted to go around searching. Another group was coming from the Karama side, and they were converging here. So when I came to tell the people in the house that they were hunting for Emabre, the other group had already arrived and it was too late. They were already taken."

Bertrude takes up the story. "The problem was that they had found Emabre's younger brother Innocent, who was hiding with another neighbor, and when they captured him, they beat him until he told them where Emabre was. When they got here, they found Serge, and they took both of them. They did not kill them here. They escorted them to their places of birth in Karama and killed them there so that the people were sure that they had been dealt with." Although most of the Tutsi families in Muhoro were slaughtered, Estephanie's stubborn defiance saved five people in her house until the RPF arrived in early July and put an end to the large-scale massacres. Low-scale killings continue.

"The situation is that the ones who did the killing were afraid that my mother would report them," Bertrude says. "The way they killed my mother, that means they can also come for us. This is the situation we are in now. If they can kill an old woman, of course they can come to kill us. The police are not providing much protection. After my mother's death, three policemen came to guard the house, but after seven days they left. And they were really just keeping company with my brother Paul who was here. He is their fellow soldier. When he left, so did they. But we can't just sit around and remain idle, so we will continue with the fields. We are afraid. We are even frightened to walk outside the house at night. I don't put a foot out that front door after it is dark. The dilemma we face in Muhoro is that the people who witnessed and survived the genocide are in greater danger than those who carried out the killings."

Silence fills the room. Emabre, Gabriel, and Bertrude stare blankly ahead. After a few moments, everyone walks out of the house back out to the grave with a small wooden cross on it. "My mother saved a few people and look what happened to her," Bertrude says. "When they found her body, it was all cut up. They never found her left arm, and her right arm was ripped apart. They slashed her to pieces."

Back in Butare, Mrs. Mukarwigema of the Association of Genocide Survivors sits in a café pondering a plate of kebabs and chips, but she does not have much of an appetite. She cannot get Estephanie's murder out of her head. "She was such a brave woman," she says. "If there were more people like her, maybe not so many people would have died." Maybe even her own husband and children. Mrs. Mukarwigema lost her husband, Jean Baptiste Rwandema, an English teacher, and four of her six children. Jean Baptiste, who hid with their eldest daughter Aline in the home of one of his former Hutu students, survived until the very day the RPF troops roared into town. His mistake was to have ventured out into the streets too early to celebrate the liberation: the retreating militias killed him minutes before the RPF's arrival.

Aline and Denise survived, but the four youngest ones—Marie Jeanne, Delphine, Jean de Dieu, and Jeanne d'Arc—died at a Catholic mission of Save where a Tutsi priest had given them shelter along with dozens of other children. Schoolteachers informed on the priest; the militia murdered him. A Hutu priest took charge and handed the children over to the *interahamwe*. Mukarwigema, who was concealed at another part of the mission station with the nuns, later found their bodies in the forest around the compound. "All the children were betrayed," she says. "Even some of the children's godfathers turned them in."

BEATRICE NYIRANSENGIMANA's children were betrayed, too, by her own brothers, and now she is demanding justice. Beatrice is a short, stout farmer, and you can feel her strength in the grip of her massive hands, see it in the sinewy muscles of her powerful arms, sense it in the unyielding penetration of her gaze. Beatrice has seen into the shadows of the human soul, has witnessed horrific things few people can even imagine, and she is standing up to do something about it no matter what the consequences. Her life and those of her remaining two children are still in grave danger, because even though the forces of genocide have been defeated for the moment, they are still very much alive in her home area of Taba, in the hills of Gitarama overlooking Kigali.

Beatrice is a Hutu, but like Nitikina and Thérèse, she is now an outcast in her community, and she's a widow, as are an estimated one-third to one-half of all women in the areas hardest hit by the genocide.[21] A striking gender imbalance is one of the most difficult long-term challenges facing Rwanda in the wake of the genocide. Women now constitute an estimated 70 percent of the population, and they face special problems beyond the trauma of the violence and the widespread rape that occurred during the crisis. They must rebuild their lives, make a living at a time when the economy has virtually collapsed, reclaim their property, and raise fatherless children, all in a society that still regards them as second-class citizens. "What is clear is that Rwanda will only rebuild itself through these women, and the international community must do everything possible to help them deal effectively with the past in order to move productively into the future," says Dorothy Thomas, director of the Women's Project at the New York–based human rights group, Human Rights Watch.

Beatrice no longer goes to church because she holds the pastors partly responsible for the killings. And when someone comes to pay her a visit, she is never quite sure if their intentions are friendly or murderous. For the rest of Beatrice's life, the genocide will never end. Her only solace is that the main leader of the gangs that killed her husband and five children, the former *bourgmestre* of Taba Jean Paul Akayesu, was arrested in Zambia and has been indicted for crimes against humanity by the International Criminal Tribunal for Rwanda sitting in Arusha, Tanzania.

Beatrice's error is to have married a Tutsi, Bernard Ntanuruhunga, although at the time of their union nearly twenty years before, she had no idea of the possible consequences. There were plenty of mixed Tutsi-Hutu marriages in Taba. After Bernard proposed, he paid the necessary dowry, and her family accepted their marriage. Her elder brothers, Jean Pierre Dushimimana and Innocent Gasharamanga, used to come around for dinner, and the extended families on both sides celebrated festivities together. That all changed after President Habyarimana's plane was shot down. "I suddenly discovered that I had married into a bad ethnic group," she says. "Then the genocide came, and everything in my family changed. I cannot explain why it happened. I think it was mostly greed." Father Oscar would call it "egoism," but it amounts to the same thing.

After sleeping in the fields for nearly a week, Beatrice and her family fled to take shelter in her parents' house. As a known Tutsi, Bernard was a marked man. Beatrice's father hid him in his sorghum field. At night they wrapped Bernard in a blanket and brought him into the dwelling for supper before returning him to the field to sleep. But her two paternal uncles, Nathan and Dayini, and her brothers Jean Pierre and Innocent, joined the *interahamwe* militias marauding in the area, and they led the gangs to their father's house in search of Beatrice's husband and children—"little rats" because their father was a Tutsi.

"Jean Pierre came to the house one day when we were preparing lunch and said, 'Give us those *inyenzis* who are here.' My mother said, 'Jean Pierre, are you going to kill your own nephews and nieces. Surely not?' Jean Pierre replied, 'What if I kill them?' The *interahamwe* chief was Silas Kubgurimana, and he said that for the Tutsi it's all over, whether they are children or not. Silas said that even [the RPF's military commander and now vice president] Paul Kagame, who was causing all this trouble, was a child when he left the country, so all the children must die. They said that the goal was that in the future, when a Hutu child was born, he would not even know what a Tutsi looked like. Their heads were hot. They said that even where you find goats and cows of the Tutsis, you must eat them immediately and kill their owners."

At first, Beatrice and her parents were able to pay the *interahamwe* to leave her children alone; but it was a constant battle. The militias would appear demanding the children, and only offers of money would keep them at bay. Beatrice took advantage of the interlude to smuggle her two oldest children, Jérôme and Rachel, out of the area to the safety of relatives' homes, but because of numerous roadblocks and constant *interahamwe* patrols, her five youngest—Martha, Silas, Séraphine, Théogène, and Etienne, who was a ten-month-old infant—had to remain behind with her parents. Innocent, Jean Pierre, and her uncles again came for the children. This time, there was to be no argument. Money could not purchase their safety. The children of the snakes had to die.

"They dragged my children away. They took little Etienne from my back, and there was nothing I could do," she said, bursting into tears. "They were sobbing and screaming for their mother, but I couldn't do anything. I felt so helpless as they were led down the road. They kept looking back at me and screaming 'Mama!' That was the last time I saw them." Innocent, who had already murdered Bernard's two-year-old niece, took the children, and together with other militiamen, hacked the youngsters with machetes and threw them into a pit latrine to die. They survived for three days; Beatrice could hear their screams at night. Two nights later, her uncle Dayini found Bernard hiding in a swamp. "There were about one hundred people, and Dayini handed Bernard over to the gang. They cut him to pieces. My brothers later told me it was a big carnival feast."

With the arrival of the RPF, the ringleaders of the genocide, such as Jean Paul Akayesu, fled south, either to Burundi or Zaire. But hundreds of others who participated in the killings remain behind, some even retaining their government posts. Among those who stayed were Beatrice's uncles and brothers, who occupied her former home and planted crops on her land. When the new authorities started arresting alleged genocide perpetrators, Beatrice stepped forward and accused her relatives, which drew the ire of her neighbors. As a result of her charges, her uncles and brothers were jailed. "My brothers are in prison, and I put them there. They belong there. Even my father supported my decision. He said that after all they had killed my children and they had no right to do that." Others in Taba disagreed, however, and soon the threats began. One councilor in Taba, Vénuste Twahirwa, launched a campaign of harassment against Beatrice. "After I helped to put Innocent in jail, Twahirwa tried to get him out. He told me that if they killed Innocent, I was finished, too."

Beatrice and Twahirwa maintain a running dispute. She, and many others, accuse him of blocking attempts to jail *interahamwe* suspects. "Twahirwa told me, 'You are always trying to imprison people. How will you testify against all of them?'" Then Twahirwa came to her house one afternoon with two policemen and arrested her. Beatrice was put in jail with the very men she had accused of killing her children and 150 relatives. "Twahirwa went around bragging to everyone in the village, 'This one has made herself an officer of the army and is arresting people. That little thug has made herself the most important person around and I finally put her inside.' He calls me the 'madwoman.' Luckily, the soldiers guarding the jail took pity on me and gave me food and water. When the *bourgmestre* [mayor] found out about it, he set me free."

The threats continue. Beatrice accused one of Twahirwa's relatives, a local man named Ndahiyo, of attempting to kidnap Rachel, her eleven-year-old daughter. "Fortunately, we heard the screams and were able to stop him. He threatened to kill her and said he would bring the *interahamwe* to finish us. I told him, 'You carried children and threw them in a pit and they were crying there for three days, and they died on the fourth. Did you think that was human?'"

Two farm workers she hired to help her in the fields fled after threats from Twahirwa, and the latest one, Jean Bosco Ngiruwonsanga, says he received a beating and a warning that he should stop working for the "madwoman." On April 8, 1996, two years and a day after the start of the genocide, her house was set on fire at midnight while she and the children were asleep inside. Beatrice refused to give in. Within a week, she had built a new one fifty yards away. When she went to tell Twahirwa that someone had burned down her house, she said he told her, "it was long overdue." Beatrice had to leave her newly built home and move in with another Hutu widow who also lost her "Hutsi" children. "There is no doubt that my life is in danger, but I put myself in the hands of God. There is nothing else I can do. I was no better than the people they killed. We are the same." Beatrice and other local officials say that Twahirwa has a son and a brother-in-law who were members of the *interahamwe*. "He says that one day they will return in a powerful way."

MEMBERS OF the *interahamwe* and the former Rwandan army eventually did return, though not in the "powerful way" they might have imagined. The spark which sent them back home, ironically, was another attempt at ethnic cleansing, this time by officials loyal to the Zairian government of Mobutu sese Seko. Their target was a community of three hundred thousand ethnic Tutsis, the Banyamulenge, who had lived for the past two hundred years on land that after independence became part of the Congo. Mobutu denied the Banyamulenge citizenship in 1981, and when the RPF seized power in Kigali, many young Tutsis from Congo crossed into Rwanda to join the new government's army. Once the Banyamulenge felt a new surge of persecution, they launched a rebellion in eastern

Congo with strong support from a Pan-African coalition which centered on Rwanda and Yoweri Museveni's Uganda and included a wide range of countries such as Angola, Burundi, Eritrea, Ethiopia, South Africa, Tanzania, Zambia, and Zimbabwe. In a matter of weeks, the Banyamulenge and their allies in the rebel Alliance for Democratic Forces for the Liberation of Congo-Zaire, led by long-time Marxist Laurent Kabila, captured wide swaths of eastern Congo. In doing so, they broke the grip of the *interahamwe* and the former Rwandan army on the refugees.

Over 1 million of the Hutu refugees piled their life's belongings on their head and marched back to the homes in Rwanda they had left two and a half years before. President Pasteur Bizimungu, a Hutu, stood at the border to welcome them back. "The Rwandan people were able to live together peacefully for six hundred years, and there is no reason they cannot live together again in peace," he said. His message, which was repeated on the national radio throughout the day, reflects the government's official policy of equal opportunity for Rwandans, regardless of their ethnic group. It has been part of the RPF's program since the days of exile in Uganda. Upon assuming power, it reversed the fateful decision of the Belgian colonizers by issuing new identity cards that do not include ethnic affiliation. But the administration's call for all Rwandans to live together in peace is a difficult one. Rare have been the cases in which the victims of massacres have been asked to live alongside those who carried them out.

Today, the only hope for peace, and it is a slim one, is to bring those guilty of crimes against humanity to justice so that the tenets of community responsibility can be restored. "The ones who were involved in these crimes must be arrested and prosecuted like anyone should be for murder," says Father Oscar. "Because they are people who were involved in criminality." Although the International Criminal Tribunal for Rwanda, which is holding court in the Tanzania town of Arusha, has indicted the ringleaders of the genocide, and the Rwandan government is holding another ninety thousand alleged participants in jail, the wheels of justice have turned slowly.

Once again, the international community has let Rwanda down. The tribunal in Arusha was riddled by incompetence, and according to a UN report released in February 1997, "not a single administrative area functioned effectively." UN headquarters, it said, was lax in providing qualified lawyers, administrators, and management guidelines. The tribunal was such a mess that Secretary-General Kofi Annan of Ghana forced the resignations of the court's chief administrator, Andronico Adede of Kenya, and deputy prosecutor Honoré Rakotomanana of Madagascar.

The first trials of 100,000 detainees inside Rwanda began in December 1996. Under a law passed the previous year, nearly two thousand of the accused are in Category One, considered leaders of the genocide. They are to receive a mandatory death sentence. Anyone in three lesser categories, which cover the vast majority of the detainees, can seek a reduction in penalties provided they confess to their involvement and furnish specific facts, including dates, places, and the names of their accomplices. With a severe shortage of lawyers and adequate courts, the trials are moving ahead slowly. International human rights groups have questioned the fairness of the Rwanda Tribunal, given that the accused often do not have access to defense lawyers and the prosecutors and judges are overwhelmingly Tutsi.

Until the guilty are tried and sentenced, however, Father Oscar believes there can be no peace in Rwanda. Like many of the survivors, he has come to regard as a dirty word "reconciliation," a term that has been repeated like a hosanna in the outside world as the solution to the Rwandan crisis. To him it implies an obligation to forgive before the crimes have been recognized and punished. As he prepares to leave for mass, Father Oscar looks out from the church near the mass grave where the reburial took place and says ominously, "This is not the beginning, and it's not the end."

An Act of Faith

It was a time of turmoil and confusion. Alarm spread among the people of the settlement at Tado on the Mono River as the reign of King Aholuho unraveled. Residents of the kingdom were particularly upset at the marriage of a princess to a foreigner. Some said the groom was a migrant from the east in what is today the land of the Yoruba people in Nigeria. Others said he was a leopard. A power vacuum was developing, and warriors loyal to various aspirants to the throne spread terror throughout the land. Clans started to split off in mass migrations, following the great African tradition of striking out in search of a new place to settle when political intrigue or land shortages at home reached the critical point. These were people of the Adja linguistic group, such as the Ewe, the Fon, and the Gun, and they were destined to build substantial societies of their own. The Fon headed east and later formed the Dahomey kingdom, which grew into one of West Africa's most powerful precolonial states. The Ewe moved to the hilly country around the lower Volta River near the future Ghana-Togo border; and the Gun settled close to the Porto Novo area, near Benin's frontier with Nigeria. After consulting their ancestors, another clan set out in a southeasterly direction.

For months this human column moved through unfamiliar territory toward an uncertain destination. No place seemed appropriate for settlement. Then one day a sparrow hawk appeared overhead, staying just ahead of the column. The senior chief said it was a spirit showing the way. The travelers followed the bird until they came upon the shores of a great lake. Tired and hungry, they stood at the water's edge not knowing what to do. They could not turn back to the violence they had escaped, but they had no means to cross the water. The sparrow hawk circled in a holding pattern above, apparently as stumped as they were. The senior chief began muttering prayers to the ancestors.

Suddenly a crocodile appeared at their feet, sending a wave of fright through the assembly. Once their initial panic subsided, the chief summoned a traditional healer to conjure some magic to enable the beast to talk. The crocodile promptly enquired what the people wanted. The chief stepped forward to recount the acts of violence which had forced them to flee their homeland in the west and to explain that they did not know how to cross the lake. Could the crocodile help? He agreed on one condition. Until the end of time, the people could never again harm the life of a crocodile. The chief conferred with the elders and they gave their assent; the deal was done. The crocodile ferried the migrants one by one over to some shallow waters in the middle of Lake Nokoue in what is now the modern nation of Benin. Over the coming weeks and months, the people moved to and fro from water to land gathering lumber to build the village they called Ganvie, or "the people who have found peace." To their land-loving neighbors, the inhabitants of Ganvie became known, not surprisingly, as the *Tofinu*, or "the water people."

The story of the founding of Ganvie might not be factually correct in all its details, but it eloquently tells, in near biblical terms, a story common to almost all African peoples. Oral histories the length and breadth of the continent are filled with migration, conquest, and assimilation. The history of Africa is literally the chronicle of the journey of man, stretching back perhaps 2 million years. The starting point was the great East African valley formed 15 million years ago when the continental crust was cracked open to form the Gregory Rift, a three-thousand-mile scar in the earth's surface that runs down from Israel to northern Mozambique.[1] The early hominids roamed to north, west, and south, and when modern man, *Homo sapiens sapiens*, appeared some two hundred thousand years ago, the journey continued, generation after generation. One of the greatest migrations saw Stone Age fishermen from the moist forests of southeastern Nigeria and Cameroon follow rivers and streams to branch out and disseminate their Bantu languages wide and far, to the point where they now dominate sub-Saharan Africa south of the equator. Without doubt, Africa is the cradle of humanity's pioneering spirit.

The story of Ganvie is also familiar in that it tells of a people who grew so dissatisfied with their home that they felt they had no choice but to withdraw. In this case, they sought security in the middle of a lake. Over the centuries, Lake Nokoue, a body of water spread out over fifteen thousand hectares, has proved to be a convenient refuge. On the land, weak communities were vulnerable to raids by powerful neighboring states, such as Dahomey, which were deeply involved in the business of selling slaves to the European ships anxiously waiting on the coast to carry African labor to the mines and plantations of the New World.

In more recent times, Ganvie became the ideal refuge from European colonialism, which came to stay in 1894 after France's extremely difficult conquest of the Dahomey, the original name of the country of Benin. After independence in 1960, the early years were unstable, with various experiments in civilian rule aborted by four military coups. The fifth, led by Major Methieu Kerekou, an anti-French Marxist, imposed a repressive order. Ganvie's only direct brush with Major Kerekou was in 1978, when he visited the village and said everyone should move to the land. Nobody did. Since 1991, Benin has enjoyed a democratic government, with a peaceful transfer of power to elected administrations, the first headed by former World Bank economist Nicephore Soglo, and then in 1996 back to Kerekou. The central government intrudes little in Ganvie. The settlement's people pay taxes, and in return the state provides primary and secondary schools. There is a health clinic, a maternity ward, and a pharmacy. Other than the fact that it sits on water, Ganvie appears to be a normal African village in the far south of Benin. Its twenty thousand people inhabit a tightly packed settlement of bamboo houses on wooden stilts rising out of Lake Nokoue that constitutes a virtual Venice in West Africa.

Just after sunrise, the small households begin to stir. The voices of thousands of children fill the air, with infants sitting on their front porches and staring in seeming wonder as their older brothers and sisters go to school. Scores of still drowsy commuters enter into spirited negotiations with water taxi drivers over the fare to the nearest point of land as a queue begins to stretch in front of the only public telephone around. The morning crackles with the cackle of women as the market traders get down to business. Loaded down with an array of wares, from fresh vegetables and fish to brightly colored cloth and stacks of cigarettes, they gather at the central marketplace to start their day of haggling. If business there is slow, groups of traders paddle through the narrow passageways, bringing new meaning to the concept of selling door-to-door.

The men head out to work their fields, although the crops the farmers tend are not the cassava, corn, and vegetables so common on the mainland. Villagers here await a harvest of a different sort; its yield is fish. Capturing fish in Ganvie is no sporting affair, although some young men can be seen from time to time whipping nets above their heads like aquatic cowboys and tossing them into the water in the hope of a quick catch. For the most part, fish farming in Ganvie, the village's main income earner, is a serious business approached with scientific calculation and a great deal of patience. What Ganvie's fishermen do can best be described as husbandry. It begins with cutting tree branches and brush on the mainland and planting them in the shallow waters in circles or rectangles. Such fish ponds, known as *akaja*, are both breeding grounds and traps. "A home for the fish," was the way one muscular middle-aged man, standing chest-deep in the lake, described his *akaja*. "And the fish like my homes," he added as a smiling assertion of his skill. With time, algae collect on the foliage and provide the ideal food for abundant species of fish, such as carp, sole, and sunfish. After several months go by, the fisherman will cast a tightly woven net around the hedge, remove the branches, and then slowly tighten the noose to nab his quarry.

Ganvie's entire culture revolves around water. Just popping in for a visit to a friend a few houses away involves a journey in a wooden *pirogue* canoe. There is even a floating fuel station, consisting of a young man in a *pirogue* loaded down with ten-gallon plastic jerricans filled with petrol for the community's few generators and with kerosene for the kitchen stoves. Ganvie has no electricity.

Maneuvering the vessels across the windy lake and through the narrow alleyways of Ganvie seems to be second nature to its residents. A *pirogue* skimming silently along Lake Nokoue's brown waters with a nonchalant preteen girl at the helm is a common sight. *Pirogues* are not for everybody, though. Their edges are only six inches above the water, and a sudden shift in weight is sure to catch the attention of any traveler, veteran or not. These days, tourists and visiting dignitaries with neither the time nor the stomach for a ride in a *pirogue* can take a motorboat from the nearest landing at Calavi. The rickety wooden pier there is always busy. Ganvie women offer fried and fresh fish in exchange for soap, soft drinks, plastic cups, and a myriad of household goods. A transaction is either a direct barter deal or involves CFA franc notes, the currency pegged to the French franc, which is used by France's former colonies in West Africa.

Despite the years of preaching by the Roman Catholic Church and Kerekou's formerly Marxist government, Ganvie, like most of the rest of Benin, has stuck to its ancestral religious roots. Benin is the birthplace of *vodu*, commonly known in the West as voodoo, which spread to Brazil and Haiti with the slave trade. The people of Ganvie remain loyal to their own particular pantheon of *vodu*, which worships *Zahun*, the fish god. The spirits of the ancestors who return to earth to speak through their descendants are central to the practice of *vodu*. In Ganvie, rituals to commemorate the death of a chief or village elder prompt dancers to enter into a trance and cover themselves with a mixture of corn flour and palm oil.

In recent years, development has taken its toll. Lake Nokoue used to be fed primarily by two rivers, the So and the Oueme, whose fresh water dominated the ecosystem. But that began to change in 1959, when the colonial government built the port of Cotonou, Benin's biggest city, and eliminated a sandbar that had prevented ocean water from contaminating the lake. The salt content is rising, and the traditional swelling of the lake by the rivers flowing into it is not as big or lasting as it once was. The process has disturbed the formation of phytoplankton, a principal fish food, around the *akaja* which the *Tofinu* plant in their patches of water. Accompanying the arrival of the ocean water from the Gulf of Guinea are tiny mollusks which attack the wooden stilts on which the *Tofinu* houses are built. So the residents of Ganvie have to spend more time and money to find enough wood to maintain their homes. Overpopulation among the polygamous *Tofinu* is another pressure. Almost three-quarters of Benin's people live in the southern part of the country, where the population density is among the highest in West Africa. Ganvie is no exception. Available space for fishing in traditional waters is scarce, and disputes over tracts of water are breaking out.

As a result, more and more young *Tofinu* are following the journeying ways of their forefathers. They are taking their fishing skills to streams and lakes in Nigeria and, ironically, to Togo near the land their ancestors fled hundreds of years ago. Opportunities to save money are greater away from the salty waters and family obligations back home. The handiwork of the *Tofinu* can be seen in the inland waters around Nigeria's commercial capital, Lagos, where *akaja* farms are plentiful. "Many of our young men go away to save money and return later to invest in a shop or a new house in Ganvie," says Celestine Ahissou, a university student. "But there are some who, after they see the world out there, never come back."

Africa is always on the move in the age-old search for economic opportunity and a more secure future. The human tide sweeps past official borders right across the continent and beyond. Just fifteen miles south of Ganvie, the coastal road from Accra in the west to Lagos in the east is one snaking stream of humanity, as merchants, fishermen, businessmen, and truck drivers ply their trades with little concern for the four border stops. In one sense, that is the idea behind the twenty-year-old Economic Community of West African States, which with nearly 200 million people is the largest such grouping in Africa. Unfortunately for the member states, much of the trade is "informal" and is not taxed or recorded, though the laws of supply and demand are in full flow. When the Nigerian military government banned wheat imports in the 1980s in a vain effort to promote local production, Benin's purchases of grain skyrocketed, fulfilling the needs of its population many times over. The rest was smuggled over the border to Nigeria's wheat-starved bakeries. Despite being Africa's premier oil exporter, Nigeria is routinely ground to a halt by fuel shortages. Sometimes this is due to a breakdown at a refinery, but often its price, among the cheapest in the world, is the culprit. It is the "informal" economy at work again. Since Benin pays world prices for imported gasoline, Nigerian gasoline is smuggled across the border and sold at inflated prices in jugs and soft-drink bottles outside reed shacks every couple of miles along the main highway.

The explosion of the "informal sector" continentwide is a strong indicator of what people think of their governments' rules and regulations. With such colorful names as *jua kali* (hot sun) in Swahili and *dumba nengue* (run for your life) in the Shangaan language of Southern Mozambique, the informal sector is massive, especially in the major urban areas. It accounts for 30 percent of employment in Abidjan, 50 percent in Dakar and Lagos, and 80 percent in Accra.[2] People everywhere are looking for ways to reestablish control over their lives. Some riot and some rebel for it, but the overwhelming majority has taken a similar road in principle to that of the *Tofinu* water people. Yet it is more than anything a journey of the mind. With few exceptions, ordinary people are not so much challenging their countries' boundaries and concepts of the nation-state as ignoring them. Claude Ake, the Nigerian social scientist, put it this way: "The state in Africa has not become a reassuring presence but remains a formidable threat to everybody except the few who control it. It is largely regarded as a hostile force to be evaded, cheated, defeated and appropriated as circumstances permit."[3]

Forty years after independence, the African nation-state has not yet proved to be the primary tool of liberation that Kwame Nkrumah dreamed of in 1957 when he led Ghana to become the first country in sub-Saharan Africa to gain independence from colonial rule. For the nation-state, the contemporary horizon is filled with peril. The threat comes in part from armed violence, such as in the Great Lakes region, but in other areas, the nation-state is increasingly irrelevant. Or is simply dissolving. The holocaust in Rwanda and the subsequent rebellion in former Zaire electrified a debate about the viability of the African nation-states created by the Europeans when they drew their lines across a map in Berlin over one hundred years ago.

The genocide and the waves of refugees moving throughout the region have prompted some observers to suggest that the time has come to ponder the unimaginable: to refashion Africa's frontiers, perhaps along ethnic lines. Professor Mazrui and other analysts have asked, "Should the legitimacy of tribalism be reviewed?" Others are more direct. "We should sit down with a square rule and compass and redesign the boundaries of Africa nations," says Wole Soyinka. ". . . Rwanda tells us that we cannot evade this challenge any longer."[4]

Calls for outright secession from established states are few, even in Rwanda. Hutu and Tutsi lived there together well before the arrival of the colonialists, and the problem is not that they want separate countries but that both want the same land. Even in Sudan, neither the Christian and animist Africans of the south nor the mainly Muslim and Arab-speaking north is asserting that the country be formally divided. Besides, there is no guarantee that ethnic homogeneity is a recipe for stability, although some credit it with helping the southern African nation of Botswana to prosper. Consider Somalia, where the existence of one Somali people, one culture, and one language has not saved it from imploding and fracturing along lines of the clan and even the subclan. Likewise, the presence of multiple cultures does not ensure instability. In Ethiopia, the central government has decided to use ethnicity as the basis for politics and autonomous territorial administration. Its citizens have their ethnic identity stamped into their ID cards, and the regions have the right, enshrined in the constitution, to secede.

It is this type of frank recognition of nations within nations which some believe could provide the basis of a new federalist order in Africa. In Nigeria, Africa's most populated and multicultural nation, the crisis over the annulled June 1993 presidential elections, in which a Yoruba from the western region won for the first time but was prevented from taking office, has prompted a new round of calls for a true regional autonomy. Decentralization, believes the jailed president of the Campaign for Democracy, Dr. Beko Ransome-Kuti, might be the only way to avoid bloodshed. "Nigeria can't stay as one country under the present circumstances. The only solution is to decentralize. Each ethnic group must be able to form a unit, no matter how small or unviable. The unviable ones will simply have to join with a bigger group," he says. "Anyone who does not accept this formula has a problem, because most people have made their minds up."

The problem in Nigeria and elsewhere is the state control over the distribution of resources and greed of those in power, what Father Oscar Nkundayezo would call "egoism." The Nigerian author Ken Saro-Wiwa led a movement to demand autonomy and compensation for ecological damage allegedly caused by the transnational oil company Royal Dutch/Shell for his Ogoni people, a tiny group of some five hundred thousand who inhabit the Niger River delta in southeastern Nigeria. Saro-Wiwa was hanged by the Abacha government in November 1995 for his supposed involvement in the murder of four traditional Ogoni chiefs who opposed the confrontational tactics of his Movement for the Survival of the Ogoni People. There are many who believe the real reason was because his campaign for autonomous control by the Ogoni over a significant portion of the oil earnings threatened the military government's revenues and could give other communities similar ideas. "The ultimate search in managing ethnic conflicts in Africa has to be for how to drastically reduce the sole dependence of all groups on the state, and, therefore, struggles over its control," writes Professor Eghosa Osaghae of the University of Ibadan. "That search has to proceed within the context of economic and political deregulation by which the state would not necessarily have to wither away, but to relinquish much of its control of the economy."[5]

Older patterns of rule in Africa are resurfacing, whether among the increasingly assertive traditional chiefs in South Africa or in Uganda, where public pressure forced President Yoweri Museveni to permit the resurrection of three kingdoms or in Ghana, where the Ashante king, the Ashantehene, continues to hold his weekly court.[6] In Zambia, the Lozi people are expressing their impatience more forcefully than ever before over the central government's failure to honor the 1964 Barotseland Agreement, which guaranteed King Litunga an independent legal system and control of the natural resources in his kingdom. They are demanding that President Frederick Chiluba's administration abolish a law that allows the government to veto King Litunga's right to distribute land among his people. Similar strains are emerging in countries where central governments are weak or where there are "pirates in power," to use Basil Davidson's memorable phrase referring to the Samuel Does, Idi Amins, Jean Bokassas, and Mobutu sese Sekos of the continent.

In precolonial times, ethnic identity was the unifying factor of government from the smallest settlements to the great West African states of Ghana, Mali, and Songhay that thrived from A.D. 900 to the end of the sixteenth century. Ancient Ghana, not to be confused with its modern namesake, rose on the back of the trans-Saharan gold trade to encompass an area of some 500,000 square kilometers and lasted nearly 300 years. It ruled over scores of communities, but its base was the Soninke people. Mali, ruled by the Malinke people, spread over 2 million square kilometers, reaching from the Atlantic Ocean to the Niger River town of Gao, and flourished for one hundred and fifty years. The Songhay, once part of the Ghana empire, emerged as the dominant group in the region after the fall of Mali.

Kingdoms and states centered on a core kinship rose and fell, sometimes as a result of invasion and sometimes of their own accord. Most rulers were subject to a complex set of checks and balances, usually in the form of a council of elders or senior religious figures, such as spirit mediums in direct contact with the ancestors. But in the eyes of important sectors of the population, the authorities enjoyed a certain critical mass of legitimacy. When they no longer did so, the rulers either were thrown out or their people deserted them. In that sense, the current wave of alienation challenging the postcolonial nation-state is part of a process that dates back centuries. Probably since the dawn of time, at moments of crisis when the established order was crumbling around them, people naturally retreated into their particular ethnic groups or kinship associations for security.

Some African scholars, such as the Nigerian historian Peter Ekeh, trace the current attachment to ethnic identity in West Africa to slavery and the failure of African states of the day to protect their people from it. "The response to the violation of the citizenry by the state in its sponsorship of the slave trade was the entrenchment of kinship corporations," he says.[7] The role of African leaders in the slave trade set into motion a process of estrangement between the rulers and the ruled that continues to the present.

The sense of moral damage which the trade inflicted on Africa is on display just a few hundred miles west of Ganvie, in Ghana, at Cape Coast Castle. Wreaths of flowers and ribbons and two empty gin bottles mark a makeshift religious shrine at the foot of steps that once led to a fifty-yard tunnel to the Atlantic Ocean. Looming behind are three huge chambers, dimly lit by thin shafts of sunlight falling through holes cut high up into the brick walls. The relentless pounding of the waves and the high-pitched voices of naked Ghanaian children frolicking in the surf make it difficult for a moment to imagine the horrors that occurred in these dark rooms. Even the ground underfoot seems at first sight to be nothing out of the ordinary, simply tightly packed earth one would expect to find in such an enclosure. But in that floor are the crushed spirits of tens of thousands of people. A layer of ancient human excrement covers the deepest recesses of the dungeons at Cape Coast Castle, a European fortress built over three centuries ago on the coast of West Africa. It was the product of thousands of slaves a year who inhabited the dungeons until they said their prayers at the shrine and walked down the tunnel to British ships waiting to ferry them to the New World. There were no toilets. "It was like a test; if you could survive down there for six to twelve weeks, then you were strong enough to be a slave," says Robert Bentril, the Ghanaian information officer for the West African Historical Museum at the castle. "The dead ones were brought out and thrown over the wall into the sea."

Cape Coast Castle is one of dozens of fortresses down the west coast built by European colonial powers from the fifteenth to seventeenth centuries to facilitate trade—some mineral, some vegetable, but much of it human—with the African states of the day. From the mouth of the Senegal River to Angola in southwest Africa, a distance of 1,300 miles, three centuries of slaving took at least 10 million, perhaps as many as 20 million, Africans to the Americas. The best estimates are that an equivalent number of people died during the march to the coast and in the raids by African armies to capture the slaves. Perhaps another 2 million more people perished on the journey across the Atlantic when for weeks, hundreds of slaves on board ship, often naked, were forced to lie with their heads between each other's thighs within the couple of feet between the ceiling and the wooden deck. The trade represented a massive drain on sub-Saharan Africa's population, which, by the time the slave raids ended, was estimated to total as little as 50 to 60 million people. In perhaps the worst case, Angola, which now has a total population of some 10 million people, lost up to 4 million to the slavers. On the scorecard of atrocities carried out by the human race, the Atlantic slave trade must rate as among the very worst.

Gold, for which modern Ghana earned the colonial name the Gold Coast, was the first major attraction to Africa for the Portuguese, Dutch, Swedish, and English merchants who arrived on West Africa's shores. Henry Caerlof obtained permission from the king of Fetu to build a lodge on the cape in 1653 on behalf of the Swedish African Company, which was muscling in on the Dutch monopoly of the coast. The Dutch had replaced the first Europeans trading in the area, the Portuguese, who built the nearby Elmina Castle in 1482. Local chiefs rankled at the highhandedness of the Europeans, and in 1661 they occupied the fort at Cape Coast for two years. The Dutch returned, only to be dislodged a year later by the English, who built Cape Coast Castle. It became the English center of operations along the coast, run by the Company of Royal Adventurers of England Trading to Africa under a royal charter. By 1672, the Royal Africa Company obtained a monopoly on trade. From there it launched a brisk business in gold, minting the famous Guineas in London, stamped on one side with the company's emblem.

With the opening of the colonies in the Americas came an insatiable thirst for labor, a demand some African chiefs were prepared to fulfill. The Europeans had already wiped out millions of the indigenous peoples of the Americas, through forced labor, disease, and outright violence, and the European indentured servants could not or would not do all of the work. So the Western world turned to Africa and its pool of proven tropical farmers and miners. Eighteen years after Columbus reached the Americas, the Spanish crown authorized the initial dispatch of fifty black slaves to Hispaniola—the island that consists of Haiti and the Dominican Republic—to work in the mines. A decade later, Hispaniola started exporting sugar.

Profits from plantations and mines in the New World provided the capital England and the rest of Europe needed to kick-start the final drive from feudalism to capitalism. And so the men and women who walked in chains down the tunnel of Cape Coast Castle and countless others along the coast to the awaiting ships became unwilling foot soldiers in Europe's Industrial Revolution. Manufacturing centers throughout England grew up on the back of the slave trade. Liverpool became a major slave-trading center, accounting for 60 percent of all the English slave ships by the end of the eighteenth century, as well as at least a dozen factories for producing rope. Manchester manufactured the cloth, Bristol the glass beads, and Birmingham the guns to meet the demands of the African market. Ronald Segal, author of *The Black Diaspora*, quotes an eighteenth-century writer on economics as describing the slave trade as "the first principle and foundation of all the rest, the mainspring of the machine which sets every wheel in motion."[8] The plantations of the Americas generated massive profits. No less an authority than Adam Smith once wrote: "The profits of a sugar plantation in any of our West Indian colonies are generally much greater than those of any other cultivation that is known either in Europe or America."[9]

Africa has never fully recovered from the trade. Whole villages lost their strongest and ablest young people, their best farmers and miners, and the battles waged by local chiefs to obtain more captives spread instability throughout the coast and deep into the interior. The European officials running the various castles and forts only rarely had slave-raiding gangs of their own. They usually had to pay rent to the resident chief and bought slaves with cheap European-manufactured goods, cloth and guns, which helped the chiefs to gather slaves more efficiently. Many fortunes were made by African chiefs selling their fellow Africans. In one year alone King Ghezo of Dahomey, who controlled the entire slave coast stretching from Accra in Ghana to Lagos in Nigeria in the mid-1800s, was reported to have earned 300,000 British pounds sterling, at the time a sizable fortune.[10]

Something else was decimated by the Atlantic slave trade and the European occupation that followed at the end of the nineteenth century. The foundations of Africa's political and religious systems—Africa's sense of itself—suffered horrible wounds. It is not that slavery was completely new to Africa. The trans-Saharan trafficking of relatively small numbers of African slaves to wealthy families in the Islamic world had been going on for centuries. Within Africa, too, almost all of the major states that existed in the sixteenth century when the European explorers arrived had institutions of servitude: from the Congo kingdom in northern Angola, Oyo and Benin in Nigeria, the Luba and Lunda states in Zaire, to the Munhumutapa state of the Shona people in Zimbabwe. These nations routinely acquired slaves through conquest. They treated them not as chattel but as members of the community, albeit the lowest class. The slaves owned property, sometimes including their own "slaves"; they married, even within the family which "owned" them; and in time they could rise up the social ladder.

With the advent of the Atlantic trade, the status of the slaves was transformed into chattel. They became *peixas de India*, or pieces of India, labor units for the West Indies.[11] They were commodities, and the chiefs exchanged them for trinkets, textiles, and guns—goods that boosted the prestige and power of the traditional rulers but had little beneficial impact on the local African economies. Britain outlawed slavery in the early nineteenth century, certainly more for economic reasons than humanitarian ones. Thanks in large part to the capital produced by slave labor in the West Indies, Britain was in the thrall of a revolution in manufacturing. Its hunger was no longer for slaves as much as markets for its manufactured goods and steady supplies of primary commodities, such as palm oil. Since its colonists in the West Indies could not compete with their European rivals in the New World still using slave labor, Britain sent its navy out to the coast of West Africa to interdict the trade.[12]

British war frigates boarded slaver ships, freed the slaves, and deposited them on the shores of Sierra Leone. Freetown was born, and the slaves who started their new lives there passionately rejected their African past, embracing the culture of their immediate benefactors, the British. Traditional Africa sold them into slavery and Europe had rescued them, although they represented a tiny fraction of the millions Europe had already enslaved. Put down in a land far from their original home, among people who spoke a variety of different languages, these "recaptives," or Saro, as they became known, embraced Western education and Christianity and played an extraordinary role in the development of Africa's postcolonial political thought. They were individuals of immense talent. They created a new language, Krio (Creole), built schools, and set up newspapers. They were businessmen, theologians, writers, and medical doctors. Among them were people such as James Africanus Horton, the physician and author of *West African Countries and Peoples* in 1868, which articulated the idea that Africans should be free to develop themselves.[13] But in their demands for greater African freedom was another, more disturbing message. To advance into the modern world, Africa must reject its past and adopt the political and cultural model of Britain and Europe. The struggle between these "modernists" and the traditional leaders was engaged.

The modernists argued that "backward and primitive," read "tribal," Africa would have to put its own developmental process on hold, give way to Christianity and Western-style constitutional systems, and accept the nation-states that the colonial powers had created when they divided Africa at the Berlin Conference of 1884–85. The great West African empires of the Songhay, Mali, and the Ashante of Ghana could be held up as proud symbols of Africa's past, as they often were, but they held no lessons to be learned for the future.

And yet, until the slave trade, and for a considerable time during it, the existing African states and Europe traded as equals. Europeans who arrived on Africa's shores to purchase gold and later slaves might have considered their African counterparts inferior, but they regularly complained of being outfoxed by them during negotiations. The tradition of trade between West Africa and the Mediterranean world dated back to the eighth century, when giant caravans began crossing the Sahara. Gold from West Africa was an important contributor to the monetary system in Europe. At least some African societies produced tremendous wealth. When Mansa Musa, the king of Mali, arrived in Cairo in 1324 en route to Mecca, he brought with him five hundred porters carrying heavy staffs of gold, and so generously did he distribute it that he temporarily ruined the value of money in the Egyptian capital. But by the nineteenth century, the Europeans were attempting to settle their own political rivalries by, in part, building empires in Africa. Powerful and developed African states such as Ashante, which had its own democratic institutions, army, police, and tax system, were swept aside. The British army occupied the Ashante capital of Kumasi and integrated the nation into its Gold Coast colony. In so doing, British military conquest halted one of the best chances for the creation of an African state on its own terms, within its own borders.

Tensions between Africa's so-called modernists and the traditional chiefs would simmer. When independence came to Ghana in 1957, it was a "modernist" Kwame Nkrumah, who was handed the reins of power by the British. The Ashante king of the Ashante state refused to attend the independence celebrations. The first sub-Saharan African nation-state to emerge from colonial occupation was born on very shaky ground. Professor Mazrui's curse of the ancestors had taken concrete form. Other new nations would emerge, all containing a myriad of sometimes antagonistic ethnic groups, such as the Fulani and Yoruba in Nigeria, and splitting others, many adopting the colonial language as their official tongue, and all dependent on a few commodities whose prices were determined in Europe. The colonies had been designed to serve the economic interests of the imperial powers, not the development of their peoples, and after independence they continued to do so.

When the new assembled nations of Africa formed the Organization of African Unity (OAU) in 1963, they decided that the modern borders, frontiers which no African ever had a hand in designing, were sacred. There were a few prominent African leaders, such as Julius Nyerere and Nkrumah himself, who argued that only a unified Africa could stand on equal footing with the outside world. Nyerere advocated an East African federation of then Tanganyika, Kenya, and Uganda, but it floundered. "I felt that these little countries in Africa were really too small; they would not be viable—the Tanganyikas, the Rwandas, the Burundis, the Kenyas," he said.[14]

The call for unity was a revival of a Pan-African ideal whose intellectual seeds were planted in the early 1900s by prominent Africans in the diaspora, such as W. E. B. DuBois and Marcus Garvey and his Back to Africa movement. "To go it alone will limit our horizons, curtail our expectations, and threaten our liberty," Nkrumah told that inaugural OAU meeting. "Unless we meet the obvious and very powerful neo-colonialists' threats with a united African front, based upon a common economic and defense policy, the strategy will be to pick us off and destroy us one by one."[15] On his deathbed in Conakry, Guinea, nine years later, Nkrumah is reported to have said, "When Africa is a united, strong power everyone will respect Africans, and Africans will respect themselves."[16]

But the majority of African politicians of the early independence period would not hear of questioning the nation-state borders. They wanted immediate independence. Their rejection had two motivations. A debate on redrawing the map, they believed, could prove an endless and potentially violent exercise. And many of the first nationalist leaders were enchanted with the financial and political possibilities that they would enjoy by occupying the offices of their erstwhile colonial overlords.

Early attempts to redraw the colonial boundaries ended often in bloodshed and in failure, whether the Igbos' attempt to secede from Nigeria in the 1960s or Somalia's bid to annex the mainly Somali Ogaden region from Ethiopia a decade later. President Nyerere's success in merging the former British colonies of Tanganyika and the islands of Zanzibar and Pemba into the country of Tanzania was a notable exception. In the 1990s, the only two countries which fractured, northern Somaliland from Somalia and Eritrea from Ethiopia, did so, ironically, along colonial lines. Somaliland was ruled formerly by Britain, while the southern part was occupied by Italy, as was Eritrea before the Kingdom of Haile Selassie threw out the Italian army after World War II.

There have been limited attempts to achieve regional integration, including the Economic Community of West African States, or ECOWAS, and the Southern African Development Council (SADC). The latter, twelve nations consisting of 130 million people, appears to have the most promising future. Created to shun apartheid South Africa, now SADC will depend on the newly democratic "rainbow" nation. Nelson Mandela's rise from political prisoner to president has reintroduced South Africa to the neighborhood. SADC now represents three-quarters of sub-Saharan Africa's total economic output, although the community groups countries of wildly divergent living standards. Mozambique is among the world's poorest countries, just emerging from a civil war that killed 1 million people and cost the economy billions of dollars. Next door is South Africa, a middle-income country with sophisticated banking and transport sectors, and with deep veins of mineral wealth controlled by giant transnational corporations, such as De Beers and Anglo-American Corp. It is a virtual land of opportunity, and each year tens of thousands of African immigrants flood in, making Africa's integration a reality on the ground. Most are from the neighboring countries of Mozambique and Zimbabwe, but they also come from as far afield as Nigeria, Somalia, and Senegal.

Black South Africans have been of two minds about the immigration explosion in South Africa's industrial heartland, the province called Gauteng, or "place of gold" in the Sotho language. Most have not felt the economic benefits of the miraculously peaceful transition from apartheid to democratic rule in 1994. Unemployment is at 45 percent, and millions of South Africans still have no adequate housing or health care. Many feel the foreigners are making it worse for them. In 1994, illegal aliens cost the South African economy about $50 million in housing, health-care, and policing costs, according to Dr. Greg Mills, the director of studies at the South Africa Institute of International Affairs. But simply trying to keep them out will not work. The key to slowing the wave is to develop the rest of Africa, he says. "Unless South Africa helps to make the region a better place to live, then the people of the region will come to live in South Africa."

On the street corners of Alexandra, the sprawling township of tin-roofed block houses in central Johannesburg, emotions alternate between compassion and fear. "Many of these people are exiled here as a result of the destabilization policies of the old South African government," says Nkele Ntingane, a twenty-eight-year-old community activist. "These countries are poor today because of the policies of our past government. It is natural that they have come to the relative safety of South Africa." Lucky Baloyi, a gruff twenty-seven-year-old taxi minibus conductor, is adamant. "The people here do not want them. They come here and work for low salaries and end up to taking jobs and land that the people of Alex need." Surprisingly there is talk again of the dreaded apartheid-era pass laws, even among South Africa's blacks who were victimized by them in the past. "Some of these people come in with better skills than South Africans and they find jobs," says Angie Pamaila. "In any country you have to control the people who are coming in. Sometimes I think we need influx control again." Angie is an energetic twenty-eight-year-old liaison official at the giant Ponte apartment complex in the mainly black neighborhood of Hillbrow. A looming circular tower block, the Ponte building has so many Congolese residents that most people just call it "Kinshasa."

In a wide room next to the ground-floor entrance of "Kinshasa," Reverend Daniel Muteba ministers each week in French to people in the building and the neighborhood. He used to be a chemical engineer at a diamond-mining company in the region of Kasai. Now he is a full-time pentacostal minister at the Missionary Church Center. He became a born-again Christian in 1980, and married a Belgian medical doctor, Emmanuelle. After earning a degree at the University of Louvain in Belgium, Muteba moved to South Africa in 1991 to study at the Rhema Bible Training College. Then God intervened.

He told Muteba to stay in South Africa. "I do not belong to myself, I belong to the Lord." Muteba has no plans to return to Congo, but he believes many of his countrymen would if "conditions there improve." The year Muteba migrated was an especially difficult one for Congo. Unrest in the army exploded into widespread riots and looting in Kinshasa. Thousands of businessmen and their families fled. Congolese of more humble origins made their way, too, and quickly found their niche in the informal sector. Today, they dominate the street markets that have sprung up around Johannesburg's major shopping centers, specializing in African curios and wooden sculptures. But it has not been easy. "They thought they would find opportunities here, find peace, and work in a developed country, but they now see jobs are difficult," Muteba said. "They feel that South African blacks do not like blacks from other countries."

With political stability anchored in the unparalleled legitimacy of the Mandela government and a relatively strong economy, the solidity of the South African nation-state is unchallenged. There are many problems—high crime and unemployment rates and massive income disparities—but the state is generally seen as a positive force. Before its fall, Mobutu's Zaire stood at the opposite end of the spectrum. As president, Mobutu used his three decades in power to systematically loot the country. During his reign, Zaire had a national flag, a seat at the United Nations, and embassies around the world, but for all intents and purposes as a national entity it had ceased to exist. There was no better symbol of the health of the state under Mobutu than the woeful performance of its poorly paid and ill-disciplined army. It collapsed like wet cardboard in the face of the rebellion by the Alliance of Democratic Forces for the Liberation of Congo-Zaire, which captured a nation the size of the United States east of the Mississippi in just seven months and installed its nominal leader, Laurent Kabila, as president in May 1997. As each town fell, Mobutu's army engaged in looting sprees before fleeing the rebel advance. The defenders of a nonexistent state had turned predators of the people they were meant to protect.

For years Kinshasa had no effective government, and for a time, in 1993, there were two parliaments and two prime ministers. So unreliable were statistics about the economy that the World Bank removed Zaire from the list of countries in its annual World Development Indicators.[17] By the mid-1990s, the formal economy, drained of its lifeblood by Mobutu's vampire state, had withered to the size it was in the 1950s. The informal market accounted for the bulk of economic activity, and some analysts believed it may have been as big as three times the official gross domestic product.[18] Hyperinflation reached a mind-boggling 9,800 percent in 1994. By some accounts, 85 percent of the national road network had succumbed to the ever voracious appetite of the African bush, and the national currency was shunned by millions of people in the interior. Mobutu remained aloof of the political and economic confusion of Kinshasa by retreating to live permanently in Gbadolite, his ancestral land in the far north, equipped with an international airport, allowing him to come and go without troubling to pass through the national capital. When he became gravely ill with prostate cancer, he traveled to his mansion on the French Riveria. In 1996, the UN Special Rapporteur Roberto Garreton wrote, "The State continues to be absent, which critically affects the enjoyment of civil rights and liberties and, moreover, economic, social and cultural rights."[19] A year before Mobutu's downfall, Mike Katambwa, the political editor of the opposition newspaper *Umoja*, laughed bitterly at the thought of the state of his homeland. "There is no government in this country, and there is no state as such. All the resources are used by the clique around Mobutu to become rich. What I can tell you is that things are not sure. Even we are not sure that tomorrow we are going to be here. This is Zaire today."

Tomorrow has come and gone, and a new Congo must be built on the ruins of Mobutu's Zaire. The African nation-state bequeathed by the Europeans faces its stiffest test in Congo, a country of 40 million people of some two hundred ethnic groups. It was carved out of central West Africa in the 1880s by King Leopold II of Belgium with the help of the journalist turned explorer, Henry Morgan Stanley. Leopold's Congo Free State was a most primitive colonial backwater. Slavery and forced labor were common, and the *Force Publique* troops routinely raided villages to enforce a law that required each community to provide four people annually to work as slaves for the state, and to turn over all rubber and ivory the peasants gathered to state agents. Failure to comply earned a visit by the *Force Publique*. To prove their work ethic, the *Force Publique* troops regularly amputated villagers' hands and had them smoked to preserve them for their superiors' inspection.

Anything King Leopold could do, Joseph Désiré Mobutu could do better. A one-time journalist and informant for the Belgian secret police, the Sûreté, Mobutu rose to power thanks to the warm embrace of the U.S. Central Intelligence Agency. The CIA provided

Mobutu with the financial wherewithal to maintain the loyalty of the army during the Belgian pullout, and it schemed to eliminate his one-time mentor turned opponent, Patrice Lumumba, whom the Kennedy administration regarded as a dangerous "Communist." The agency hired at least two assassins, one "a foreign citizen with a criminal background," the other described by the CIA itself as an "essentially stateless soldier of fortune, a forger and a former bank robber."[20] Not satisfied, a CIA scientist, Dr. Sidney Gottlieb, put together an assassination kit that included a poison designed, as he later told a congressional committee, "to produce a disease that was indigenous to that area and that could be fatal. . . ."[21] In January 1961, Lumumba was taken prisoner by Mobutu's soldiers and sent to the mineral-rich province of Katanga, then in rebellion against the central government, where he was murdered by thugs loyal to the secessionist leader Moishe Tshombe. According to Dr. Gottlieb's own testimony to Congress, the poison was dumped unused into the Zaire River.[22]

The Kennedy administration was enamored of Mobutu. When he visited Washington in May 1963, President Kennedy gushed: "General, if it hadn't been for you, the whole thing would have collapsed and the Communists would have taken over." So taken with Mobutu was Kennedy that he provided him with an airplane and a U.S. Air Force crew to fly it.[23]

In death Lumumba became greater than life and to this day he is regarded as a martyr to African resistance to foreign domination. In 1964, his followers who had dubbed themselves the Simbas, or lions, launched a violent attempt to set up an alternative, left-wing government in Stanleyville, later named Kisangani. The rebellion was crushed with the help of 600 Belgian paratroopers flown in by the U.S. air force. One fighter for the Simba cause and passionate Lumumba supporter was Laurent Kabila. After the collapse of the revolt, Kabila, then twenty-five, fled with his comrades into the mountains west of Lake Tanganyika around Kivu. Kabila's guerrillas survived by trading gold and ivory and by collecting $40,000 in ransom in 1975 for three Stanford University students and a Dutch friend who were taken hostage while studying the behavior of gorillas.[24] During their early days, the Argentine revolutionary Ernesto Che Guevara visited Kabila's men, but he left despairing of their commitment to revolution. It took thirty years, yet when the revolution eventually did come, Kabila's men and their Banyamu-

lenge Tutsi allies swept down from the mountains and literally overran the Congo.

In 1965, a year after the Simba revolt, Mobutu declared himself
president and remained in power for thirty-two years. Congo, despite its enormous deposits of cobalt, copper, and diamonds, has become the fourth poorest country in the world. Mobutu fared far better by plundering the country's wealth to finance various palaces he
built around Congo and the purchase of mansions in a host of European countries. Estimates of his personal wealth ran up to $5 billion,
and some commentators joked that Mobutu could have cleared his
country's entire foreign debt with a personal check. Unfortunately,
even Mobutu's wallet was not big enough. Under his rule, Africa's
potentially wealthiest country chalked up a $14 billion debt to ex-
ternal creditors.

As autocrats went, Mobutu was in a class of his own. A manip-
ulator par excellence, Mobutu deftly applied the tools of repression
and bribery to marginalize his opponents and astutely played the
anti-Communist card to woo the West. In 1971, he tapped into the
nostalgia for precolonial Africa by launching an "Africanization"
campaign known as *authenticité*. He ordered all nationals to drop
their Christian names in favor of African ones, forced all foreigners
to relinquish their ownership of businesses, which he handed over
to his associates, and adopted a new name, Zaire, for the country
and the mighty Congo River. It came from a mispronunciation by
the early Portuguese explorers of the Kikongo word *nzali*, which
means "the river that swallows all rivers."[25] His newfound commitment to tradition did not stop him from running to the Europeans
when he needed them. Like the African chiefs who engaged in the
slave trade, Mobutu could always count on the West's military support to keep him in power just as long as he ensured its untram-
meled access to his country's considerable resources and allowed
Zaire to be used as a staging point for covert operations against
neighboring states, such as Angola. Armies from Belgium, France,
and Morocco intervened in the 1960s, 1970s, and 1980s to crush secessionist rebels, mainly in Shaba province.

Joseph Désiré Mobutu changed his name to Mobutu sese Seko
wa za Banga, which according to one official translation means "the
all powerful warrior who, because of his endurance and inflexible
will to win, will go from conquests to conquests leaving fire in
his wake."[26] There have been some conquests, especially those that

fattened his treasure chest lodged safely in Swiss bank accounts, but the overwhelming legacy Mobutu has left is a country whose infrastructure has collapsed, where living conditions are among the most wretched on earth, punctuated by outbreaks of cholera, bubonic plague, AIDS, and even the dreaded *Ebola* virus, and where corruption has become a way of life. As UN Special Rapporteur Garreton wrote in January 1996, "The right to life continues to be at the mercy of military bodies and the police, whose impunity is intact; judges impose the death penalty on a regular basis and the President does not decide on petitions for clemency; pillages, torture, cruel, inhuman and degrading treatment, rape of detained women or victims of pillages have not stopped; public demonstrations are punished with disproportionate violence. . . ."[27]

Survival in the political and economic maelstrom of the Mobutu era required imaginative experiments in self-reliance, sometimes to the extent of entire regions trying to run their affairs largely on their own. The most striking example occurred in the Kasai Oriental region, situated in the lush rolling hills where East and West Africa meet. In the latter years of the regime, when it became apparent that Mobutu was "a wounded leopard," in the words of Mike Katambwa, the *Umoja* newspaper editor, the Luba people attempted to tap into a sense of community spirit to rebuild Kasai Oriental, regardless of what was happening in the rest of the country. Like the *Tofinu*, the Luba turned their backs on a hostile environment and sought their own solutions. In doing so, they fostered demands for greater regional autonomy that the government of the new Congo will have to address.

A CONVERTED chicken farm on a hot, humid morning six hundred miles east of Kinshasa was an unlikely setting to witness the stirrings of a phoenix straining to rise from the ashes of the Zairian state. But there it was, a compound of half a dozen unfinished single-story cement block buildings, where the Luba people decided to build a university and, hopefully, a better future for their children. The crippling anarchy of the capital, Kinshasa, seemed like the reality of a distant planet. Initially, a stroll through the university grounds, which featured a lone manual water pump and untidy piles of stones and scraps of wood, gave little hint of a local intellectual explosion. A step through the threshold of a rugged warehouse–turned–campus bookstore revealed stacks six feet high of old texts and often-outdated journals sent from libraries and universities around Europe and North America. The books were in a variety of European languages—French, English, Dutch, and German. Some of them were twenty years old, but as Monji Tchibanza, the spry store manager, quipped with a wink, you have to start somewhere. "Our two biggest problems are a lack of space, and the books we are receiving are very, very old," he said. "We have very few modern texts, it's true, but many of the principles contained in the old ones remain valid. Besides, when you take the decision to receive donated books, you can't refuse what they send."

Rows of wooden benches facing a chipped chalkboard filled a second room, a lecture hall that can accommodate three hundred and fifty students. In a third, workmen busily sawed wooden planks and produced bricks to fill out the rest of the other classrooms, most of which still had no windows. The laboratory equipment for the medical and chemistry departments was clean but ancient, and on display at the computer center were several ten-year-old IBMs. Clearly, the University of Mbuji-Mayi had a long way to go to enter the era of the World Wide Web. It did not even have a functioning telephone. Yet evident on the faces of the students of English studying without much reading material or even a radio to tune in to foreign broadcasts in English was an insatiable will to succeed.

"The students from an intellectual point of view are very good," said Jean-Francis Debongnie, a visiting professor from the University of Liège in Belgium who taught a three-week course on mechanical technology. "The problems are obvious. The students often don't have enough to eat, their housing is very poor, they must walk to class, and in my course, we teach five hours a day. They have to learn too much too quickly with too few resources. Also, there is the question of the economic situation—will they find jobs when they graduate? But as the province has started to rely on itself, the economy has improved. This university is a basis of hope. It is, I would say, an act of faith."

The idea of the University of Mbuji-Mayi was born in December 1990, when leading religious and business figures in Kasai realized that they could no longer count on the collapsing educational institutions in Congo's other major cities, Kisangani, Kinshasa, and Lubumbashi, capital of Shaba province, to train their future businesspeople, engineers, and doctors. "When this province was set up at independence in 1960, we did not have one secondary school. So we built them, but the graduates had to travel to Kinshasa and

Lubumbashi to further their education. The importance of having a university in Kasai is self-evident. It will stimulate cultural and intellectual development and we hope it could be a center around which the province can be built," said Joseph Tshibangu Mutamba, secretary general of the university council. "The Luba people have been kicked out of other regions and have encountered discrimination at other universities, primarily because the Luba are bright and industrious. The solidarity of the Luba is being strengthened because of the persecution we have suffered from [the Mobutu] Government. But we don't want to close ourselves off. We are open to the outside world, even to those regions which kicked us out. If someone comes here from the outside and prospers, we respect that."

The university, which offers courses in law, medicine, economics, and applied sciences, was the result of a unique partnership between the Roman Catholic Church and the all-powerful diamond company, Minière de Bakwanga, or MIBA, where Reverend Muteba worked before he migrated to South Africa. "Over the past ten years, the Church has become aware that it must play a role to substitute for the state, to assist in the field of development," said Abbot Jean Marie Ciamalakanda, the Catholic diocese director of development programs. "Only when we are free in our minds can we move forward. People here have to count on their own efforts, and there is a great reservoir of energy to channel."

While the Church donated the chicken farm as the university premises, MIBA provided a $10,000 per month cash grant and supplied electricity from its power generators. Contributions also came in from the Luba diaspora in Europe and Canada. MIBA used its plane to transport visiting professors free of charge from Kinshasa, and the two functioning hotels in the city, Tanko Hotel and Motel Nkumbikumbi, donated two rooms per academic year for visiting lecturers.

Biselela Tshimankinda, a cheerful professor of English at the university, is that too rare example in Africa of someone who at great personal sacrifice chose not to join the continental brain drain. The son of a mechanic, Tshimankinda alone among his fourteen siblings obtained a university education, and instead of opting for a teaching post abroad, he decided to return to Kasai. Born in Shaba province forty-seven years ago, he completed his B.A. in 1977 in the town of Bukavu on the Rwanda border and was appointed an assistant at the Teachers Training College in Mbuji-Mayi. After six years, Tshimankinda won a scholarship to study for his M.A. at the University of Durham in England and continued on to complete his Ph.D. in 1990. At that point, the University of Singapore tried to recruit him. "I couldn't go because I had many financial problems with my family back here and I wanted to return to teach at the Teachers College. They had no professor at the time," he said. Two months after coming back to Mbuji-Mayi, he won a fellowship to study at the University of Missouri, which he accepted but returned home the following year.

"My first thought after the United States was to go to South Africa, because I had many friends there. But then I decided to come back, to stop moving about, and to try to do something for my people." His decision to forego a career abroad has been a financially costly one. At the university in Mbuji-Mayi, he earns $3.50 an hour, and at his modest home he is unsure each morning if he will have water and electricity. "I have six children, and when I was abroad I could send money for everything because what people earn here is nothing. My first child has just completed her B.A. in English. My second is going to get his B.A. this year. I'll try to get them to study abroad," he said with false confidence, and then reconsidered. "I'll try, but it's very difficult. Without any money, it's really impossible."

Not everyone would make the same choice to remain in Kasai, though Tshimankinda's case is certainly not an isolated one. But most of those at the university have nowhere else to go. The majority of the 1,600 students are refugees from recent ethnic violence in Shaba, and that has put strains on the university's fragile revenue base. "One of our most pressing problems is that the students of displaced families are not integrated into the economy, so only part of them can pay the one hundred and fifty dollars in school fees. Even that will not cover the costs of maintaining the school and paying the professors," said Joseph Mutamba. "That's why the contributions of MIBA and the Church have been so important."

The university was one of many signs in Mbuji-Mayi that Kasai Oriental had become virtually an independent province. The national currency, the "new Zaire," was shunned after opposition leader and son of Kasai, Etienne Tshisekedi, called for a boycott. Instead, people in Mbuji-Mayi continued to trade in the "old Zaire" notes, which Kinshasa officially abolished in 1993, and in U.S. dollars. The province had its own small airline, and often consumer goods were flown in directly from Europe and South Africa. Even the notoriously ill-disciplined government troops were on better behavior; when the comrades engaged in widespread looting sprees, known as *pillages,* throughout the rest of the country in 1991 and 1993, Mbuji-Mayi remained remarkably calm. Hyperinflation, which had made the new "Zaire" currency a national joke, hardly existed in Kasai.

"For us to survive, we have to assume that the state does not exist," said Professor Tshimankinda. "With all this chaos, it goes without saying that people have to rely on their own efforts." That view is something of a motto for the Luba people, who see themselves as the "Jews of the Congo" because of their industriousness and a history of persecution. "The problem is that other people think of us as being apart from the rest of the country," said Tshimankinda. "For example, if you are on a bus and someone asks how many people there are, the response could be, there are ten people and a Luba, as if a Luba does not belong to those people. In Shaba sometimes we even had to change our names to go to school. You just change some vowels. For example, my name is Biselela. If I just change it to Bisalela, it sounds like a Ligala name."

The autonomous tendencies aside, almost no one in Mbuji-Mayi advocated the type of bloody secession declared in the early 1960s by the emperor Albert Kalonji, when Kasai mimicked Shaba's attempt to break away from the newly independent state of the Congo. They pushed the envelope of autonomy quietly.

Their determination stems from a deep feeling of injustice. In the early 1990s, the Luba were victims of the brutal policy of ethnic cleansing carried out by the authorities in Shaba where Luba immigrants had come to dominate the teaching and medical professions and held up to 80 percent of the jobs in Gecamines, the giant copper and cobalt mining company. The violence flared after 3,000 delegates meeting in a national conference intent on fostering multiparty democracy elected Tshisekedi, a Luba, as interim prime minister. In retaliation, President Mobutu, deftly employing the divide-and-rule strategy, set his two most troublesome provinces against each other and encouraged Shaba Governor Gabrile Kyungu wa Kumwanza to unleash the security forces on the Luba. Thousands died in ethnic clashes and in concentration camps; by 1994, an estimated one hundred thousand people had returned to Kasai, where many ended up in barren refugee camps. It was the last straw for many Luba all over Congo who decided to return home and make something of their homeland.

In an ironic twist, Shaba's loss has been Kasai's gain. Technicians and engineers from the now-ailing Gecamines Company have returned to Kasai to strengthen MIBA, 80 percent of which is owned by the state and 20 percent by Sibeka, a subsidiary of the Société Générale de Belgique. After several years of decline, production at the company is rising, reaching an estimated $70 million in 1996. A liberalization program begun in 1983 opened mining outside the MIBA concession to syndicates, and since then individual mining, both legal and illegal, has exploded. As a result, income from diamond production from the province rose to between $300 million and $400 million a year. While copper production has plummeted in Shaba, falling from a position of providing 60 percent of Congo's export earnings to 12 percent, the share of foreign exchange income from diamonds in Kasai rose to 35 percent. Due to the ethnic cleansing in Shaba, Mbuji-Mayi has swelled to over 1 million people.

By the eve of the launch of Kabila's rebellion in November 1996, other regions had only minimal ties with Kinshasa. In Shaba, the Lunda people maintained close links with their kin in Angola and Zambia, and the province depended on South Africa for imports of butter, sugar, and toothpaste. The far eastern region of Kivu, the first to fall to Kabila's forces, traditionally looked to Kenya, Uganda, and Tanzania. But none attained the degree of autonomy of Kasai Oriental.

"The worth of a man is measured by the obstacles he is willing to confront. We have been pushed around, but the Luba people refuse to die," said Abbot Ciamalakanda, who also lectures at the university in economics and rural development. "The history of this people is unique. At first there was a tendency to leave. The intent of the Belgian colonialists was to exploit the riches of this region, and they expelled the African people so that they could have clear access to the diamonds. In a way, this helped the Luba. They were able to travel, gain experience, and learn skills from people in other parts of the country. In Shaba, they became professors and technicians. But when the Lubas suffered persecution, they focused anew on the importance of their origins and decided to return to Kasai.

"What is happening in this region," he went on, "is the creation of the people themselves. Now we have a class of businessmen who make the region thrive. We are effectively an enclave, but the businessmen have taken the initiative to trade with the outside world to ensure that Kasai receives essential supplies. They realized that there was no one else to save them. The state certainly would not do it. There developed a spontaneous understanding between the Church and the business community to survive and live together."

Behind the provincial surge were two main powers: Jonas Mukamba Kadiata Nzemba, MIBA's president and a founder of the university, and the Roman Catholic Church, headed by Monsignor Tharcisse Tshibangu, the bishop of Mbuji-Mayi. Mukamba was a major player in the Mobutu system. A former ambassador, with stints as governor of Kasai and Shaba, he was rare among the Congolese elite because he reinvested some of his earnings. In Mbuji-Mayi, he owned a restaurant, a cooking gas company, several bakeries, and the Coca-Cola bottling plant. As the influence and attention of central government faded, Monsignor Tshibangu and Mukamba set up a think tank called the Conference for the Economic Development of Kasai Oriental to fill the vacuum and to draw up a regional development plan.

Everything in Mbuji-Mayi pivoted on the imposing figure of Mukamba, a huge man with a booming voice skilled in the delicate art of straddling the perilous high wire of Congolese politics. He described himself as "a friend" of Mobutu, whose name is the subject of universal loathing in Kasai, while he called Tshisekedi, a fellow Luba, "my brother." Mobutu appointed him as president of MIBA but could not remove him because the Luba would not accept anyone else. One senior diplomat in Kinshasa attributed Mukamba's leverage to his ability as MIBA president "to feed" Mobutu with the increased diamond revenues that accrue to the state while at the same time discreetly funding Tshisekedi.

The depth of Mukamba's influence was evident at his home, in the leafy center of Mbuji-Mayi. It was one of several dozen immaculate stone mansions built by the Belgians during the colonial days and later passed on to MIBA for its senior staff. Not surprisingly, this section of Mbuji-Mayi is commonly known as "MIBA town." At dusk, streams of people, mainly businessmen and governmental officials, lined up on Makumba's wide veranda for a chance of meeting with him to seek his advice or help, often waiting for three or four hours before he arrived from his day at the office. When he sat down to dinner, he was usually joined by a dozen important local personalities, including the military commander. Mukamba was clearly proud of Kasai's achievements in recent years and echoed the view of his fellow Lubas that waiting for Kinshasa to provide support was a waste of time. "The state does nothing for us, we have to do everything here. We have to press for federalism," he said.

But if the region is to survive on its own, there is still plenty to do. Outside of MIBA town, the roads are atrocious, and water and electricity supplies are sporadic at best. Mukamba said his most pressing project was to secure $13 million in investment to expand the mine's hydroelectric plant on the Mbuji-Mayi River to provide power for the entire city. Without it, new industries will be stillborn, and Kasai's rampant unemployment, swollen by the arrival of refugees from Shaba, would worsen, threatening the entire enterprise.

Mukamba's own position was thrown into jeopardy by the arrival of Kabila's rebel forces in Mbuji-Mayi. He tried again to adjust to the shifting political landscape. "We're not calling Kabila in, but we can't do anything to stop him if he comes," Mukamba said in March 1997, just days before the guerrilla army reached the city. "If Kabila arrives and he is the new boss, I would obey him. I obeyed Mobutu when he was boss, but he is not immortal. I would cooperate with anyone who succeeds him."[28] Kabila did not return the gesture. Soon after the alliance's military occupation of Kasai, Mukamba was fired from his post and disappeared. In June, Amnesty International issued an "urgent action" demanding that the new authorities disclose his whereabouts.

Always a controversial figure because of his links with both Mobutu and Tshisekedi, Mukamba was widely rumored to have been involved in the murder of Patrice Lumumba. It was a charge he always denied, but it was unlikely to have aided his cause when Kabila, the arch Lumumba supporter, assumed power.

Mukamba's motivation for aiding Kasai's economic autonomy drive, most residents of Mbuji-Mayi believed, was complicated, inspired more by how he wanted to be regarded by the Luba people than out of personal gain. "The university will only survive on the condition that Mukamba stays here," said Tshimankinda. "If he goes away, I think it's going to collapse, because he's the only one to my knowledge who's sponsoring it without any hope of getting something back. I think he's trying to win back his people, because most of them say he's pro-Mobutu. He knows it because many people have told him. So I think he is trying to win us back."

The vibrancy of Mbuji-Mayi was tangible along Inga Road, a wide rolling dirt tract that cuts through the heart of the city and is jammed with dozens of diamond buyers, including Sediza, owned by the South African giant De Beers, willing to pay U.S. dollars with no questions asked for stones brought in by wildcat miners.

Even beer joined in the spirit of Kasai's revival. A new beer factory built by the French-owned company Onibra opened in March 1996 with an ad campaign that appealed to the Lubas' heightened sense of ethnic solidarity by urging residents to "drink the beer of Mbuji-Mayi!" Freshly painted signs around the city—KAMANA MPATA SKOL—YOU WON'T GO WRONG WITH SKOL—told the story of Kasai's new economic opportunities. With an investment of $3 million and the creation of one hundred and fifty new jobs, the beer factory initially started producing 1.5 million bottles a month.

Again, Kasai profited from the demise of Shaba, the source of Simba beer, which used to enjoy great popularity in the region until the ethnic pogrom. To keep costs down, Onibra cannibalized equipment from several derelict factories around Congo, including Kinshasa and Lubumbashi. The milling plant came from Shaba, as did most of the management, and the storage vats, from a plant in Kinshasa, took four months to reach Mbuji-Mayi after a hazardous journey across Zaire's collapsing infrastructure—a boat ride on the Zaire River, a train excursion, and a final run of several hundred miles by truck along routes that are roads in name only.

Onibra officials say they expect a quick return on their investment, given the captive market of consumers who are both thirsty and flush with diamond dollars. "This is the one place in the entire country where it is worth building something new," said Benôit des Camps, a Belgian technician who was born in Mbuji-Mayi but emigrated to Brussels. "Compared to the rest of the country, Mbuji-Mayi is moving ahead. The diamonds and big population make it a perfect market for beer."

Diamonds are the lifeblood of Mbuji-Mayi. Before their discovery at the turn of the century, the area was dotted with small settlements and homesteads. Development of the mining sector in the 1920s laid the groundwork for the modern city of Mbuji-Mayi, whose very name encapsulates an attempt by African residents to settle their own internal disputes. "Originally, the place was known as Bakwanda, which was the name of a local clan," said Professor Tshimankinda. "The people decided to change the name because there were a lot of conflicts among the clans. So they tried to find a name that did not have to do with any particular clan. They chose mbuji-mayi, which literally means 'the goat in water.' In the Luba language, 'the goat in water' symbolizes the first diamond which was found in the river. It was believed here that there was a goat in the river with a big diamond on its head. So they gave the name Mbuji-Mayi to the town, and to the river, too."

Up and down the river valley, thousands of wildcat miners, known locally as clandestines, waded through crocodile-infested pools of water and knee-deep pits of mud in search of high-quality gems and the more common industrial diamonds. Officially, no one except authorized personnel was allowed into MIBA's expansive mine, which was guarded by a combination of Belgian and British security firms. At the entrance each day, policemen could be seen dragging away shirtless young men with their hands tied behind their back. "*Clandestines*," said Kazadi Bakeba, a mine guide. They were caught attempting to infiltrate the complex and could expect three months in jail for their effort. Along the wide, muddy tracks that lead to the various digging, cleaning, and sorting installations, however, there were signs that the *clandestines* were not so clandestine. Gangs of young men in tan shorts and shirts, apparently the standard-issue uniform for the *clandestines*, popped up everywhere. As soon as they heard a vehicle, they dashed out of sight, but quickly returned when they realized it was not the police. "You see that hill there," Kazadi said, pointing to a ridge fifty yards away; "that is the border of the mine and they can work there legally. So what do they do? When no one is looking they simply come into the mine, pick up some diamonds, and as soon as they detect our presence, they run back up the hill."

In fact, security at the mine appeared incredibly lax, and it was a wonder why MIBA did not dismiss the companies they contracted to keep out the *clandestines*. Over at the new dredge provided by De Beers under MIBA's modernization scheme, however, it became clear that something else was at work. The dredge, an awkward metallic monster several stories high, sucked up earth from a pool of brown water next to the Mbuji-Mayi River, while fifty or so men and women swam around and walked in the shallows as if on a Sunday picnic. The tiny metal tin cans in their hands suggested their true intent. When asked why there were so many *clandestines*, Kazadi said, "We can't shoot them, can we? It's not worth shooting a person for diamonds."

President Mobutu had other ideas, of course. Shooting was precisely what the army did in July 1979 when its troops attacked a group of *clandestines* and reportedly killed ninety-seven people. Not surprisingly, Mobutu took strong issue with the revelation of the murders by two Belgian human rights groups at the time. Only three people had died in the assault, he irately declared.[29] That massacre is another reason that Mobutu was so hated in Kasai.

MIBA's decision to turn a blind eye toward the *clandestines* and their diamond-scrounging ways went beyond simple humanitarian concerns. It in fact constituted a sort of unspoken welfare policy, to allow some of the jobless young men to earn something for their families, perhaps to finance their futures or their marriages to young women sitting anxiously at their parents' home or engaging in day-to-day market trading awaiting the time when their beloved will find the goat with the diamond on its head, the *mbuji-mayi*, to pay for their hand. In a city where formal employment was down to a single-digit figure and where so much wealth was concentrated in so few hands—mostly those who retired each evening into the beautiful houses of "MIBA town" with their small armies of servants and satellite dishes—MIBA's slack policy toward the *clandestines* seemed positively enlightened from the point of view of self-preservation. "They don't really find so many as to damage the company's earnings, and it's important for the community to feel they have a stake in the riches of Kasai," Kazadi said. "Otherwise, one day there could be real trouble." A British security guard who worked at the diamond-sorting center said he could not understand MIBA's indifference to the *clandestines,* but that to him it was nothing new. "I have been working in Africa thirty years, in Angola, Sierra Leone, just about everywhere, and it is always like this. Everywhere there is a mine, the locals gather around, sneaking in and stealing," he said. "This would not happen in Europe." No, it would not.

As the presence of the *clandestines* confirmed, for thousands of people in Kasai economic prosperity was elusive. At the lowest rung of society were those refugee families from Shaba who were unable to find work at the mine, the beer factory, or in the scores of small businesses that opened up in recent years. Most vulnerable among them were the artisans and construction workers who were employees at Gecamines, were used to cash salaries, and had no experience in living off the land. They survived in resettlement centers on the outskirts of town in makeshift waddle-and-daub homes, dependent on aid from the Catholic Church and international relief agencies, and whatever else they could earn by engaging in petty market trading. Many were still traumatized by the violence in Shaba and by the loss of loved ones during the ethnic cleansing there. One of them was Yombo Pierre Kabasele, a tall, strong man who lived with his wife and six children in a settlement camp with nearly a thousand other families seven miles outside Mbuji-Mayi. He sat in the shade of his hut one afternoon with his eighteen-month-old daughter, Bashala, and eight-year-old son Yombo, whiling away the day.

Sitting idle did not come easy to Kabasele, whose powerful arms and massive hands betrayed his former profession as a mason at Gecamines. "I have tried farming, but as you can see I'm not very good at it," he said, glancing with a sheepish smile at his tiny garden of a few cassava plants and several drooping corn stalks. "I need work, but there are no jobs right now. My main task is to look after the children." Once a salaried employee for the biggest company in Congo, Kabasele joined 90 percent of the country's 16-million-strong workforce, eager for work but with little chance of a job in the so-called formal sector of the economy. Even in Kasai, with its modestly expanding opportunities, finding employment is difficult, and for a displaced person, virtually impossible. For Kabasele and his family and millions of others, the informal sector or the black market was the only market.

His descent into impoverishment began in 1992, when the Shaba politicians embarked on their policy of ethnic cleansing to ingratiate themselves with President Mobutu, who was angered and threatened by the Luba upstart Tshisekedi and his campaign for democracy and good governance, which inspired the young and the opposition. Mobutu was particularly displeased that the national conference chose Tshisekedi as prime minister.

Tension in Shaba had been rising for weeks following speeches by Governor Kyungu wa Kumwanza demanding that Tshisekedi's supporters be driven from the province. "We were all following his speeches very closely," Kabasele said. "He said something like 'Since Tshisekedi wants power for himself, then all the Lubas should leave Shaba.' I remember him saying that if Tshisekedi was not willing to share power, then he should be content to be president of his own region, meaning Kasai. 'This region is ours,' Kyungu said. That's when he sent the army out to set fire to everyone's houses. You see, they were jealous of the people from Kasai because the Lubas had the best jobs in the big companies, the courts, and the hospital."

Kyungu wa Kumwanza knew that he could find enough people in Shaba to carry out the violence, by either bribing or coercing them, especially if there was the prospect of financial gain. As the Hutu extremists in Rwanda were to realize two years later, and for that matter as the Nazis discovered in Germany, normally decent people can be enticed into participating in ethnic cleansing and even genocide when there is loot to be had. "As I was heading home from work," Kabasele recalled, "I saw that all my Luba neighbors were running away from their homes. I was told that we must go straight to the train station. There were groups of soldiers and civilians armed with bows, arrows, and *pangas* [machetes]. 'If you don't comply, you will be beheaded,' they told us. I was frightened because we could see everyone with their luggage on their heads and the houses were on fire. Everyone was running to the train station."

Kabasele's wife Masenge had already packed their belongings and was heading for the trains which the Shaba government had organized to send the Lubas home. While they were on the road, their five-month-old daughter Mbuyie, who was born on June 30, the Congo's independence day, was killed. "The Katangan soldiers were trying to take the baby from my wife," Kabasele said. "The soldiers grabbed Mbuyie and smashed her on the ground." Together with his mother Tshitolo and his wife's parents, Kabasele headed for Kasai. "There was nothing when we came. We were sleeping in the open air. Some aid agencies came with some food, tents, and firewood. At first we did not feel welcome here. There was a great deal of resentment because we had good jobs in Shaba. The local people said, 'You felt more civilized and believed that we were peasants involved in witchcraft, but now you see you are back.'"

As bad as conditions were in the refugee camp, Kabasele and his family had no intention of trying to return to Shaba. There was no work at Gecamines, and he lost all his property. "I have very bad memories of Shaba now. The time when everyone was living together is long past. Now for me Shaba is a place of pain. It's where my daughter died. For me, the future is here in Kasai. It's the same for all of the Luba. This is our home and we have to start our lives again."

The family depended on what Masenge earned selling paints and dyes at the market. She left early in the morning to walk the four miles to town and returned after dark. On a good day, she could earn about 50 million old Zaires, or $3.50, enough to buy some corn and cassava flour to which Kabasele added cassava leaves from the few surviving plants in his failed garden. He was the family cook as well. But for the family to have a chance of leaving the camp, Kabasele needed to find work. For a time he was employed on a construction site, but the Mobutu-appointed governor who owned it was sacked for selling plots of state land, and Kabasele was never paid. "I want to work for individuals now. Working for the government is no good. I would like to go around town to search for jobs, but there is no one to look after the children. If my wife doesn't go to the market, we don't eat. I am not a farmer. What I know is building houses. I have always been a mason and I will always be a mason."

The Catholic Church has been caring for families like Kabasele's and one thousand others who returned from Shaba, but its emphasis is on self-help, not handouts. Seeds and tools are favored over bags of corn and rice. This was part of the Church's decision to sponsor development work in the 1980s, when the devastating effects of Mobutu's misrule and the *authenticité* program were all too apparent. Traditionally patron of most of the still-functioning schools and health clinics, the Catholic hierarchy embarked on a campaign to promote small-scale empowerment. It established development bureaus in each diocese to support projects in agriculture, animal husbandry, and infrastructural improvement. Special attention is focused on educating women in income-generating schemes to produce and sell practical consumer goods, such as textiles, soap, salt, and dyes. "On the ground, we assist the people to help themselves, so that they take responsibility for their lives," said Abbot Ciamalakanda. "Our method is participation—for the people to participate in decision making and in carrying out the decisions." In Kasai, that philosophy dovetailed nicely with the region's go-it-alone strategy.

In the post-Mobutu era, the fate of Congo and perhaps central Africa will depend on the Kabila administration's ability to convince its people that they have a greater stake in the new order than they did in the old one. That should not be difficult given the abysmal record of the Mobutu government. But to succeed, the new government will have to tread carefully and take into account all the various coping mechanisms people have built to survive the age of Mobutu, whether it be locally run schools, traditional forms of justice, or more assertive regional aspirations. Mobutu's Zaire might have died, but Congolese civil society never did.

Though a Luba himself, from Shaba province, President Kabila has found Kasai Oriental a troublesome region, not the least because he did not include the much-loved Mobutu critic, Etienne Tshisekedi, in the first cabinet. Within a month of taking office in May 1997, there were reports of demonstrations in Mbuji-Mayi and a passive resistance campaign to protest the alleged occupation of the area by mainly Banyamulenge Tutsis, who formed the cutting edge of Kabila's army.

The taste of local autonomy Kasai Oriental enjoyed in Mobutu's last years will be difficult to erase. "The majority of people want federalism and respect for the feelings of the region," said Abbott Ciamalakanda. "The population has become aware and more determined." Treated with political sensitivity and a healthy dose of investment, Kasai could harness its diamond wealth with local ingenuity to become an economic engine of central Congo and a key to helping the government rebuild the national economy. If Kinshasa acts with an iron hand, Kasai is likely to retreat into itself and seethe with hostility.

Asked before Mobutu's fall how the people of Kasai would react to attempts from Kinshasa to snuff out Kasai's autonomous pretentions, the responses of Abbot Ciamalakanda and his assistant Florent Mulumba carried a warning that remains valid today. "We are not prophets but in politics there are always surprises," said the elderly and more cautious Abbot Ciamalakanda. The younger Father Mulumba was more forthright. "Let's not lose sight of the determination of the people to set themselves free."

Circling Spirits of the Age

Three days before his arrest, Dr. Beko Ransome-Kuti was perched behind a desk cluttered with papers and books, his high forehead bent down slightly in a somber pose. The phone rang. His body heaved a light sigh of fatigue. Limply cradling the receiver at such a distance from his face as to suggest a faint fear that it might bite him, he muttered low at first, then louder when no one on the other end responded. The line was dead. Replacing the phone, he clicked his tongue in disgust.

Nigeria's telephone system brings new meaning to the word "awful." Minutes later came another call, successful this time, and he sent the fax machine humming into action to transmit to human rights groups letters from political detainees that had been smuggled out by sympathetic prison guards. The detainees were in secret jail cells on charges of plotting to come to power the same way the current military regime did—by *coup d'état.* Few believed the allegations. Among the prime suspects was Olusegun Obasanjo, the only general in Nigeria's history to return power from the military to a democratic government.

Throughout the afternoon, Dr. Ransome-Kuti alternated between transmitting the letters and attending to relatives of the prisoners who stopped by to see about publicizing their cases to the local newspapers, to the foreign press, to anyone who would listen. There was a special urgency in their pleas. Just two days before, the military authorities publicly executed forty-three armed robbers outside Lagos' notorious Kirikiri maximum-security prison and disposed of their bodies in a garbage truck. Now there was growing concern that the firing squad was just warming up. "They do not care about human life," said Beko, as Dr. Ransome-Kuti is universally known by friend and foe alike. "It just shows they would not blink an eye if they killed the alleged coup plotters. This is a brutal and very dangerous regime."

Another one of the military's periodic clampdowns against opponents, real or imaginary, was in full flow, and as usual Beko was fighting from the metaphorical trenches, his only weapon the spoken and written word. This time the stakes had reached new heights. Obasanjo, the former head of state, and thirty-nine other prominent personalities and military officers were arrested and convicted by a secret tribunal of planning to overthrow the regime of General Sani Abacha. No one knew who might be picked up next. When one of Obasanjo's associates, Mrs. Titi Ajanaku, who was detained for four months on suspicion of links to the alleged rebellion, was finally released, she summed up the fleeting nature of individual freedom in modern Nigeria. "Over four months incarceration over something I know nothing about. I was miraculously picked up on March 9 and was miraculously released on July 13. God is wonderful."

It was a typical day in the life of Beko, an unassuming medical doctor who was sucked into the maelstrom of Nigerian politics and emerged somewhat reluctantly as a leader of the pro-democracy movement. A gentle, slender, at times frail-looking man, Beko appears physically overmatched in the contest of wills he has chosen to engage with the military. With a voice so soft that it is often difficult to hear what he is saying, it seems unfathomable that he poses a threat to the rulers of sub-Saharan Africa's most populous nation. He has never been in the best of health, and the months of detentions, the constant late-night arrests, the telephone threats have taken their toll. As the years of his running confrontation with Nigeria's military rulers pass the decade mark, he becomes thinner and paler. In seventy-two hours from now, he would be behind bars once again, but if he did not suspect his fate, it would not have surprised him.

When his late brother, the Afro-beat superstar Fela Kuti who died of AIDS on August 12, 1997, composed a song about standing up for one's beliefs, about the man who refuses to run—"I no go run, Na man dey stand, Na goat dey run"[1]—he could have been singing about Beko. Since he threw himself into the human rights campaigns and the pro-democracy movement in the mid-1980s, Beko has never run. The military authorities have threatened him,

attempted to bribe him—a common practice known in Nigerian parlance as "settling"—and repeatedly jailed him, but to no avail. They
cannot break him. Beko remains standing, *Na man dey stand*. He is
the president of the Campaign for Democracy, a pesky alliance of
human rights groups, women's associations, and student organizations that keeps snapping relentlessly at the generals' heels no matter how much repression it faces.

That day, though, as he sat in his office chain-smoking cigarettes,
Beko seemed distracted, from time to time rolling his huge brown
eyes and shaking his head at the chaos swirling around him. "They're
crazy," he said. "They won't stop until they destroy everything."

Foreign leaders and personalities from Nelson Mandela and
Pope John Paul II to the British and U.S. governments urged General Abacha to show clemency to Obasanjo and the others, but the
appeals rang hollow. It was a familiar pattern. The same thing happened in June 1993, when Chief Moshood Abiola, the Muslim millionaire, won the country's first free elections in a decade. The military regime decided it did not fancy the outcome, so it annulled the
entire electoral process in the name of promoting democracy. When
Abiola was arrested for declaring himself president, the outside
world complained, but nothing happened, and Abiola remained in
jail. Like most of those involved in the human rights movement,
Beko was growing embittered by the outside world's failure to go
beyond words and take action against the regime. "Maybe if they
kill Obasanjo," he said with a sarcastic smile, "then the international
community will finally do something."

It was July 1995, and Nigeria, 100 million people strong, resem-
bled one of those massive creaky "mammy wagons" that ply its
streets and highways, hurtling down the road hopelessly packed
with goods and passengers, riding on bald tires toward probable disaster with the driver all but asleep at the wheel. Long gone are the
days when the giant of Africa was supposed to lead the continent to
economic and political deliverance and to shine as a symbol of pride
for the African race. That role has passed to Nelson Mandela and his
multiracial South Africa. Nigeria today hangs like a millstone around
the neck of West Africa, its entrenched military junta giving spiritual
succor to a host of petty dictators who rise and fall in neighboring
states. As Pierre Sane, the Senegalese secretary general of Amnesty
International, wrote: "When Africa threw off the chains of colonialism, Nigeria was looked to as a beacon of hope and progress by all
Africans. As a young Senegalese man, I shared this enthusiasm. A

country of enormous energy and potential, Nigeria seemed destined to lead the people of Africa to a better future. Thirty years later, Nigeria is looked at with despair, as successive governments have become locked into a cycle of contempt for human rights. Nigeria has instead been the inspiration for those African leaders who oppose justice and freedom."[2]

As it heads toward its fortieth year of independence from Britain, Nigeria's very name has become synonymous in the outside world with corrupt military leaders, multi-million-dollar business fraud, drug mafias, imprisonment of pro-democracy activists, lawyers, union leaders, and a host of other unsavory practices. A laughing-stock of the international community and a source of shame to most Africans, Nigeria symbolizes all that is said to have gone wrong in postcolonial Africa. Those once proud universities, Ibadan, Ifè, and Ahmadu Bello, have degenerated into dilapidated shells of their former selves, literally robbed of the excellence that spawned a generation of highly trained professionals and once attracted students and professors from Europe and the United States. Chinua Achebe captures the despair in his classic book, *The Trouble with Nigeria*: "Does it ever worry us that history which neither personal wealth nor power can pre-empt will pass terrible judgment on us, pronounce anathema on our names when we have accomplished our betrayal and passed on? We have lost the twentieth century; are we bent on seeing that our children also lose the twenty-first? God Forbid."[3]

Other than its marvelous Gold Medal victory in soccer in the 1996 Olympics, Nigeria's biggest claim to fame today is its position among the leading heroin traffickers into Europe and the United States, even though not one poppy plant grows on its soil. Nigerians are natural traders. As their economic fortunes have declined, many of Nigeria's financial wizards and professionals have turned their considerable talents to the lucrative trade of supplying the industrialized world with the cocaine and heroin its youth demands.

Sophisticated drug-trafficking syndicates operate in Nigeria, often involving highly efficient Igbo dealers from the east, where commodity trading has a long tradition. Entire villages have been reorganized into drug-running schools. The syndicates obtain their heroin supplies mostly from Thailand, their cocaine from Brazil, and smuggle both to the West. A favored method of trafficking was to hire poor men, women, and children, all desperate to earn hard currency, purchase the round-trip air tickets to Europe and the United States, and before their departure have them consume 500 to 900 grams of heroin or cocaine in balloons or condoms, washed down with thick okra soup. These Nigerian couriers were dubbed "swallowers" in U.S. drug enforcement circles. Fifteen thousand Nigerians were arrested worldwide for drug trafficking in the 1980s, but the trend has worsened dramatically in the 1990s. As Robert Nieves, the U.S. Drug Enforcement Agency's chief of international operations, testified on Capitol Hill in March 1995, "Nigerian traffickers are pivotal to the worldwide trafficking" of heroin.

To suggest the involvement of senior Nigerian officials in the drug trade can be dangerous. In October 1986, journalist Dele Giwa, editor of the popular magazine *Newswatch*, was killed by a parcel bomb after he mentioned to his colleagues the idea of investigating the widely rumored but unproven involvement of former dictator General Ibrahim Babangida's wife Maryam in the drug trade. A day before his murder, according to a leading human rights group, the Constitutional Rights Project, Babangida's national security adviser telephoned Giwa's wife to ask for directions to their home. When the package arrived, it was marked: "From the office of the C-in-C." As Giwa opened the parcel over breakfast, he said, "This must be from the president." Those were his last words.

The most depressing thing about Nigeria is its unrealized potential. Everything is possible, yet nothing is possible. It is a country of frenetic hustle and bustle; of unflagging confidence and industriousness; of brilliant writers, such as Chinua Achebe, Ben Okri, and the Nobel prize-winning Wole Soyinka; of music stars such as King Sunny Ade, Fela Kuti, and his son Femi; and of athletic prowess on the world's football pitches. It is also a land whose people race around furiously just to stay in the same place, not to lose ground to the rising waves of poverty, of dirt, of despair about the future for their children. All the while, a tiny wealthy elite hovers around a sumptuous banquet set by a clique of military officers with unbridled access to the fruits of Nigeria's multi-billion-dollar oil-exporting industry.

To understand the challenge Beko and others face, consider the history of Nigeria. Its creation out of three hundred ethnic groups by the British colonizers can only be described as slipshod. Its formation in 1914 as a distinct entity was carried out in the interests of the British Empire and not the region's African inhabitants, who were already deeply traumatized by centuries of slave trade and European occupation. The modern state of Nigeria was born in 1960, supposedly as a federation of three relatively autonomous regions: the north, where the mainly Muslim Hausa-Fulani people of the precolonial Islamic state, the Sokoto Caliphate, ruled over hundreds of minority ethnic groups; the east, where the largely republican and Christian Igbo people dominated dozens more minorities; and the west, where the Yoruba people reigned supreme. Political leaders vying for power resorted to inflaming ethnic and religious passions. The death knell of the federation came in 1966, when the military staged its first fateful intervention in politics, killing Prime Minister Tafawa Balewa and the premiers of the northern and western regions. That set the stage for the launch of the three-year secessionist war by the Igbo people of the east, to set up their own independent state of Biafra. The conflict cost a million lives, but the federal army won in 1970, and the east remained part of Nigeria.

Since then, Nigeria gradually but relentlessly came to be lorded over by generals ruling in the name of maintaining national unity. "The military used to have some mystique, but everybody now realizes that they are just armed robbers in uniform," Dr. Suleimanu Kumo, a Muslim lawyer, said one afternoon over tea at his home in the northern city of Kano. "They are doing it openly, brazenly." Except for a brief spell of democratic government from 1979 to 1983, a succession of military strongmen have built brick by brick a centralized state that has mimicked the divide-and-rule tactics of the colonial era to undermine all autonomous civilian institutions—from the associations of medical doctors and lawyers to students' and workers' unions—and to divert the country's considerable resources into foreign bank accounts and property in European capitals, particularly London. As Claude Ake has written, "Somehow Africa succeeded in crystallizing the form and the content of the colonial state, reproducing it in personal rule, the single-party state, and military rule."[4]

Nigeria's petroleum industry has earned over $200 billion in export revenues over the past twenty years, but the country has almost nothing to show for it except a $34.7 billion foreign debt. A per capita income of $240 remains unchanged from the pre-oil days. Those who have attempted to protest against the regime of the day have been jailed, threatened, bribed, or killed. Nigeria is bereft of a unified opposition to military rule. "There is this big chasm between the military and the rest of the country," says Mathew Kukah, the outspoken Roman Catholic priest. "There is nothing in between. Because, whether it is the labor, the lawyers, the doctors, all these associations, have all been scuttled, deliberately scuttled."

The result, Beko often says with typically wry sense of humor, is that Nigerians are "demented people," who believe they have "no future, no tomorrow." You can judge the prevailing mood of Lagos' residents by the way they relieve themselves in public, says Sully Abu, former editor of the respected weekly magazine, *African Guardian*. Men urinating in broad daylight in the city's streets have always been a common sight in Lagos, so normal in fact that on the walls of many government buildings warnings are painted boldly: DON'T URINATE HERE. Few Lagosians are proud of the fact, but the reality is that there are no public toilets to cater to the millions of people who spend their entire day locked in traffic jams or hawking on the streets. It must be said, however, that one never sees women relieving themselves in public.

In recent years morale has plummeted to such depths that men defecate in full view of street market vendors and passing vehicles. "It shows the depression of our society, how far the standards have fallen," Sully says. "During the 1980s, when the petty corruption started to become really obvious, I always prided myself on never giving a bribe to the police, or at the airport. I remember telling my friends that I bribed no one for a telephone or for housing or to pick up my own luggage. Now I can't say that. No one cares anymore."

What has gone wrong in a country that many Nigerians firmly believed would reach Europe's level of development within a few decades? Nigeria's problem, Chinua Achebe has written, is its spectacular lack of principled leadership:

> The trouble with Nigeria is simply and squarely a failure of leadership. There is nothing basically wrong with the Nigerian character. There is nothing wrong with the Nigerian land or climate or water or air or anything else. The Nigerian problem is the unwillingness or inability of its leaders to rise to the responsibility, to the challenge of personal example which are the hallmarks of true leadership. . . . I am saying that Nigeria *can* change today if she discovers leaders who have the will, the ability and the vision. Such people are rare in any time or place. But it is the duty of enlightened citizens to lead the way in their discovery and to create an atmosphere conducive to their emergence. If this conscious effort is not made, good leaders, like good money, will be driven out by bad.[5]

Achebe's diagnosis of his own country's ills could apply to much of the rest of the continent. The pattern has been repeated over and over. The wealthy and the powerful appropriate their nation's income and send it abroad, leaving the rest of the country to stagnate. Hospitals, schools, universities, and the general economy are starved of financial resources until they are on the brink of collapse. It is of little consequence to the wealthy, however, since the elites simply fly their families to Europe for medical treatment or to continue their studies. That used to be the pattern, and to some extent it still is.

But the 1990s have seen a countervailing dynamic at work. No country has made a more dramatic turnaround than Uganda under President Yoweri Museveni. Long remembered for the economic devastation and unspeakable atrocities carried out by dictators Idi Amin and Milton Obote, Uganda is now a leading light on the African horizon. Museveni's government might not be strictly democratic, but the stability and rapid economic development it has brought speaks of a successful administration. Since assuming power after a guerrilla war against the Obote government, Museveni has shed his leftist leanings and pursued free market economics with vigor. He believes in "no-party democracy," which means that candidates for local and national office must stand on their own. Political parties in the Ugandan context, without economic growth and the emergence of a middle class, will simply descend into ethnic and religious rivalries that hold the country down, Museveni maintains. The press is freer than it has ever been, and stories criticizing ministers and officials for corruption are published routinely. Rising agricultural production, increased foreign investment, and limited infrastructural development has had the economy running at a 6 percent growth rate for the past decade.

Museveni calls his ideology simply "modernization." Like-minded leaders include President Issayas Aferworki of Eritrea, another country devastated by years of war, the result of its secession from Ethiopia, and Paul Kagame in Rwanda.

Aferworki, another former leftist pursuing a capitalist road to development, has allowed the formation of political parties as long as they are not set up along ethnic and religious lines. Whether Laurent Kabila's new administration in the Congo will become the latest convert to the model of decent government, no-party politics, and an open economy pioneered by Museveni remains an unanswered question. But no foreign leaders have more influence over Kabila than Museveni and Kagame because of their strong backing of the rebellion which toppled Mobutu.

The initial stirrings of Africa's new democracies occurred in the former French colonies of West Africa, such as Benin and Mali, where popular protests forced entrenched dictatorships to give way to democratic governments. "National conferences" gathered thousands of delegates who negotiated new constitutions that enshrined the basics of democratic rule, such as free speech, a separation of powers, and regular multiparty elections. Since then, Benin, once ruled by a Soviet-style government, has celebrated two peaceful transfers of power to elected administrations, the last one, ironically, back to the former dictator, Mathieu Kerekou, who shed his Marxist ideology and repackaged himself as a born-again Christian. Mali has become a showcase following the downfall of the dictator Moussa Traoré in 1991. With the election of President Alpha Oumar Konaré the following year, Mali won high marks both at home and abroad for the establishment of a democratic culture and an effective economic reform program.

Another important breakthrough took place in October 1991 in the southern African nation of Zambia, when twenty-seven years of authoritarian rule by President Kenneth Kaunda came crashing down in the first free and fair elections in two decades. Kaunda's was the first one-party government among the former British colonies to taste defeat at the ballot box. As the partial results of the polls were broadcast over Zambia's national radio on the night of October 31, celebrations erupted throughout the country. The scene at a bar in Kalingalinga, a poor township on the edge of the capital, Lusaka, was one of euphoria. Shouts of "He's gone! He's gone!" and "The hour has come" erupted as the crowd savored the landslide victory by Frederick Chiluba's Movement for Multi-party Democracy, the MMD. Over the din of chaotic celebrations and dancing to rhumba music, Edward Mwanza, a thirty-year-old market trader and part-time construction worker, bellowed, "It was the people's wish. Twenty-seven years is too long, and people were just tired of a one-man show. We wanted change."

In many ways, it was in Kalingalinga that Kaunda's regime began to unravel the year before. In June 1990, the government raised prices for the nation's staple, maize meal, and students from the University of Zambia, just five hundred yards from the township, marched into Kalingalinga. Together with local residents, they looted state-owned shops. The ensuing rioting, which spread to the rest of Lusaka, marked the first time that students and unemployed youth had joined forces, and the protest took on a decidedly political tone.

"The MMD had formed some months earlier, but those riots were the beginning of the end for Kaunda," said Robinson Makayi, editor of the independent newspaper *The Weekly Post.* "It succeeded because it was never planned, and Zambia would never be the same. Kaunda did not know it then, but power was reverting to the people." At the end of that month, a lone soldier briefly occupied the national radio station and announced, incorrectly it turned out, Kaunda's ouster. Thousands of people poured into the streets, singing and dancing for several hours until the security forces restored order. From then on, the MMD and Chiluba, a former trade unionist, went from strength to strength, forcing the government into repeated concessions. A new constitution ensuring multiparty democracy was written, the High Court forced the state-controlled media to broadcast opposition propaganda, and all political detainees were released. "We Zambians could just not take it anymore," said Steven Phiri, a forty-six-year-old bricklayer in Kalingalinga. "The old man just had to go."

After the results were official, Chiluba sat in a friend's house in the center of Lusaka, savoring his victory and waxing eloquently about how he would ensure that democracy took root in Zambia. He also promised not to harass Kaunda. "I want the fears to vanish, to disappear from his mind," he said. "There will be no witch-hunting. Kenneth Kaunda is the father of this country so we must show him respect." Sadly, after moving into the State House, Chiluba broke his word on both counts. Over the ensuing years, his government repeatedly attempted to muzzle the independent press and orchestrated the approval of an amendment to the constitution that banned Kaunda from contesting the 1996 general elections. Eleventh-hour pleas from Nelson Mandela and former President Jimmy Carter to allow Kaunda to run failed to move Chiluba. All foreign election monitors refused invitations to scrutinize the election. Not surprisingly, Chiluba was reelected with 82 percent of the vote in a low turnout. As soon as the elections were over, police raided the offices of the Zambian election monitors, and several prominent opposition figures went into hiding. Right now, democracy in Zambia is decidedly weak.

Since Chiluba's first victory in 1991, however, the rest of southern Africa has gone through a sea-change. South Africa celebrated its first-ever democratic elections in April 1994, and Mozambique sealed the end to its civil war with a free and fair vote in October. That same year in Malawi, a democratic system replaced the thirty-year dictatorship of Hastings Banda. In Zimbabwe, where President Robert Mugabe's ZANU party has won all local and general elections since independence, there are voices demanding change. None has struck a deeper popular chord than Margaret Dongo, a former guerrilla fighter in the war for independence who defected from ZANU after accusing party officials of corruption. Dongo won a parliamentary by-election in November 1996 and remains a fiery critic of the government.

The raw courage it takes for an individual to cross the line into opposition politics in Africa is difficult to exaggerate. The decision of the Kenyan businessman Kenneth Matiba to support calls for multiparty democracy in 1988 cost him a term in jail, where he was beaten and suffered a stroke. The prodemocracy movement which emerged with such promise and enthusiasm in the tiny West African state of Togo was literally beaten into the ground by President Gnassingbé Eyadèma. A "national conference" of democratic forces had, like their counterparts in Benin and Mali, met in July 1991 to restore constitutional rule after twenty-five years of Eyadèma's dictatorship. The conference stripped Eyadèma of many of his powers and set up a transitional government headed by Joseph Kokou Koffigoh. Several months later, the army took over the national radio station and kidnapped Koffigoh from his office in Lomé, the capital, at gunpoint. Then came an assassination attempt on the strongest opposition presidential candidate, Gilchrist Olympio, son of Togo's first president, Silvanus Olympio, who was killed in the 1963 *coup d'état* that brought Eyadèma to power. After a year-long strike in support of democracy, Eyadèma organized presidential elections in August 1993 but banned Gilchrist Olympio from contesting them. The opposition boycotted the polls; Eyadèma won 93 percent of the votes. Only one-third of the electorate bothered to vote.

In Nigeria, the seeds of democracy and good government have found the soil almost impenetrable. Anyone actively supporting an end to military rule can count on threats and an extended time in jail. Democratic spokesmen such as Wole Soyinka have fled into exile for fear of their lives. Beko Ransome-Kuti has never been short of courage. Resistance to tyranny literally flows in his blood. He grew up in the town of Abeokuta, about thirty miles northwest of

Lagos, which the first European missionaries described as "a sunrise in the tropics." Abeokuta is a city with a remarkable history, where the "modernist" ideas of the freed slaves in Sierra Leone mixed with the more traditionalist local African chiefs to produce a revolution in political thought. A list of personalities who have emerged from Abeokuta in the modern era reads like a Nigerian *Who's Who*: Wole Soyinka; Chief Moshood Abiola, the businessman who became a presidential candidate and later the country's best known political prisoner; Olusegun Obasanjo, Nigeria's only Yoruba president; Beko, his brothers Fela Kuti the singer and Professor Ulikoye Ransome-Kuti, a former health minister; and the Harvard-trained industrialist Chief Ernest Shonekan.

Abeokuta was founded in 1829 by Sodoke, a chief of the Egba clan, who led a group of refugees in flight from the wars and banditry that followed the collapse of the Yoruba state at Oyo. Civil wars raged among the various clans that made up the Yorubas, who were under pressure simultaneously from the expansionist Islamic Sokoto Caliphate to the north and the powerful slave-trading Dahomey kingdom to the west in the modern-day republic of Benin. Warriors roamed the countryside, and fighting broke out for control of the nearby city of Ibadan. Within twenty years of the founding of Abeokuta, there came a new influx of refugees, this time Yoruba ex-slaves freed by the Royal Navy and originally deposited in Freetown, Sierra Leone, as well as some returning from Brazil and the Americas. Among them was Beko's grandfather. The settlers of Abeokuta were open to new ideas and alliances. Into the mix stepped Britain's Church Missionary Society (CMS), which saw the ex-slaves, alienated from the traditional African rulers who had sold them into bondage, as the ideal recruits to spread their message throughout West Africa. By 1854, four CMS stations were established and began to run catechist classes. Five years later, Abeokuta gave birth to Nigeria's first newspaper, the Yoruba-language *Iwe-Irobin*, and the missionaries developed an orthography of Yoruba to translate the Bible that is still in use today.

The ex-slaves brought with them from their stay in Sierra Leone the belief that the only way Africa could move ahead in the modern world was to embrace Western concepts of constitutional government. Despite their attraction to Western culture, however, they wanted to govern themselves, and they were horrified when Britain declared Lagos a colony in 1861. The discovery of quinine helped to combat malaria, a major barrier to European penetration, and whites started arriving in West Africa and replacing Africans in the Church. Four years later, the traditional chiefs united with the Christian-educated African elite in Abeokuta to set up in effect an autonomous government, known as the Egba United Board of Management. The heady cocktail of African and Western ideas, Christianity and traditional Yoruba religion—the Ifá divination system— had carried Abeokuta and its favorite sons to the forefront of the anticolonial struggle. For many historians, that moment marked the beginning of West African political thought of the modern, postcolonial era.

Fearing that the European churchmen were the beachhead of British imperialism, Abeokuta expelled the missionaries in 1867. "Christianity was domesticated, with many different versions," Soyinka said in an interview at his Abeokuta office before his flight into exile. "The political rebels of the last century were also rebels from Christianity, who broke away and formed their own independent, heavily Africanized churches." And parallel to Christianity, Yoruba religion survived. "There is something very democratic about the Yoruba pantheon," Soyinka added in his resonant voice. "The Yoruba allocates to every deity some kind of flaw. It brings them down to mortal level, makes them accountable, makes them undergo penance. It is very sophisticated, which is one of the reasons this religion survived in the Americas."

The unique experiment with self-government was to endure for half a century. In 1914, the British, with the consent of the Alake, a particularly conservative traditional ruler who feared Abeokuta's revolutionary ideas, called in troops of occupation, and the city succumbed to colonial rule. But the tradition of education and political awareness lived on. Before independence, Abeokuta was often at odds with the remnants of the Sokoto Caliphate, which ruled in northern Nigeria until the British troops invaded the area and killed the Sultan. After the end of British rule, Nigeria's succession of northern-dominated military governments saw Abeokuta as an opposition stronghold. "Very often we find ourselves being accused by the rest of the nation of being the ones always causing all the trouble. The country would be unified except for the arrogance of Abeokuta, the Egba people," Soyinka said facetiously. "We think we know too much; we think we are too clever. Then we are accused of taking all the plum jobs, in the judiciary, for instance. We were the first lawyers to come out, so we sort of monopolized the judiciary. Natural litigants. It is part and parcel of our general cantankerousness."

As a youngster, Beko did not share his parents' interest in politics. His father, the Reverend Israel Oludotun Ransome-Kuti, patriarch of the Kuti clan, as principal of Abeokuta Grammar School formed the Nigerian Union of Teachers and led a campaign to demand British recognition of the teachers' right to strike. But by all accounts, his mother, Funmilayo, was the real family firebrand. She organized women to fight for their right to vote and waged many battles against indiscriminate taxation of women by the traditional ruler, the Alake. One of her campaigns forced the Alake to abdicate in 1948.

Like that of Abeokuta itself, Beko's is a hybrid culture, a sometimes uneasy blend of Yoruba beliefs, Christianity, and Islam. "My father was running a school, but he never really discriminated between Christians and Muslims. If you passed the exam, you passed the exam. What he could not stand was to bear only an Arab or Christian name. You have to bear your own indigenous name, like, instead of Suleiman, you should bear Adisa. His whole philosophy was that the good in native culture should be encouraged and the bad should be discouraged. But how you chose the good from the bad became a problem. Because one of the things was that we were not supposed to prostrate for anybody. I presume that came out of two things: hygiene and servility. You should just put your hands behind your back and bow, and the way you carry on will show your respect rather than degrading yourself by lying on the ground and things like that." Abeokuta's openness to foreign cultures is succinctly described by Kole Omotoso, a Nigerian novelist and professor of comparative literature in South Africa, when he writes about Soyinka: "He was born into a culture of celebration, public and private, a culture of dance and song in such a variety it could be bewildering. But also he had been born into a culture that had always made a virtue of taking from others what it thought useful for its continued self-expression and survival."[6]

Beko grew up among a generation of West Africans that was fanatical about education, and his prime concern was to decide whether to become a lawyer or a medical doctor. "The value of education was widely respected, and people strove by all means to get themselves educated." Eventually he chose medicine, and after grammar school his parents scraped together the money, bought him passage on a cargo boat, and sent him to study in Britain, where he completed his medical degree at the University of Manchester in 1963. At the time, Nigeria was brimming with optimism. "We thought that in ten years' time we would have surpassed the UK. The way we saw it, the UK then was just coming here and taking all our resources away, and that if we could use those resources here, the sky was the limit."

After returning to Nigeria, Beko took up posts first at the Lagos University Teaching Hospital and then at the University College Hospital in Ibadan. For the next ten years, he focused on his medical career, and in 1972 joined the Nigerian Medical Association. The dreams of Nigeria overtaking Britain had been shattered by the civil war and rising levels of corruption. It was Beko's work at the medical council which provided his first real taste of how supposed ethnic hostility and regional rivalry between the largely Muslim Hausa-Fulani of north and mainly Christian Aerobes and Igbos of the south was used as a ruse for self-enrichment. Northern hospitals, ostensibly fearing domination by the Yorubas and Igbos, wanted to hire foreign doctors rather than to employ qualified physicians from the south. "I thought it was because people were not confronting each other. Why did they need to bring people from outside Nigeria? I later found out why. They went around recruiting so they could get money. People in India, the Philippines, used to bribe the recruiting team."

A turning point came in 1977, when his mother Funmilayo died after the military authorities raided the home of his rebellious brother Fela. "Fela had a running battle with the army for a few years. They attacked the house, and they threw my mother out the window. She broke her leg. She just never recovered from it. She could not eat or drink. They had to put her on drips and so on for months. I think probably what might have affected her was the fact that after all her hopes to achieve independence the country could degenerate to such a point where people might just come, surround your house, set it on fire, and throw you out the window. It must have been a big shock."

The man who headed the government of the day was General Olusegun Obasanjo, another Abeokuta product. In 1979, he became the first Nigerian military leader to hand over power to an elected administration, a move that won him great respect both at home and abroad. Nigeria's experiment with civilian government would prove to be short-lived, however. Corruption under the elected civilian government was rampant, and when it was reelected in the 1983 polls, which were marred by widespread rigging, the military stepped in again.

The incoming military administration enjoyed wide popularity in its early days. Its bold anticorruption drive, known as the "war against indiscipline," found deep resonance among a population that had seen billions of dollars in petroleum revenues disappear and felt the onset of an economic crisis caused by the collapse of world oil prices, the source of 90 percent of the country's foreign exchange earnings. It was not long, however, before the regime revealed a more repressive side. State Security Decree 2, which allowed indefinite detention without trial, was promulgated in 1984, and the following year the medical association was banned. Beko spent the first of his repeated spells in prison. He was picked up by Nigeria's secret police, the State Security Service, and put in solitary confinement. After a hunger strike, he collapsed and was taken to the hospital.

Nigeria's foreign debt crisis had become so severe by 1985 that the military ruler, General Ibrahim Babangida, opened negotiations with the IMF on a "structural adjustment program," commonly known as SAP, which brought about a massive devaluation of the *naira*. The *naira*, which had been worth twice as much as the U.S. dollar, so strong in fact that taxi drivers would throw foreign currency back in the face of visitors and demand *naira*, went into a free fall from which it has never recovered. Opposition to military rule grew, especially in Beko's home region in the west. Beko left the medical association and took a fateful step across the threshold into politics. "It was not possible to stand on the side anymore when everything was falling apart all over the place," he said. "It started when the hospitals began breaking down. Doctors were complaining that nothing was being done about it. So something just had to be done. At that time, the feeling among the senior doctors was that confrontation was not the way, and they favored lobbying and collaboration. Those of us who did not believe in that just stepped down." In 1989, he joined with a core group of lawyers to set up the Committee for the Defence of Human Rights, which he still heads today.

Despite General Babangida's repeated promises to give way to a civilian government, by 1990 the only people who believed him were foreign diplomats and segments of the Western press. He set up two political parties, the Social Democrats—"a little to the left"—and the Republicans—"a little to the right." Domestically, the soccer-mad Nigerian public gave General Babangida the nickname of "Maradona" after the Argentine football star Diego Maradona, for his fancy political footwork, which left opponents bedazzled. Still willing to work within the system, Beko accepted a controversial government appointment in January 1991 as chairman of the Lagos University Teaching Hospital, where he had first worked after graduating from medical school twenty years before. He did so at the urging of his brother Ulikoye, then the minister of health, but the decision drew criticism from antimilitary activists who feared Beko was selling out. He lasted nine months on the job. When Beko refused to desist from his human rights activities, General Babangida fired him.

The military authorities were particularly irked by the demands by the mushrooming number of human rights groups, almost all of them based in Lagos, for a "national conference," modeled on similar exercises in Benin and Mali, to negotiate Nigeria's political future. By then, Beko's medical clinic in Lagos was transformed into the headquarters of the civil rights movement. Student activists, relatives of prisoners seeking news of their loved ones, and journalists all queued to see him. Satisfactory conversations with him were almost impossible because of the constant ring of the telephone and fax or the repeated interruptions by someone next in line. In November 1991, the fledgling pro-democracy movement met in the southeastern city of Port Harcourt to form the Campaign for Democracy, a broad umbrella of human rights, students', and women's groups, but with little support outside the Yoruba-dominated west. Six months later, the campaign held its first convention in the northern city of Jos. Within days, Beko was again detained. "Babangida had started to clamp down. He had exhausted his nice side by then," Beko recalled with a sly smile.

General Babangida's nasty side emerged in May the following year, 1992, when his troops opened fire on protesters who took to the streets of Lagos to demand an end to military rule and a reversal of the government's austerity measures. The National Association of Nigerian Students called the demonstrations to denounce severe fuel shortages and rising prices. The students launched their protests three days after Beko issued a statement for the Campaign for Democracy saying, "Under the present circumstances, to save our country from total collapse, General Ibrahim Babangida should resign and make way for a sovereign national conference composed of all social groups. We call on the Nigerian people to rise up to the challenge and take the necessary steps to retrieve their sovereignty." The protests quickly turned into riots taken over by street thugs known as "area boys." The city was shut down for two days.

The first signs that something was amiss on the morning of May 13, 1992, were the tree branches sticking out of car windows and tied to their engine hoods. The green leaves were a sign of solidarity with the student protesters, but in effect they were also a safe-conduct pass. All over the huge metropolis, vegetation was ripped from the ground by passing motorists and pedestrians desperate to steer clear of the running battles between the marchers and the anti-riot police. One truckload of off-duty soldiers even had a bundle of green leaves tucked under the windshield wiper. At the first rumor of unrest, drivers pulled over, tore off a branch, and stuck it on their vehicle, before heading off toward a potential trouble spot. It certainly made life easier for journalists. All they had to do to find the protesters was to follow cars and trucks sporting branches of green leaves.

Unfortunately, because everyone was so panicky, the method was not an altogether reliable one. Police manning roadblocks sometimes viewed the foliage as an insult to their authority and angrily pulled such vehicles over, so many drivers hid the leaves until they passed through the checkpoints. Lagos' always resourceful street traders, mainly young men in shorts and T-shirts who weave in and out of traffic jams selling everything from cold drinks to portable telephones, took immediate advantage of the new market opportunity. A handful of green leaves went for one *naira*, more than the price of one liter of petrol.

Throughout the day, hundreds of youths vented their anger, smashing windows of banks and offices along the main thoroughfares of mainland Lagos and in the financial district on Lagos Island. Most shops and businesses were closed down, and several major roads looked like war zones, littered with burning tires, barricades, and cement blocks that had been used as missiles. Large sections of the city became no-go areas, as marauding gangs of unemployed youths looted shops, attacked vehicles, and extorted money from passersby. The riot police responded in typical fashion, firing on the protesters, first with rubber bullets, then, when their patience wore out, with live ammunition.

For those determined to make their way through the city, the best thing about the protests was that they cleared the roads of Lagos' usual daunting traffic jams, the hours-long gridlocks known as "go-slows." A trip from Lagos or Ikoyi islands to the mainland, which on normal days could take anything from one to three hours, became a leisurely twenty-minute drive, provided one could avoid the protesters and the police checkpoints. On the second day of the riots, Beko was sitting at his office in the clinic adjacent to his two-story home in the Anthony Village neighborhood. Just two blocks away, protesters battled with the riot police, but Beko sat calmly behind his desk in near-total darkness. There was a power cut in the area; or as Lagosians liked to joke at the expense of the chronically inefficient Nigerian Electricity Power Authority, "NEPA done quench."

As the running battles of the first day ran into the second, at least eleven deaths were reported. Beko shook his head. "Why don't they let them march and leave them alone? Instead, they have to shoot them and create confusion." For a man who had seen his supporters defy the military and paralyze Lagos, Beko was very unhappy. He abhorred violence but saw that more was coming. The antigovernment protests would go on, he was confident. "The only hope is that they are controlled, and not spontaneous with a lot of killing."

Five days later, two hundred armed police agents forcibly entered Beko's home at 4:15 A.M. and took him away in his pajamas. For nearly a month, the government refused to disclose the whereabouts of Beko and several other prominent rights activists, including the maverick lawyer Chief Gani Fawehinmi, Baba Omojola, Femi Falana, and student leader Olusegun Mayegun. Vice President Augustus Aikhomu initially claimed rather implausibly that the government had no part in the detentions, which he said were the work of the security agencies. Only in Nigeria would the vice president seek to avoid responsibility by blaming his own security forces. Justice Minister Clement Akpamgbo later contradicted him, however, announcing that Beko and the others were being held under the military's 1984 State Security Decree 2, which allowed indefinite detention without trial. The detainees, he charged, harbored a "secret plan to illegally engineer a change" of government. It was a refrain that would be heard frequently over the next four years as the military sought to silence its opponents.

Throughout early June, a Lagos High Court repeatedly ordered the military to produce the prisoners, and the regime ignored it. The Nigerian Bar Association retaliated by launching a boycott of the nation's courts, an ineffectual move if there ever was one since the military government worked tirelessly to undermine the courts' authority. Finally, a month after their arrest, the detainees appeared in a magistrate's court five hundred miles north of Lagos in the central village of Gawgawdala, near the new capital, Abuja. The police drove them there from Lagos in the dead of night like a gang of kidnappers. By this time Beko's fragile health was waning and police had to help him into the courtroom. The magistrate agreed to the detainees' request for medical attention, which their jailers refused. The trial dragged on inconclusively for several months until the charges were dropped. Beko and the others returned to Lagos, sick and tired but not subdued.

General Babangida, who had already postponed the military's withdrawal from politics twice before, was about to do so again by missing his self-imposed deadline of January 1993. He played the civilian politicians like yo-yos, scheduling presidential primaries and then justifying their cancelation by blaming corrupt electoral practices which the military permitted in the first place. "Babangida started an advert on television, 'Handover is here, where is takeover?'" Beko later remembered. "In other words, there was nobody to take over from him. I had a dog called Larry then. I told my brother Ulikoye, the minister, that if Babangida did not have anybody, he should just hand over to Larry." Beko was again detained on December 31, a month before Babangida was scheduled to leave office.

By the time Beko emerged from jail, the handover had been rescheduled to August 1993, the eighth anniversary of General Babangida's military coup. Beko and his fellow human rights activists began canvassing the politicians of the Social Democratic Party (SDP), the one "a little to the left." The SDP was generally considered to be slightly more sympathetic to the south, while the other party, the National Republican Convention (NRC), was seen as a more conservative force, with stronger backing from the Muslim north. The candidate who eventually won the SDP nomination was Chief Moshood Abiola, a flamboyant millionaire businessman who, in what would later become a great irony of the unfolding crisis, was particularly close to General Babangida and the military.

Chief Abiola's considerable wealth—the owner of an airline, a shipping line, and a publishing house, he is believed to be one of the richest men in Africa, worth $2 billion—was inextricably linked to the military. Chief Abiola was the quintessential Nigerian "big man," a true *oga,* in Yoruba parlance. He started to build his fortune in the mid-1970s, when as a vice president for the International Telephone and Telegraph Corporation (ITT), he negotiated a billion-dollar contract with the military government of the day to install a telephone system in Lagos. The exchange was renowned for its grave deficiencies, and for many, Abiola symbolized the civilian elite's complicity with military rule. He was the target of a popular song composed by Beko's brother, Fela Kuti, entitled "ITT, International Thief Thief." Chief Abiola freely admitted his tie with the army, often explaining it with a proverb: "To kiss somebody, you have to get near them; to bite them, you have to get near them, too."

Yet in the topsy-turvy nature of Nigerian politics, the poor and working people of Lagos enthusiastically supported Chief Abiola precisely because he was so wealthy. Kayode Sukoya, a car hire businessman, explained it this way: "He is a very rich man, and I think he got rich from the military. I don't know the details but I am sure he must have been in a romance with the military. Now we are not really interested how he got the money. We have the belief that the man is so rich that what he needs to do is to help the poor masses." In Nigeria, logic dictated that you voted for the rich because their wealth was so great they would not need to steal from government coffers, and perhaps, just maybe, some crumbs would fall the people's way.

In the end, the elections went ahead on June 12, 1993, and as the returns rolled in from the thirty states, Chief Abiola's victory became certain. He was poised to become the first elected Nigerian leader from the Yoruba west and the first candidate to have scored victories across religious and regional barriers. International observers judged the vote as the cleanest election in the country's history. It was not to be. Before the final results were announced, General Babangida annulled the exercise, citing voting irregularities. The Campaign for Democracy actively backed Abiola's cause, however reluctantly. "You cannot describe me by any stretch of the imagination as a pro-Abiola man," Beko explained. "Before the election, there was no difference between Abiola, the military, Babangida. One viewed him as part of the problems of the country. But we had a running battle with Babangida and he just had to go. The military had to go."

As the protests against the cancelation of the elections grew, Beko was arrested again on July 6 and taken to Abuja. While he and several others languished in jail, Chief Abiola, saying that he feared for his life, dramatically fled to London aboard his private jet. The pro-democracy movement attempted in vain to convince Abiola to return to Nigeria and lead his supporters as the country's elected leader, but for months he refused. When he eventually did return, his credibility was severely shaken. Beko stayed in jail for two months, until General Babangida stepped down in favor of a military-backed transitional council headed by an old friend of Beko's and a fellow native of Abeokuta, Chief Ernest Shonekan. The number two man in the council was the wily coup master General Sani Abacha, the infantry officer who was a key figure in the rise of General Babangida. "Emissaries from Abacha had come to speak with me," said Beko, "to ask me my opinion about the state of the nation, about what to do. I said the army should not come in. Unless we had a national conference, this country would not settle down." Beko's advice was ignored. In November, General Abacha staged his own coup, announcing, "Any attempt to test our will will be decisively dealt with." He was true to his word. In the violence that followed in subsequent weeks, the police shot dead at least one hundred and fifty people.

A week after the Abacha coup, the mood at Chief Abiola's mansion in Ikeja was one of defeat. The dozens of paintings and pictures of himself with world leaders and Nigerian politicians and military rulers—including General Babangida, the man who halted his presidential ambitions—betrayed an ego as huge as Nigeria itself. In the context, they seemed like a sad joke. Chief Abiola continued to meet with his supporters, screened by securitymen called Mandela and Qaddafi, but their numbers were fewer than during the early post-election days. There were a handful of traditional rulers and cronies from around the country who came to pay their respects and, as several of his aides suggested, to pick up funds to maintain their public support for the failed presidential candidate.

Usually a man with something to say on any occasion, Chief Abiola was remarkably mute that day. Typically, he resorted to a proverb to describe his situation: "When the music changes, the dancer must step to a different tune." Others already had. Abiola's running mate in the June 12 election, Baba Gana Kingibe, delivered a telling blow to Abiola's dampened hopes of still becoming president by joining General Abacha's new twelve-man Provisional Ruling Council. "Don't give up hope yet," Abiola told a telephone caller, in a passionless tone of voice that clearly revealed he already had. He put the phone down and said he was planning to return to London to consult his physician. A few days later, the symbol of Nigeria's yearning for democracy jetted off to London.

On the street level, the pro-democracy movement defied the odds by keeping the dream of June 12 alive; and on the second anniversary of his aborted election victory, Abiola with renewed vigor declared himself president, saying, "Let the heavens fall." Unfortunately, what fell was the strong arm of the military. Within days Abiola was arrested and, treading the well-worn path of Beko and his human rights colleagues, was moved by the secret police to Abuja. General Abacha ignored international appeals for Abiola's release from the West and from African leaders, Nelson Mandela included. Chief Abiola was guilty of treason, the military said, for having declared himself president. A six-week pro-democracy strike in July and August was crushed and trade union leaders and human rights activists rounded up. Three major newspaper groups, Chief Abiola's *Concord, Punch,* and the highly respected daily, *The Guardian,* were closed for nearly a year. Beko was detained at least four times in 1994.

By mid-1995, the government had lifted its closures of the newspapers, most notably *The Guardian,* historically one of Africa's best dailies. But the price *The Guardian* had to pay, a humiliating apology to General Abacha by senior editors and reporters, was high. The longtime reporter and editor of the publishing house's weekly magazine, Sully Abu, resigned in protest. Chief Abiola still languished in detention in Abuja, and his doctor said he had lost weight and occasionally all sense of time itself. The Ogoni rights leader, Ken Saro-Wiwa—who had campaigned against the transnational oil company, Royal Dutch/Shell, for its pollution of Ogoniland in southeastern Nigeria—along with several of his close aides, was in prison on murder charges. General Abacha gave a speech to the War College in which he promised to restore democratic government "as quickly as possible," but added rather ominously that the military was "a unifying force for all time."

BEKO HAS NEVER BEEN under any illusions. He knows that Nigeria's solution must come from within. The international community's response to the military's human rights violations has been feeble. With its huge economic interests involved, especially the massive investments of its transnational oil companies, there is little chance that the West will repeat its intervention in Haiti, where American negotiators and troops removed a military junta that, like the Abacha regime in Nigeria, thwarted the democratic will of the people. Nigeria is simply too far away to warrant military action or the imposition of tough economic sanctions.

The dilemma for the democratic movement is how to bring about a peaceful solution. Beko echoed an increasing number of Nigerians, both southerners and northerners, who believe that decentralization—allowing the major ethnic groups a greater latitude of political autonomy while agreeing to share national resources—is the only road to a stable future. A return to the federal system that was originally designed to govern Nigeria is, however, a pipedream as long as the military rules. Centralization goes to the very heart of the military order. Top-down, vertical control is part of the generals' mind-set, integral to the myth of the great African giant which longs for a seat on the UN Security Council, which dreams of being a Third World superpower. General Babangida and his successor, General Abacha, repeatedly spurned calls for a national conference to negotiate far-reaching political change. An election which the generals set up and which had seen one candidate, albeit one from the south, win nationally, was halted too. What was coming next, Beko did not want to contemplate, because there is little chance that it would be anything but violent. There seemed to be no alternative.

Beko is part of the generation of Nigerians who were the first Africans to taste the horror of civil war with the armed bid to create Biafra. But the new generation, those frustrated young unemployed men who struggle to make a living on the streets of Lagos, Ibadan, and Kano, the "area boys," are too young to remember what a disaster full-scale conflict can bring. It is a frightening thought but an accurate forecast that by the year 2000, Nigeria will be the home to somewhere around 50 million children, sixteen years old or younger, half of whom will live in the cities, with less than a one in a thousand chance to reach university, and will be faced with job opportunities limited to street hawking and other black market activities. Some will attempt to reach Europe or the United States, or perhaps even South Africa. The ones who stay behind are growing angrier by the day. They might end up in gangs or join radical Muslim sects in the northern cities of Kaduna or Kano.

Demonstrating, letterwriting, holding press conferences, mounting legal challenges, engaging in debate—these are the tactics Beko learned, from the time when his mother organized women against onerous taxes in Abeokuta. Yet as Nigeria heads toward the millennium, its neck still firmly under the boot of the generals, Beko's liberal agenda looks to be frighteningly irrelevant, and he knows it. "Trouble will eventually start unless the problems are resolved peacefully. The people are so desperate," he said sullenly. "If people want to get guns, they will find them. I never could imagine thinking about guns, but at the stage we are at now, I don't know anymore." In the back of his mind were the tragedies that have unfolded in the southern African nations of Mozambique and Angola, in the nearby West African states of Liberia and Sierra Leone, and most worrying of all, in the Great Lakes region. "It is getting to the point where people might just lash out. It would be anarchy, like the Rwanda nightmare."

It was late in the afternoon, and Beko readied his fax machine to send off another set of statements from the detainees. He smiled and said, "I hope the SSS [secret police] didn't follow you."

Three days later, the police came for him. After a fifteen-minute trial, Beko was sentenced by the secret tribunal on August 2, 1995, his fifty-fifth birthday, to life imprisonment for faxing defense statements of the other detainees with, in the words of the court, "a view to having the British and various governments invade Nigeria." Like Obasanjo and many of the other alleged coup plotters, Beko's sentence was later reduced to fifteen years in prison. He was sent to the far northern city of Katsina and held in isolation.

Worse was in store for Ken Saro-Wiwa, the Ogoni rights leader. On November 11, 1995, Saro-Wiwa and eight other Ogoni activists were hanged in a prison in Port Harcourt after a trial that international jurists described as politically motivated and lacking in basic legal standards. In June 1996, Chief Abiola's senior wife, Kudirat, was gunned down in Lagos. A series of unexplained bombings began. The government accused Wole Soyinka in absentia and eleven pro-democracy campaigners of involvement and charged them with treason.

Beko Ransome-Kuti celebrated his fifty-sixth birthday as he did the year before: in jail. Odds are that he will celebrate his next one, too, in the Katsina prison. He could be there a long time. General Abacha has announced a new transition to civilian rule program and refuses to deny rumors that he will be a candidate. Deprived of reading material, regular visits by his family, and proper medical care, Beko's health continues to deteriorate. The abiding image of him sitting in his office, comforting victims of human rights abuses and plotting to bring democracy to his Nigeria, brings to mind the opening passage in Ben Okri's book, *Songs of Enchantment*, about the song of the circling spirits: "We didn't see the chaos growing; and when its advancing waves found us we were unprepared for its feverish narratives and wild manifestations. We were unprepared for an era twisted out of natural proportions, unprepared when our road began to speak in the bizarre languages of violence and transformations. The world broke up into unimaginable forms, and only the circling spirits of the age saw what was happening with any clarity."[7]

Postscript

It was a typical Sunday afternoon in Kinshasa. Luckily, there was just enough of a breeze to ruffle the blanket of humidity rolling in from the Zaire River and to ensure the day would be a pleasant one. Without the normal workday traffic of cars and trucks, the air was unusually fresh and quiet. Thousands of young people walked along the sides of the streets, all heading in one direction—the giant oval sports stadium. The excitement built, the volume of the laughter rose, as the crowd drew near. For it was game day, and local favorites Vita Club of Kinshasa were scheduled to do battle against Inter from the neighboring country of Burundi.

A bit of confusion arose at the entrance gates as police and soldiers on duty raised their batons to threaten pedestrians who were trying to slip by. After one vehicle made its way through to the parking lot, the police shut the gate and waited for a few minutes to let the next one in. Everyone trying to get through pleaded with the police that there was no reason to keep the gate so tightly controlled. But the people's expressions of misunderstanding rang hollow. They knew it was a potential roadblock, a point where a few armed men could hopefully make some extra money and if nothing else at least demonstrate their authority. Neither the police nor the army receive salaries sufficient to feed their families. Their performance reminded me of a group of street kids I had seen the day before who placed a makeshift toll of thick tree branches at fifty-yard intervals across one suburban road and demanded, though far too meekly to succeed, money for the cars to pass. Few passersby paid the boys, but the traffic jam was only beginning to gorge itself on the incoming cars; within an hour or so, when the line would stretch around the bend, someone might pay. The soldiers at the soccer stadium did not seem to be having much more luck. Each time a car entered, a handful of legitimate ticket holders slipped through the cordon, and the frustrated troopers slammed the gate shut, only to turn to face dozens more cars revving their engines and angling to penetrate the barrier. When the crowd of pedestrians became too rowdy, a few swift smacks with the hard black batons quickly restored order, albeit temporarily.

Inside stood Kinshasa's impressive Kamanyola Sports Stadium completed in 1992 by a Chinese construction team. The ten thousand fans on the eastern side began a series of rolling "Mexican wave" cheers, while the equally numerous crowd on the western side remained strangely quiet. Most of them were followers of another local club, Mapewa Pembe, and because Vita Club was their main domestic rival, they supported the Burundians. The near-equal division of the stadium into opposing sides was the purest manifestation of the dictum: "The enemy of my enemy is my friend." As the teams were warming up, the rival fans invented spontaneous songs to insult each other. It was all in good humor. The Vita supporters initiated the serenades by roaring with a melodic chant claiming that Jesus Christ was backing their side. To that their rival fans stood in unison, turned their backs, and hissed. When it comes to soccer in Africa, even Jesus Christ pulls little weight.

A coterie of local dignitaries emerged from a tunnel to parade around the deep red synthetic rubber running track, and the fans on both sides of the divide suspended their melodic war. This was a new target for their attentions. That was of course the celebrities' intention, but they received a good deal more than they had bargained for. The big man of the day was Sports Minister Kisombe Kiaku. He stood beaming before the crowd, his hands above his head in a clench like a prize-fighter. What better place to show one's face, do a little politicking, and catch a game at the same time. His appearance sent a wave of silence over the throng. It was to prove a momentary lull. At first the voices were few, sporadically erupting before falling back. Individuals offered up chants to see if the crowd would take them, and after a few tries went silent again. Then something took hold, building slowly, just a rumble you could feel before hearing it. Within seconds the voices united into one giant chorus that filled the stadium with the strength and purity of a massive church choir. The hymn was powerful, mournful, rising and falling like an outpouring of collective lamentation. The confident smile on the minister's face melted into a frown of disbelief. *"Moyibe aye, moyibe aye,"* they sang. "The thief has come."

The minister's hands fell down lazily to his sides in resignation, and he turned to walk on. The rest of the dignitaries hustled behind him, realizing that whatever it was they were offering, this was the wrong audience. They reached the midpoint of the stadium to greet the respective team coaches and shake hands with the referees. The crowd, though, was not yet finished with the minister. The heckling started, and the line which won the honor of admiration through imitation went, "It's because of you and Mobutu that the country has such a bad image."

They were, of course, hollering about their president, Mobutu sese Seko, the architect of a pyramid of corruption that drained the Congolese people of their riches and denied an entire generation the chance of enjoying a decent life. Mobutu, ill with prostate cancer, was increasingly regarded by the public as "a wounded leopard" in the words of Mike Katambwa, the editor of the *Umoja* newspaper.

Fourteen months later, the Kamanyola Stadium was filled again with tens of thousands of people. They were not there to enjoy an afternoon of soccer. They assembled to witness the dawn of a new order. Standing before them was Laurent Kabila, the man who had vanished into the eastern mountains before the majority of Congolese were even born, and who had reemerged thirty years later at the head of a guerrilla army that drove Mobutu into exile and swept his hated regime onto the scrap heap of history. As Kabila took the oath of office before twenty-two justices dressed in red robes trimmed with leopard skin, he said, "We should start from the beginning."

The once unthinkable had happened. Mobutu was gone. The death of his friend, Rwandan President Júvenal Habyarimana, had set off the horrific genocide by his allies, the Hutu extremists, and the resulting shockwaves eventually shattered Mobutu's ossified regime. His departure was a seminal event in Africa's postindependence history. Despite repeated calls for Western intervention, especially by his friends in Paris, supposedly on humanitarian grounds to protect Rwandan refugees, Mobutu's ouster was planned and executed by an African coalition of Congolese opponents and neighboring countries fed up with his destabilizing antics. Through his Zaire had flowed arms and insurgents wreaking havoc in Angola, Burundi, Rwanda, and Uganda. Their leaders decided Mobutu was a blight on the continent and had to go.

After the collapse of apartheid and Mobutuism, the focus will inevitably shift to the West African colossus of Nigeria, where the brooding military regime is virtually at war with its own people. The generals rule by force of arms and are seen by the vast majority of Nigeria's population as "pirates in power," and like Mobutu, hypocritical perpetrators of the very economic and political chaos they say they are in power to prevent. But surely their time will come, too.

Nigerians suffer from a confusing mix of problems related to extreme poverty, declining living standards, and the country's own pyramid of corruption but being easily cowed by authority is not one of their weaknesses. The point was driven home to me during a visit I made to the southeastern river town of Abonnema in December 1991 with a delegation of the National Population Commission. We arrived in an aluminum dingy after a half-hour ride from the city of Port Harcourt, and immediately set off to pay our respects to the local authorities. The commission members led us not to the local government representatives but to someone far more important. Lawrence Karibi Bob-Manuel, the eighty-year-old Alabo, or paramount chief of Abonnema, was sitting in his living room enjoying a leisurely Sunday morning when we entered. His back slightly hunched over from age, the Alabo welcomed us as if we were long-lost sons. It was 10:00 A.M., but with visitors to attend to, he broke out a fresh bottle of Scotch whiskey and poured drinks for everyone. Straight up, no ice. Before anyone could put glass to lips, however, Alabo Karibi Bob-Manuel walked to his front door and leaned gingerly out over his front steps and with his trembling hands sprinkled a few drops of whiskey on the front stoop. He was making an offering to a local goddess worshipped by villagers who inhabit the winding sea canals near the Niger River delta.

Abonnema, which Alabo Karibi Bob-Manuel said translated roughly as "Love your own," was in a festive mood that day. The national census had gone well, the river town had just been upgraded to a local government area, with the expectation that Abonnema's port would retake its one-hundred-year-old place as a prime palm-oil exporting gateway. "Now that the federal government has recognized our importance as a local government area, we are hoping that Abonnema will return to its former glory," Alabo Karibi Bob-Manuel said proudly.

No visit to Abonnema was complete without a tour of the rusty palm-oil processing plant and three huge storage tanks situated at the water's edge. The Alabo dispatched a couple of junior chiefs to accompany us. To get there, we walked through the town literally on periwinkles, those small snails that seem to be everywhere in the delta. Nothing of the periwinkle is wasted. The snail's meat is the base of a popular soup and its shell is mixed with asphalt to form city streets. Massive piles of periwinkle shells lie gutted by the roadside, the discarded husks from countless meals.

It was during an intense discussion with one of the chiefs about the importance of the periwinkle that a young man approached and began inquiring sternly what a foreign journalist was doing in Abonnema. I was a bit taken aback, considering the warm welcome from the Alabo, but I answered his queries willingly. He wanted my passport number, nationality, and press ID—a reporter's equivalent of name, rank, and serial number. The man said he worked for the State Security Service, Nigeria's secret police. Clearly, he was not very well trained, since the one thing security personnel are not supposed to do, at least initially, is reveal who they are.

Our hitherto amiable discussion erupted into a heated argument when the security man demanded to see my notes. I said that he could see anything but the notes; not that there was anything controversial in them, unless he considered notations on periwinkles a threat to national security. But I had no intention of letting him see them. It was a matter of principle, and I knew that if he got his hands on them, I might never see them again. The discussion grew more agitated, until he committed a grave mistake. He started shouting. I assumed, of course, that I was headed for trouble and would probably spend the day at police headquarters answering all kinds of time-wasting questions until everyone became bored enough to let me go. It turned out rather differently. Our private brouhaha drew the attention of the other Nigerians in our party, and in particular the Alabo's junior chiefs. Within seconds there unfolded a scene that would have been unthinkable, or so I thought, in a country ruled by military dictatorship. As one, the Nigerians rounded on the not so secret policeman.

Defiant at first, he quickly crumpled under the sheer force of collective reprobation. "I am just doing my job," he said feebly, to which one of the chiefs literally spat out, "What job? You people are capable of nothing." A chorus of "stupid man" and "you are embarrassing" rang out from all quarters. The agent slowly backed away, cowering under the wave of insults, until one voice rang out. "Disappear!" shouted a chief. "Disappear from here!"

The last time I saw the embattled police agent, he was dejectedly shuffling down the beach and tossing periwinkle shells into the sea, probably all too aware that he had blown his chance to sample a wonderful lunch of grilled fish, pounded yam, and explosively hot pepper soup.

I think it is fair to say that in Africa, more than anywhere else, the gulf between the rulers and the ruled, or misruled, as the case may be, is astonishing. I am not referring here to a gap in wealth or lifestyle, which is usually immense as well. The point is that they inhabit two almost separate realities, and therein lies the root of so many problems. Perhaps Africans are too kind to their leaders, allowing them too long a stretch in power, even when they are clearly not up to the job or do not have the people's interests at heart. Perhaps they are simply too forgiving. It is an honorable trait, and one that is in evidence across the continent—from South Africa, where the white minority continues to enjoy a lifestyle built from the blood and sweat of the African majority, to Rwanda, where survivors of the genocide are being asked to live next door to the very people who carried out the slaughter. In the future, perhaps Africans should be a little less forgiving and hold their leaders a great deal more accountable.

For responsibility and accountability are the bedrocks of any just society. In this book, I tried to portray the lives of people who must confront tremendous odds each day solely to survive. Hopefully, I have been able to highlight some extraordinary catalysts for change; that there is a new generation of Africans armed with the values and drive of their forefathers, who are ready to tackle the challenges of the future. It can be a difficult task, as demonstrated by the case of a unique man I met in Lagos who refused to disown his principles in the face of temptation.

There was no doubt that Adebayo Aremu was a truly remarkable individual. That much was clear from the nickname he had acquired in the local press: "the honest Nigerian." His story was written about in the newspapers and talked about in the street with a breathless amazement, as if this one man alone among 100 million people had managed to embody two seemingly irreconcilable concepts: Nigerian and honesty. Aremu, a hardworking taxi driver who struggled each day to make ends meet, was an exception, and for that he had caught the nation's imagination, at least for a while. The first time I heard about him in early 1992, Aremu was the butt of a joke. My friend and regular guide in Lagos, Kayode Sukoya, was laughing in his deep baritone one day, telling a story he had just heard. Despite the obvious ridicule, however, Kayode could not hide his sneaking admiration for the man who had done the unimaginable: Found money that did not belong to him and returned it to its rightful owner. If Kayode had not read about it, he would never have believed it possible. But there it was in black and white. The *Concord* newspaper, owned by the Muslim millionaire Chief Moshood Abiola, who would later tumble down the vortex of Nigerian politics, had published a three-paragraph story about the exploits of "the honest Nigerian." Together, Kayode and I decided to track down this modern-day wonder.

The point of departure for our hunt was a makeshift taxi rank in the teeming Surulere section of Lagos. Like the rest of Lagos but even more so, Surulere is dirty, smelly, crowded, and chaotic, but enchanting all the same, alive with a mass of humanity pushing and shoving just to survive another day. We pulled in just before midday and approached a crowd of drivers sitting in rows on wooden benches in the shade, wiping the sweat from their brows and fanning themselves with rolled-up newspapers to provide momentary relief from the sapping ninety-degree heat and humidity levels that defied measurement and, for a good part of the day, movement. Our repeated inquiries about Aremu drew blank stares of incomprehension until we said, "You know, the honest Nigerian." Immediately everyone started laughing. "That crazy boy, you mean," said one. "He's out on a job, but he'll soon be at home for lunch." Kayode listened carefully to the directions to Aremu's house given by one of the drivers in Yoruba, the language of the dominant ethnic group in southwestern Nigeria. Once Kayode had the address right, there was much cackling and snickering. "What did they say?" I asked. "That they would never do what Aremu did," Kayode replied. Another man shouted cheerfully in English for my benefit, "A stupid boy!"

Aremu's home was just several streets away, but because the snarled traffic had ground to a near halt in Surulere's mazelike streets, it took us fifteen minutes to arrive by car. We could have walked the distance in five, but in Nigeria no rightminded person would walk when a car was available. It just was not done. We stood for a few minutes chatting to his neighbors until Aremu arrived. He seemed depressed. He led us through a dank cement hall, where naked children were playing in pools of water, and by the smell of it, their own urine, into a compound where a dozen families lived, sharing a communal toilet and a kitchen. Aremu's home, in which he lived with two wives and four children, consisted of one room slightly bigger than the double bed that filled it. The reason for Aremu's despair soon became obvious. Honesty, in his view, simply did not pay in Nigeria. In fact, it was ruining his life.

Driving was everything to Aremu. He started in the business when he was sixteen years old, and at thirty, he knew nothing else. Despite his long experience, however, he had still to reach the pinnacle of his trade: owning his own car. It was his dream, everything he had worked for. "Unless you have your own car, most of the money you earn from clients each day goes to the boss," he explained. On a good day Aremu's take could reach the equivalent of $10, and although his two wives chipped in with profits from their market trading, it was impossible to save enough money to purchase a vehicle.

Aremu's big chance to revolutionize his life came one morning while he was driving around the Lagos suburb of Ikeja looking for a fare. He picked up a woman who was going to the sprawling Idumota market in the central business district of Lagos. Minutes before their arrival, however, gangs of "area boys" had swept through the market extorting protection money from the traders, mainly Igbos from the east who dominated the retail trade. By the time Aremu and his client pulled into the narrow alleyways that sliced through the rows of wooden market stalls, a full-scale riot was under way. The thugs attacked the taxi and smashed the windshield. Aremu and the woman fled for their lives.

When the dust settled, Aremu made his way back to the taxi, and to his astonishment found that the woman had left behind a pile of goods and a bundle of cash worth 21,000 *naira,* or about $1,000 at the time, which was as much as he could earn in eighteen months under the best of circumstances. For an hour he waited in vain for the woman to return. When she did not, he found a receipt for the goods she had bought earlier in the day at the bottom of one of her bags, and with it, Aremu was able to trace the shop in which she had made the purchases. He left a message at the store, and three days later, the woman came forward to claim her belongings. Aremu handed it all back.

Did he not think of keeping it, perhaps to make a substantial down payment on a car? No one would have blamed him. Aremu, a devout Muslim, considered the question for a moment and said,

"There is nothing I am going to do with someone else's money. The thought never crossed my mind. If it happened again, I would look for the owner. It's not in my nature to steal." The response sent Kayode into an uproar of laughter. "A real honest Nigerian, heh-heh."

Aremu shrugged his shoulders, in silent recognition that everyone considered him a fool for doing the right thing. Then he resumed the story. The woman handed him 1,000 *naira* as a reward, which, given the amount he had returned, was a mere token. Yet aside from that insubstantial bonus, initially at least, everything went well. A reporter for the *Concord* newspaper picked up the story and published it. Readers were so touched that they sent him 4,000 *naira* in private donations, and the prestigious John F. Kennedy International School in the eastern city of Warri wrote to offer his eldest daughter, ten-year-old Mutiyat, a full scholarship to secondary school once she finished her primary studies.

After that his luck changed for the worse. The owner of the taxi blamed him for driving into a riot and ordered him to pay for the damages to the vehicle, which cost more to repair than the 4,000 *naira* he had received from well-wishers. Then Aremu was fired. Next, his second wife promptly left him. "She said I have been a driver for fifteen years and have never been able to get my own car. When I had the opportunity, I just gave it away." His disappointment deepened on March 7, 1992, when he was invited to be a guest at the Performing Musicians Association of Nigeria annual awards ceremony in the capital, Abuja. There he met then-president Ibrahim Babangida, who praised him for his honesty, shook his hand, and left without offering him anything else. Aremu returned to Lagos with no work and hefty bills to pay. He sent his four children to live with his mother. He took any odd jobs he could find. He was bitter. "The country will be honest if everyone sees it as a duty," he said. "But if there is no reward for being honest, people like me are seen as being stupid."

So it went for two months. It was the worst time Aremu could remember. He had lost his job and one of his wives, he could no longer support his children, and friends were laughing at him. Then his roller-coaster ride with principled behavior took an upturn. A neighborhood police inspector who owned an extra car and was in need of some additional income decided to put it to good use as a taxi. He had heard about Aremu and decided that there was no one better suited to be his driver than the honest Nigerian. After a brief interview, he gave Aremu the job.

The best was yet to come. A British lawyer in London had read my story about Aremu's plight in *The Independent* newspaper and decided to send a gift of £300 (about $500), in recognition of his honesty. Kayode and I returned in May to Aremu's house and acted as if we were simply paying a visit. When we placed a bag filled with 10,000 *naira*, the converted value of the lawyer's donation, on a small table by his bed, Aremu was at first dumbfounded. Then he burst into uncontrolled laughter. "In a miraculous manner, Allah has come to help me," he shouted. "It's true that honesty pays."

Three years later, Kayode and I set out once again in search of Aremu. I was preparing to leave Nigeria, and before I did, I wanted to see how Aremu was getting along. We found the taxi rank where he worked. Just as they were three years before, the drivers were sitting around in the shade, chewing kola nuts, and fanning themselves with newspapers to make the unbearable, stinking, humid air of Surulere somehow more bearable. Aremu had left for lunch but was expected back at any moment. "The honest Nigerian," one of the other drivers said, laughing. We waited fifteen minutes and had decided to leave just as Aremu darted through the traffic toward our car. We shook hands and Kayode explained that we had returned to see how he was getting along.

"No good, no good," he said, shaking his head. The policeman who had hired him had sold the car, and now he had no vehicle to drive. He hung around the taxi rank hoping to stand in for a driver who was off sick or to pick up odd jobs, nothing steady. The money sent by the lawyer in Britain had run out long ago, and he was relying on the meager profits from his wife's market trading. The children were still with his mother, because he could not afford to take care of them, and Mutiyat would not be going to the Kennedy School in Warri until next year, when she finished primary school. But the scholarship still stood.

After he finished sketching out his situation, we asked him, would he do it all again, give the money back? "I could use that money now," he said. "It would be very helpful." But would he give it back? "I don't know anymore," he said. "I'm not sure." We bid good-bye and I promised to see him the next time I was in Lagos. Kayode started the engine, and suddenly there was a tapping at the window. It was Aremu. He wanted to say something. "I think I would do it again," he said. "I think so."

Notes

Preface

1. Claude Ake, *Democratization of Disempowerment* (Lagos: Malthouse Press Ltd., 1994). Available from WN.APC.ORG/MEDIATECH/PUBLISH/AARSOOO.HTM. Updated September 12, 1995.

2. Basil Davidson, *The Black Man's Burden. Africa and the Curse of the Nation-State* (London: James Currey, 1992), p. 295.

Glorious Light

1. Ali Mazrui, *The Africans—A Triple Heritage* (Boston: Little, Brown, 1986), p. 11.

2. UNICEF estimates that sub-Saharan Africa would need $2.4 billion above current spending levels to reach universal primary education. See *The Cost and Financing of Primary Education. Options for Reform in Sub-Saharan Africa* (New York: UNICEF, 1996), p. 3.

3. Davidson, *The Black Man's Burden*, p. 38.

4. Ronald Segal, *The Black Diaspora* (London: Faber & Faber, 1995), p. 5.

5. Claude Ake, *Democratization of Disempowerment*.

6. James C. McKinley, Jr., "African Statesman Still Sowing Seeds for Future," *New York Times*, Sept. 1, 1996, p. A3.

7. Karin Davies, "Congo Good Neighbors," the Associated Press, Kinshasa, June 1, 1977.

8. "African Visionaries Mandela and Museveni to Meet," Reuters, Johnnesburg, May 25, 1997.

New Roads Taken

1. Chinua Achebe, *The Trouble with Nigeria* (London: Heinemann, 1983), p. 1.

2. Adebayo Adedeji, Lecture in Kaduna, reported in *West Africa* magazine, Nov. 11–17, 1991, cited Michael Barratt Brown, *Africa's Choices: After Thirty Years of the World Bank* (Harmondsworth, UK: Penguin Books, 1995).

3. Frank Willett, *African Art* (London: Thames & Hudson, 1993), p. 69.

4. Ibid., p. 73.

5. Ibid., p. 35.

6. Oliver Sultan, *Life in Stone, Zimbabwean Sculpture—Birth of a Contemporary Art Form* (Harare: Baobab Books, 1994), p. 17.

7. Cited in ibid., pp. 35–36.

8. Ibid., p. 8.

9. Ibid., p. 6.

10. "African Trailblazer Begins to Falter," *Financial Times Survey* (Ghana), July 9, 1996, p. 1.

11. World Bank, *A Continent in Transition: Sub-Saharan Africa in the mid-1990s*, cited in *Africa Confidential*, vol. 36, no. 9 (1995), p.4.

12. "African Trailblazer Begins to Falter," p. 2.

Spirit of Peace

1. See Thomas Blakely, Walter van Beek, and Dennis Thomson, eds., *Religion in Africa* (London: Heinemann/James Currey, 1994), p. 17.

2. Michael Crowder, *West Africa Under Colonial Rule* (London: Hutchinson, 1968), p. 388.

3. Mazrui, *The Africans*, p. 45.

4. Quoted in *Conspicuous Destruction, War, Famine and the Reform Process in Mozambique* (New York: Human Rights Watch/Africa, 1992), p. 23.

5. Cited in ibid., p. 170.

6. Christian Geffray, *La Cause des Armes au Mozambique. Anthropologie d'une Guerre Civile* (Paris: Editions Karthala, 1990), p. 31.

7. J. S. Mbiti, *African Religions and Philosophy* (London: Honeymoon Books, 1969), p. 132.

8. Quoted in Joseph Hanlon, *Mozambique: The Revolution Under Fire* (London: Zed, 1984), p. 138.

9. See *Conspicuous Destruction*, p. 38.

10. Text of a radio message dated July 7, 1988, found among documents captured by Frelimo forces at the Renamo presidential base at Nhamagadoa, in Maringue, on April 18, 1991.

11. David Lan, *Guns and Rain* (Harare: Zimbabwe Publishing House, 1985), p. xvii.

12. S. I. G. Mudenge, *A Political History of the Munhumutapa Empire c. 1400–1902* (Harare: Zimbabwe Publishing House, 1988), p. 63.

13. Ibid., p. 68.

14. Allen Issacman, *The Tradition of Resistance in Mozambique* (London: Heinemann, 1976), pp. 158–76.

15. Claude Ake. *Democracy and Development in Africa* (Washington: The Brookings Institution, 1996), p. 15.

The Healing Touch

1. Rajendra Kale, "South Africa's Health, Traditional Healers in South Africa: A Parallel Health Care System," *British Medical Journal*, May 6, 1995, pp. 1182–85.

2. Ibid.

3. Kenyan Vice President George Saitoti, speaking at October 17, 1996, launch of *AIDS in Kenya: Socio-economic Impact and Policy Implications.*

4. Florence Sigauke, "Conflicting Signals on the Cost of AIDS in Zimbabwe," *The Herald* (Harare), May 1, 1997.

5. Richard Rigby, "Out of Control," *British Medical Journal,* June 3, 1995, p. 1475.

6. Chenjerai Hove, *Shebeen Tales* (London: Serif, 1994), p. 76.

7. Laurie Garrett, *The Coming Plague* (New York: Penguin Books, 1995), p. 370.

8. Lawrence Vambe, *An Ill-Fated People* (London: Heinemann, 1972), p. 198.

9. Ibid., pp. 199–200.

10. See Garrett, *The Coming Plague,* p. 383.

11. Ibid., p. 452.

12. John Nkoma, "A Question of Relevance," *New Scientist,* October 7, 1995, p. 52.

13. Letters to the Editor, "In-vitro Resistance of Plasmodium Falciparum to Qinghaosu Derivatives in West Africa," *The Lancet,* April 2, 1994, p. 850.

The Battle for the Mind

1. *Education News,* UNICEF, New York, Issue 16, vol. 6, no. 2 (1996), p. 8.

2. Kevin Watkins, *The Oxfam Poverty Report* (Oxford, 1995), p. 25.

3. Nkoma, "A Question of Relevance," p. 61.

4. Watkins, *Oxfam Poverty Report,* p. 25.

5. *Public and Private Costs of Primary Education,* UNICEF Staff Working Papers, No. 15, April 1996, p. 44.

6. Crowder, *West Africa Under Colonial Rule,* p. 372.

7. Ibid., p. 373.

8. Roland Oliver, *The African Experience* (London: Pimlico Books, 1991), p. 101.

9. Alphonse Gouilly, *L'Islam dans l'Afrique Occidentale Français,* cited in Crowder, *West Africa Under Colonial Rule,* p. 373.

10. Crowder, ibid., pp. 384–85.

11. *Education in Sub-Saharan Africa.* A World Bank Policy Study (Washington, DC: World Bank, 1988), p. 12.

12. Keith Richburg, "Decay 101: The Lesson of 'Africa's Harvard,'" *The Washington Post,* August 11, 1994, p. A1.

13. *Conspicuous Destruction, War, Famine and the Reform Process in Mozambique,* p. 154.

14. *Education in Sub-Saharan Africa,* p. 12.

15. Ibid., p. 74.

16. Richburg, "Decay 101," p. A1.

17. Watkins, *Oxfam Poverty Report,* p. 39.

18. Nkoma, "A Question of Relevance," p. 61.

19. *Education News,* UNICEF, p. 4.

20. Nkoma, "A Question of Relevance," p. 61.

21. Wande Abimbola, "Ifá: A West African Cosmological System," in Blakely, van Beek, and Thomson, eds., *Religion in Africa,* p. 102.

22. Cited in *Education in Sub-Saharan Africa*, p. 74.

23. Lawrence Cockcroft, *Africa's Way—A Journey from the Past* (London: I. B. Tauris, 1990), p. 44.

24. Segal, *The Black Diaspora*, p. 153.

25. Crowder, *West Africa Under Colonial Rule*, p. 373.

26. Segal, *The Black Diaspora*, p. 153.

27. Cockcroft, *Africa's Way*, p. 47.

The Universal Soldier

1. *An Assessment of Children and Youth in Renamo Zones*. Creative Associates International for UNICEF. May 1994, p. 37.

2. Rachel Brett, and Margaret McCallin, *Children: The Invisible Soldiers*. Rädda Barnen (Swedish Save the Children), Stockholm, 1996, p. 43.

3. *The State of the World's Children*, UNICEF (Oxford: Oxford University Press, 1996), p. 14.

4. Neil Boothby, Peter Uptson, and Abubacar Sultan, *Children of Mozambique: The Cost of Survival*. Duke University, Institute of Policy Sciences and Public Affairs, February 1991.

5. Mozambique News Agency (AIM) report, June 15, 1990.

6. *Angola: Alliance for Life*, UNICEF. Document prepared for *The State of the World's Children* (Oxford: Oxford University Press, 1996), Luanda, July 1995, p. 4.

7. *The Impact of Armed Conflict on Children*. Draft of report for the United Nations by Graça Machel, July 1996, p. 12.

8. Paul Richards, *Fighting for the Rain Forest, War, Youth and Resources in Sierra Leone* (London: Heinemann/James Currey, 1996), p. 81.

9. Brett and McCallin, *Children: The Invisible Soldiers*, p. 149.

10. Robert Kaplan, "The Coming Anarchy," *The Atlantic Monthly*, February 1994, pp. 43–76.

11. Stephen Riley, *Liberia and Sierra Leone—Anarchy or Peace in West Africa?* Research Institute for the Study of Conflict and Terrorism. London, February 1996, p. 5.

12. Richards, *Fighting for the Rain Forest*, pp. 57–59.

13. Ibid., p. 37.

14. See Boothby, et al., *Children of Mozambique*.

Heroes of the Apocalypse

1. *Rwanda: Death, Despair and Defiance*. (London: Africa Rights, September 1994), pp. 455–56.

2. Davidson, *The Black Man's Burden*, p. 13.

3. Ibid., p. 11.

4. Gérard Prunier, *History of a Genocide. The Rwanda Crisis* (London: Hurst & Co., 1995), p. 16.

5. Ibid., p. 31.

6. Ibid., pp. 30–31.

7. Ibid., p. 39.

8. Ibid., p. 85.

9. The Steering Committee of the Joint Evaluation of Emergency Assistance to Rwanda, *Historical Perspective: Some Explanatory Factors*, ed. David Millwood, Vol. 1 of *The International Response to Conflict and Genocide: Lessons from the Rwanda Experience* (Odense: Strandberg Grafsk, 1996), p. 17.

10. *Rwanda: Killing the Evidence, Murder, Attacks, Arrests and Intimidation of Survivors and Witnesses.* (London: Africa Rights, March 1996), p. 39.

11. Prunier, *History of a Genocide*, p. 222.

12. *Rwanda: Death, Despair and Defiance*, p. 688.

13. Prunier, *History of a Genocide*, pp. 352–53.

14. Human Rights Watch/Fédération Internationale des Ligue des Droites de l'Homme, Sept. 24, 1996. New York and Paris.

15. The Steering Committee of the Joint Evaluation of Emergency Assistance to Rwanda, "Synthesis Report," p. 34.

16. Ibid.

17. The Steering Committee of the Joint Evaluation of Emergency Assistance to Rwanda, *Re-building Post-War Rwanda*, ed. David Millwood, Vol. 4 of *The International Response to Conflict and Genocide: Lessons from the Rwanda Experience* (Odense: Strandberg Grafsk, 1996), p. 92.

18. Cited in *The State of the World's Children*, p. 14.

19. *Rwanda: Death, Despair and Defiance*, p. 708.

20. Ibid., p. 345.

21. The Steering Committee of the Joint Evaluation of Emergency Assistance to Rwanda, *Re-building Post-War Rwanda*, p. 61.

An Act of Faith

1. Richard Leakey, and Roger Lewin, *Origins Reconsidered* (London: Abacus, 1992), p. 9.

2. Brown, *Africa's Choices*, p. 218.

3. Claude Ake, *Democratization of Disempowerment.*

4. Richard Dowden, "The Return of the Kings," *Prospect* (London), July 1996, pp. 61–65.

5. Eghosa Osaghae, *Ethnicity and Its Management in Africa* (Lagos: Center for Advanced Social Science, 1994), p. 44.

6. Dowden, "The Return of the Kings," p. 64.

7. Peter P. Ekeh, "Social Anthropology and Two Contrasting Uses of Tribalism," quoted in Davidson, *The Black Man's Burden*, p. 226.

8. Segal, *The Black Diaspora*, p. 23.

9. Adam Smith, *An Inquiry into the Nature and Causes of the Wealth of Nations*, cited in ibid., p. 41.

10. Ibid., p. 27.

11. Ibid, p. 17.

12. Crowder, *West Africa Under Colonial Rule*, pp. 27–28.

13. Cited in Davidson, *The Black Man's Burden*, p. 37.

14. McKinley, "African Statesman Still Sowing Seeds for Future," p. A3.

15. Kwesi Kafrona, *Organization of African Unity: Twenty-five Years On. Essays in Honour of Kwame Nkrumah*, Afroworld, 1988, cited in Brown, *Africa's Choices*, p. 2.

16. Baffour Ankomah, and Mike Afrani, "If I Fall, I Fall as a Man," *New African*, April 1997, p. 14.

17. *Economist Intelligence Unit Country Profile, 1995–96*, [Zaire] London, p. 12.

18. Brown, *Africa's Choices*, p. 128.

19. Report on the Human Rights Situation in Zaire. Presented by Special Rapporteur Roberto Garreton, in Compliance with Resolution 1995/69 of the United Nations Human Rights Commission. E/CN.4/1996/66 Jan. 29, 1996.

20. Jonathan Kwitny, *Endless Enemies. The Making of an Unfriendly World* (New York: Congdon & Weed, 1984), p. 69.

21. Ibid., p. 65.

22. Ibid., p. 71.

23. Sean Kelly, *America's Tyrant. The CIA and Mobutu of Zaire* (Washington: American University Press, 1993), p. 2.

24. Kwitny, *Endless Enemies*, p. 80.

25. Blaine Harden, *Africa—Dispatches from a Fragile Continent* (New York & London: W. W. Norton, 1990), p. 41.

26. Ibid., p. 37.

27. Report on the Human Rights Situation, Jan. 29, 1996.

28. Michela Wrong, "Rebels Poised to Control Zaire Diamonds," *Financial Times* (London), March 12, 1997, p. 4.

29. Kwitny, *Endless Enemies*, p. 88.

Circling Spirits of the Age

1. Fela Kuti, *Fear Not for Man* (Afrodisia: Decca, 1997).

2. Pierre Sane, *Nigerians Deserve a Better Fate*, Amnesty International, London, Nov. 6, 1996.

3. Achebe, *The Trouble with Nigeria*, p. 3.

4. Claude Ake, *Democratization of Disempowerment*.

5. Achebe, *The Trouble with Nigeria*, pp. 1–2.

6. Kole Omotoso, *Achebe or Soyinka, A Study in Contrasts* (London: Hans Zell Publishers, 1983), p. 53.

7. Ben Okri, *Songs of Enchantment* (London: Jonathan Cape, 1993), p. 3.

Acknowledgments

It would be impossible to thank all of the people who have made this book possible, although the stories of many of them have appeared in these pages. I would like to make special mention of Gil Lauriciano and Carlos Mhula, who gave generously of their time to help me understand Mozambique, and Kayode Sukoya, without whose guidance and patience I would have found Nigeria a far more difficult place with which to come to grips.

Special thanks to colleagues at *The Independent* newspaper for their support, including the former Africa Editor, Richard Dowden, Heather Kerr, and the late Nicholas Ashford, and to Michael Holman, Rakiya Omar, Patrick Smith, and Alex Vines. I am deeply appreciative to Emily Loose, my editor at John Wiley & Sons, for seeking me out to write this book, to my agent, Gloria Loomis, and to Brennon Jones who provided valuable comments on the draft.

Index